# Thinking about Language

## Helping Students Say What They Mean and Mean What They Say

A Landmark School Teaching Resource

Roberta Stacey

Landmark School, Inc.
Prides Crossing, MA

© 2003 Landmark School, Inc.

All rights reserved. No parts of this publication may be reproduced in any form without permission from the publisher.

Published by Landmark School, Inc.
P.O. Box 227
Prides Crossing, MA 01965

Library of Congress 2003101657

ISBN 0-9624119-9-x

Printed in the United States of America

*Landmark School, Inc.*

# Alice's Lesson in Oral Expression

"Come, we shall have some fun now!" thought Alice. "I'm glad they've begun asking riddles—I believe I can guess that," she added aloud.

"Do you mean that you think you can find out the answer to it?" said the March Hare.

"Exactly so," said Alice.

"Then you should say what you mean," the March Hare went on.

"I do," Alice hastily replied; "at least—at least I mean what I say—that's the same thing, you know."

"Not the same thing a bit!" said the Hatter. "Why you might just as well say that 'I see what I eat' is the same as 'I eat what I see'!"

"You might just as well say," added the March Hare, 'that I like what I get' is the same as 'I get what I like'!"

"You might just as well say," added the Dormouse, which seemed to be talking in its sleep, "that 'I breathe when I sleep' is the same thing as 'I sleep when I breathe'!"

Lewis Carroll, *Alice's Adventures in Wonderland*

Landmark School, Inc.

# Contents

| | |
|---|---|
| Preface | ix |
| Acknowledgments | x |
| About Landmark Outreach | xi |
| About the Author | xii |
| Landmark Teaching Principles | xiii |
| Introduction | xvi |
| Auditory Attention and Recall | xx |

**Chapter One: Phonology** — 1

| | |
|---|---|
| Introduction | 1 |
| Phonological Awareness | 6 |
| Auditory Discrimination of Phonemes | 8 |
| Articulation of Phonemes | 12 |
| Articulation of Multisyllabic Words | 14 |
| Responding to Unintelligible Speech in the Classroom | 16 |
| Responding to Processing/Production Errors in the Classroom | 18 |
| Bibliography of Instructional Materials | 20 |

**Chapter Two: Morphology** — 21

| | |
|---|---|
| Introduction | 21 |
| Regular Noun Plurals | 25 |
| Noun-Verb Agreement | 27 |
| Definite and Indefinite Articles | 29 |
| Noun Possessives | 31 |
| Irregular Noun Plurals | 32 |
| Present Progressive Tense of Verbs | 35 |
| Third-Person Singular, Present-Tense Verbs | 36 |
| Past Tense of Verbs | 38 |
| Irregular Past Tense of Verbs | 40 |
| The Irregular Present-Tense Linking Verb "Be" | 45 |

*Landmark School, Inc.*

| | |
|---|---|
| Present-Tense Linking Verbs | 47 |
| The Irregular Present-Tense Verbs "Have" and "Do" | 49 |
| Modals | 52 |
| Auxiliary (Helping) Verbs and Modals | 54 |
| Contractions | 57 |
| Future Tense of Verbs | 61 |
| The Six Verb Tenses | 63 |
| Comparative and Superlative Forms of Adjectives and Adverbs (Regular and Irregular) | 68 |
| Suffixes | 71 |
| Prefixes | 76 |
| Bibliography of Instructional Materials | 81 |

## Chapter Three: Syntax    83

| | |
|---|---|
| Introduction | 83 |
| Word Order in Simple Sentence | 89 |
| Simple Sentences with a Noun Phrase and Action Verb | 91 |
| Simple Sentences with *Where* Phrases | 93 |
| Simple Sentences with *When* Phrases | 95 |
| Simple Sentences with *Where* and *When* Phrases | 97 |
| Simple Sentences with Adjectives | 99 |
| Simple Sentences with Adverbs | 101 |
| Simple Sentences with Negatives | 103 |
| Passive Voice | 105 |
| Yes-No Interrogatives | 107 |
| Indirect Requests | 109 |
| *Wh-* Interrogatives | 110 |
| Basic Sentence Types, Classified by Purpose | 113 |
| Conjunction Deletions | 115 |
| Phrases with Verbals: Participles, Gerunds, and Infinitives | 117 |
| Compound Sentences with Coordinating Conjunctions | 120 |
| Compound Sentences with Conjuncts (Connectives) | 122 |
| Sentences with Correlative Conjunctions | 124 |
| Complex Sentences with Subordinate Adverbial Clauses | 126 |

| | |
|---|---|
| Sentences with Right-Branched Adjective Clauses: Subordinate Clauses as Object-Related Adjectives | 129 |
| Sentences with Embedded Adjective Clauses: Subordinate Clauses as Subject-Related Adjectives | 132 |
| Complex Sentences with Noun Clauses: Relative Clauses as Subjects, Objects, Predicate Nominatives, or Objects of Prepositions | 135 |
| Statements with Quotations | 138 |
| Sentences with Structural Ambiguities | 140 |
| Bibliography of Instructional Materials | 142 |
| **Chapter Four: Semantics** | **143** |
| Introduction | 143 |
| Vocabulary: Action Verbs | 149 |
| General Vocabulary | 151 |
| Vocabulary: Adjectives That Describe Quality | 155 |
| Vocabulary: Adjectives That Tell Which or How Many | 162 |
| Vocabulary: Adverbs | 164 |
| Word Retrieval | 168 |
| Locative, Directional, Spatial, and Temporal Prepositions | 172 |
| Instrumental and Idiomatic Prepositions | 175 |
| Personal, Reflexive, and Intensive Pronouns | 177 |
| Demonstrative, Indefinite, and Indefinite Negative Pronouns | 180 |
| Categories | 182 |
| Antonyms | 184 |
| Synonyms | 188 |
| Homonyms: Multiple-Meaning Words | 192 |
| Analogies | 195 |
| Temporal-Sequential Relationships | 197 |
| Directional Words | 200 |
| Figurative Language | 202 |
| Making Inferences | 210 |
| Literature | 212 |
| Bibliography of Instructional Materials | 216 |

*Landmark School, Inc.*

| | |
|---|---:|
| **Chapter Five: Pragmatics** | **217** |
| Introduction | 217 |
| Discourse: Presenting a Topic | 221 |
| Discourse: Summarizing an Event or a Selection from Literature | 223 |
| Discourse: Sharing Descriptive Information | 225 |
| Discourse: Expressing Comparisons and Contrasts | 230 |
| Discourse: Explaining a Process | 234 |
| Discourse: Describing Cause and Effect | 237 |
| Discourse: Expressing Opinions | 239 |
| Discourse: Eliciting Comments from Students Who Give No Response | 242 |
| Discourse: Encouraging Students to Expand on Minimal or Incomplete Responses | 244 |
| Discourse: Accommodating Students Who Exhibit Slow Processing or Delay in Formulating a Response | 246 |
| Social Communication: Ritualizing | 248 |
| Social Communication: Requesting Information or Assistance | 250 |
| Social Communication: Conversation and Discussion | 252 |
| Social Communication: Classroom Discussion | 254 |
| Resolving a Conflict | 256 |
| Social Communication: Resolving Conflicts in a Residential Setting or during Free Time | 259 |
| Paralinguistic Communication: Articulatory and Prosodic Features | 261 |
| Paralinguistic Communication: Volume and Pitch | 262 |
| Paralinguistic Communication: Register | 264 |
| Paralinguistic Communication: Nonverbal Skills | 266 |
| Paralinguistic Communication: Disfluency/Dysfluency | 269 |
| Bibliography of Instructional Materials | 271 |
| | |
| References | 272 |
| Glossary | 277 |
| Bibliography | 284 |
| Appendix | 287 |

# Preface

I have been associated with Landmark School for children with language-based learning disabilities in numerous capacities since its founding in 1971, my most important roles being those of instructor and speech-language pathologist. I work with children daily, learning what works and doesn't in my own classroom laboratory.

Teachers new to the practice are often frustrated when they behold a sea of glazed eyes in response to a carefully prepared lesson. The problem is in assuming too much prior knowledge on students' part. It has taken me years to make an accurate judgment about presenting a lesson at a level that is accessible to the student, rather than one that is too difficult.

In its original form, this was my personal "recipe" book for developing curriculum and writing goals and objectives for Landmark students' individual education plans. A number of Landmark teachers and speech-language pathologists also found it a useful resource for lesson planning. At this juncture, the book has evolved from personal experience as well as from study. The micro-united objectives under each goal roughly follow a developmental order. This structure makes it easier to plan each step in the teaching process.

It is my hope that this book will be a useful guide for other instructors who are dedicated to leading their students toward a happier place in the world of oral language. It should help new and experienced teachers alike accomplish no-fail presentations of new skills. Finally, parents actively involved in their child's learning, especially in home-schooling, have found earlier drafts of this book helpful in locating their child along the learning spectrum and in setting realistic expectations for the next level. Excellent reading for parents who want to understand how their children learn is *A Mind at a Time*, by the renowned pediatrician Mel Levine (2002).

# Acknowledgments

The 1997-1998 Landmark Elementary and Middle School faculty, whose names appear below, contributed in a most important way to the strategies presented here. Their contributions are based upon actual, rather than theoretical, classroom experience.

### 1997-1998 Landmark Elementary and Middle School Faculty

| | | | |
|---|---|---|---|
| Kathie Babcock | Tina Estes | Sharon Majewski | Jen Schoen |
| Suzy Bernier | Jill Flemming | Rich Mangano | Ken Schulman |
| Ellie Bertolino | Jenny Hanchett | Joan McLaughlin | Nell Schwechheimer |
| Debby Blanchard | Scott Harlan | Bruce Miller | Dottie Seiter |
| Santo Brillati | Martha Heddon | Mollie Mitchell | Colleen Shaw |
| Larry Bulloch | Susan Hedman | Deirdre Mulligan | Ellen Slade |
| Janice Burgert | Sharon Hudzik | Phil Murphy | Beth Sucic |
| Debbie Chandler | Terrill Jennings | Sandi Nadeau | Kirk Swanson |
| Amy Clemens | Julie Jones | Lisa Nichols | Wendy Taylor |
| Cynthia Colbourne | Mary Kahn | Brett Oakes | Freddi Triback |
| Amy Corkins | Rob Kahn | Eva Oliveira | Charlene Williams |
| Heather Crossen | Rick Keesler | Jen Osborne | Scot Wilson |
| Susie Dillon | Gretchen Korb | Allen Pickwick | Sophie Wilson |
| Chuck DiPietro | Leon Lemure | Karl Pulkkinen | Chris Woodin |
| Charlie Eberhart | Julie Littlefield | Cathy Roy | Jen Woodin |
| Charlotte Eliot | John Lyons | Matt Rutter | Wendy Zimmerman |
| Larry Eliot | Beth Mahoney | | |

Special appreciation is extended to the late Charles Drake, founder of Landmark School; Rob Kahn, who provided strong encouragement throughout the project; Charles Haynes, a gifted instructor who was instrumental in developing the oral expression program at Landmark; Martha Heddon, a valued colleague; and Don Stacey, my husband.

# About Landmark Outreach

Established in 1977, the Landmark School Outreach Program provides professional development programs and publications that offer practical and effective strategies that help children learn. These strategies are based on Landmark's six teaching principles and on over thirty years' experience in the classroom. Members of the Landmark faculty deliver graduate courses and seminars at the Landmark Outreach Center and on site at school districts across the country. For more information about professional development opportunities and publications, visit our website at *www.landmarkschool.org* or contact the Landmark School Outreach Program at (978) 236-3216.

## *About Landmark School*

Founded in 1971, the Landmark School is recognized as an international leader in the field of language-based learning disabilities. The school is a co-educational boarding and day school with students, age seven to twenty years old, from across the United States and around the world. Within its highly structured living and learning environment, Landmark offers individualized instruction to elementary, middle, and high school students. The school's program emphasizes the development of language and learning skills. Landmark students learn strategies for managing their learning differences so that they can realize their full potential both socially and academically.

*Landmark School, Inc.*

# About the Author

Roberta Stacey, Ed.M., S.L.P., has been associated with Landmark School since its founding in 1971. She has served as tutor, classroom instructor, and speech-language pathologist. Ms. Stacey is currently cochair of the oral expression/literature department at Landmark's elementary-middle school campus and consults as a speech-language pathologist.

Ms. Stacey received her B.A. from the University of Colorado and her master's degree in human development from Harvard Graduate School of Education. She has presented numerous workshops to fellow professionals and graduate students in speech-language programs.

*I did not write xiii, xiv, or xv Landmark School stuff*

# Landmark Teaching Principles

**Imagine** an instructional hour in which all students are interested and involved. The teacher motivates students by making the material meaningful to them. Information is presented in a variety of interesting ways that engage the range of learning styles in the class. The teacher builds opportunities for success by presenting information in small, sequential steps, and offers positive feedback as soon as students learn and apply a relevant new skill. The teacher provides examples and clear directions for homework, and sets aside a few minutes at the end of class for students to begin the homework assignment. During this time, the teacher answers questions and makes sure each student understands the task. In short, the teacher structures the hour so each student is challenged, works at an appropriate level, and leaves the class feeling successful and confident.

The Landmark School was founded in 1970 to provide this type of structured, success-oriented instruction to students with learning disabilities. For more than thirty years, Landmark teachers have continually enhanced and refined teaching strategies to help students learn more effectively. Landmark has shared its teaching strategies with public- and private-school teachers from all over the world through Landmark seminars. All students can and do learn from Landmark's structured, success-oriented instructional models.

At the heart of Landmark's instructional strategies and programs are six teaching principles. They are summarized below.

## *Teaching Principle #1: Provide Opportunities for Success*

Providing students with opportunities for success is key. Failure and poor self-esteem often result when teachers challenge students beyond their ability. Landmark begins teaching students at their current level of ability. This approach improves basic skills and enhances confidence. As Landmark teachers introduce each new skill, they provide basic examples and assignments to build confidence and keep students from becoming overwhelmed. As the information becomes more challenging, teachers assign students easier problems to supplement the more difficult ones. In this way, those students who are having trouble with the material complete at least part of the assignment while they work at understanding and learning to apply new information. Teachers provide students with whatever struc-

*Landmark School, Inc.*

ture is necessary to help students be successful, such as study guides for tests, templates for writing, and guidelines for projects.

Only with a solid foundation of basic skills and confidence can students make progress. That is why it is key to provide them with opportunities for success.

## *Teaching Principle #2: Use Multisensory Approaches*

Multisensory teaching is effective for all students. In general, it means presenting all information to students via three sensory modalities: visual, auditory, and tactile. Visual presentation techniques include graphic organizers for structuring writing and pictures for reinforcing instruction; auditory presentation techniques include conducting thorough discussions and reading aloud; tactile presentation techniques include manipulating blocks and creating paragraphs about objects students can hold in their hands. Overall, implementing a multisensory approach to teaching is not difficult; in fact, many teachers use such an approach. It is important, however, to be aware of the three sensory modes and to plan to integrate them every day.

## *Teaching Principle #3: Micro-Unit and Structure Tasks*

Effective teaching involves breaking information down into its smallest units and providing clear guidelines for all assignments. This is especially important for students with learning disabilities. Micro-uniting and structuring are elements of directive teaching, which Landmark consistently uses with students. *Micro-uniting* means analyzing the parts of a task or assignment and teaching those parts one step at a time. Teachers organize information so that students can see and follow the steps clearly and sequentially. As students learn to micro-unit for themselves, they become less likely to give up on tasks that appear confusing or overwhelming. Consequently, these strategies enable students to proceed in a step-by-step, success-oriented way.

## *Teaching Principle #4: Ensure Automatization through Practice and Review*

Automatization is the process of learning and assimilating a task or skill so completely that it can be consistently completed with little or no conscious attention. Repetition and review (spiraling) are critical. Sometimes students appear to understand a concept, only to forget it a day, week, or month later. It is not until students have automatized a skill that they can effectively remember and use it as a foundation for new tasks. Teachers must therefore provide ample opportunities for students to repeat and review learned material. For example, the Landmark writing process emphasizes practice and consistency. Students always brainstorm, map/outline, draft, and proofread in the same way. This provides them with an ongoing, consistent review of learned skills.

## Teaching Principle #5: Provide Models

Providing models is simple, yet very important. It is one of the most effective teaching techniques. Models are concrete examples of what teachers expect. They do not mean that teachers are doing assignments for students. They are standards to which students can compare their own work. A model or example of a completed assignment serves as a springboard for students to begin the assignment. For example, teachers should give students a model of a sequential paragraph when teaching basic sequential paragraph writing.

## Teaching Principle #6: Include Students in the Learning Process

Students are not passive receptacles to fill with information. They come to class with their own frames of reference. Their unique experiences and knowledge affect them as learners and should be taken into account. Therefore, during every exercise, teachers should accept student input as much as possible. They should justify assignments, accept suggestions, solicit ideas, and provide ample time for students to share ideas. Teachers should include students in assessing their own progress by reviewing test results, written reports, and educational plans. Creating and improvising opportunities to involve students in the learning process allows students to become aware of how they learn and why certain skills benefit them. As a result, students are motivated and more likely to apply those skills when working independently. In short, an included student becomes an invested student who is eager to learn.

# Introduction

From infancy, and in some respects even the womb, the child absorbs information from different linguistic areas simultaneously. For example, a baby registers intonation, as in the rising pitch at the end of a question; rhythm; tone of voice; gestures; and different phonemes. Because children are bombarded with linguistic stimuli, teachers should become familiar with each student's skills and needs in each linguistic area. For example, a student might discriminate speech sounds with ease (phonology) but have extreme difficulty summarizing the plot of his favorite movie (pragmatics).

A special student population exhibits a degree of language disability when assessed under sufficiently demanding conditions. A "subtle dysphasia" is evident when such students are confronted with complex tasks of naming or producing syntax to formulate their thoughts, especially under time constraints.

Children who display clear-cut disabilities in oral language competence require direct intervention. These children know and understand more than they can express. They struggle with time and their own organizational and expressive language deficits. The impact upon their academic experience is major. To avoid frustration or the embarrassment of delays, errors, misarticulation, disfluencies, or circumlocution, they resort to avoidance techniques (such as getting kicked out of class) or even give up.

Children with normally developing verbal skills can build metalinguistic awareness, an ability to reflect upon language itself. Given exposure to language early in life, they possess intuitions about the structure of language and its components. Four-year-old youngsters busily try out rules they discover, such as adding *-ed* for past-tense verb forms and *-s* for plurals. That these children are not just parroting back what they hear is evident in the logic of their errors, which reflects their realization that our language is governed by rules. They are not copying their parents when they say, "I comed," "I heared," "mouses," and "sheeps." It's that they learn the exceptions to the rules later.

Metalinguistic knowledge serves as a scaffold for orderly processing and storage of information. It allows for concise, coherent delivery of information as well. Difficulty comprehending and using the underlying structure of language affects a child's ability to process or share information accurately, whether listening to a lecture, reading literature, or participating in discussion.

*Landmark School, Inc.*

## A Case in Point: Annie

Annie entered Landmark at nine years of age. From her records, we knew of a significant discrepancy between Annie's poor verbal skills and superior nonverbal skills. She was a budding artist with a strong sense of hope and optimism. She was well-organized and worked conscientiously. But Annie was almost completely mute in the classroom.

It was our job to help Annie realize her potential in the areas of receptive and expressive language skills. The task was daunting, as Annie seemed unable to describe the simplest experiences in a way that we could understand. Although inaccurate articulation was one barrier, her desperate efforts to recall words and formulate sentences were the main obstacles to satisfying conversation.

I met weekly with Annie and her tutor. Initially, her tutor served as a scribe while Annie and I talked. From the tutor's notes and my observations, I categorized Annie's errors into the five linguistic categories.

## Examples from Annie

| What Annie Said | What Annie Meant | Type of Error |
|---|---|---|
| /akuh/ | Because | Phonological |
| /thum/ | Some | Phonological |
| /buluts/ | Bulbs | Phonological |
| I broken | I broke | Morphological |
| Doesn't supposed to be | Isn't | Morphological |
| Amy shared me with the stuff she had. | Amy shared the stuff she had with me. | Syntactical (word order) |
| She has a grandmother to feel her much better. | She has a grandmother who makes her feel much better. | Syntactical |
| Keep on finding | Keep on looking | Semantic |
| Thermometer | Calendar | Semantic |

*Landmark School, Inc.*

| What Annie Said | What Annie Meant | Type of Error |
| --- | --- | --- |
| A paper thing like toilet paper, like paper stuff. It's almost like "towel" – oh, yeah, paper towel. | Paper-towel tube | Semantic |
| You hear like my mother when you yawn. | You sound like my mother when you yawn. | Semantic |
| In describing a picture of firemen putting out a building fire, Annie described details, beginning with what she saw in the upper right-hand corner of the picture ("I see a bird way up here.") but did not describe the main action in the picture. | A building is on fire. Firemen are putting out the fire. | Pragmatic (prioritizing information) |

Annie's tutor and I determined the highest priority goals for Annie, since it would be impossible to address every single need. For Annie, it was most important that she learn how to share her thoughts in a coherent manner. At Landmark, Annie was immersed in a structured curriculum for receptive and expressive language skills the entire academic day. In her written expression class, her oral expression/literature class, and her individualized tutorial, Annie used organizational templates to express what she knew.

Annie's story is one of the most heartening and dramatic in terms of success. She is proof that the strategies we use at Landmark can succeed. Annie is still a budding artist. She has come to love writing as well. Although she is not loquacious, Annie can express herself coherently, and her verbal skills have shown substantial gains in standardized testing. Annie needed to be taught step by step at levels accessible to her.

## About This Book

*Thinking about Language* is intended as a diagnostic and teaching tool for professionals who work with elementary- and middle-school children in language development: special-education instructors, speech-language pathologists, and classroom teachers who are interested in learning about the linguistic structures underlying our language. Although my teaching experience has been with children with language-based learning disabilities, some students in every "normal" classroom are trying to cope with difficulties in isolated areas of language. These students can be helped by teachers who understand the linguistic elements.

The particular focus of this book is oral expression. Students learn not only through listening and reading, but also through self-expression. Listening to their own voices often clarifies their thoughts, and their comprehension might reach a higher level as a result. The more they talk, the greater their self-confidence, in many cases. Bernice Cullinan (1987) argues most persuasively for "talk in the classroom."

The receptive and expressive language skills presented here are divided into the five linguistic areas for purposes of structure and convenience:

- phonology (speech sounds)
- morphology (meaningful word parts)
- syntax (sentence structure)
- semantics (vocabulary, meaning)
- pragmatics (social communication, discourse)

Within each linguistic area, the book's sequence roughly follows a developmental order from simpler, or first learned, to more complex. The chapters on morphology and syntax reflect the work of Wiig and Semel in *Language Assessment and Intervention for the Learning Disabled* (1984). The chapter on pragmatics draws its goals from several sources. Landmark's program for academic discourse is based upon Simon's *Evaluating Communicative Competence* (1994). Other resources for communication skills include Weinrich, Glaser, and Johnston (1986) and Kreidler (1997).

*Thinking about Language* should be valuable as a:

- diagnostic tool
- guide for teaching receptive and expressive language skills
- resource for strategies used by Landmark School faculty
- desk reference
- resource for organizational templates
- resource for word lists

# Auditory Attention and Recall

The significant issue of auditory attention and recall is relevant to every chapter of this book. Many Landmark students appear to lack adequate auditory attention and recall, which are essential for efficiently gathering information. These students might have difficulty:

- screening out ambient noise in the classroom, such as a fan, furnace noise, the flickering hum of a fluorescent light, or even the ticking of a watch

- focusing upon and recalling more, as opposed to less, relevant information (i.e., main ideas as opposed to details)

- developing efficient rehearsal strategies, as in trying to recall a string of words rather than efficiently chunking the information

- processing verbal information from oral presentations delivered at a normal speaking rate

- maintaining the stamina necessary to focus upon oral information; in other words, they might suffer from mental fatigue and be unable to concentrate once they hit overload

Can memory be improved through exercise? The claims of companies selling herbal supplements and educational publishers selling books are most persuasive. However, even if a student is trained to recall a series of five oral directions or seven digits, does the student generalize these splinter skills into overall improvement of short-term memory? Proof is not so clear.

It does seem prudent to explore what a classroom educator can do to help students who don't seem to remember what they just heard. The focus should be on practical, real-life tasks and strategies.

- All Landmark students are required to write down their daily homework in assignment notebooks, which are especially designed to conform with their daily class schedule. Many students would be lost in homework limbo without these assignment books. In fact, Landmark runs a homework makeup session each day after school for students who "forgot" to do their homework. Assignments are presented both verbally and on the board.

- Students with attentional or processing deficits are often asked to retell directions that were just delivered to them. Comprehension of the directions might be an issue.

*Landmark School, Inc.*

- Younger students are expected to practice their home addresses and important telephone numbers until they are memorized.

- In phonemic development classes, students are taught to write dictated sentences of gradually increasing length, from five words to eleven words or more. Sentences are dictated only once. Students are encouraged to repeat the sentence quietly, if they wish. Over the years, students have improved their ability to write sentences of increasing length verbatim. Remembering words in context, as in a sentence, as opposed to remembering isolated word strings, is demonstrably easier for students.

- In oral expression/literature classes, students memorize several poems each year. They use a variety of strategies for memorization. One successful strategy is to draw a picture for each verse as a mnemonic cue. Gestures to accompany each verse also help. One instructor asked each of her students to describe the most helpful strategy. Students were quite specific in reporting the number of lines they attempt at each trial, and how many times they practice each verse.

- In content courses, students are taught to write two-column notes as they read or listen to the text. The left column is for the main idea, and the right column is reserved for writing details relevant to the main idea. Therefore, students are chunking information for mastery, a strategy for memorizing that they might not recognize as such.

What else can the instructor do?

- Speak intelligibly. In the 1950s, instructors were required to pass an articulation test before they were granted a teaching license. Intelligible speech was mandatory, to the extent that a relatively minor lisp might stand in one's way of getting a license. In these more liberal times, such restrictions are no longer part of the licensing process; however, too many educators mumble. Teachers must self-monitor for intelligible speech.

- Provide interactive lessons. The lecture format is fatiguing to these students.

- Speak slowly. Many instructors, otherwise excellent, simply talk too fast. The ongoing frustration is that they rarely reduce their rate of speech, even with the best of intentions. Rapid speech is as automatic as breathing to them. A normal rate is between 130 and 250 words per minute (Emerick and Haynes

1986); 250 words per minute is far too rapid for successful processing by a typical Landmark student. Reading orally to students at about 130 to 140 words per minute is successful. Delivering verbal information, as in a lecture, should definitely be under 200 words per minute.

CHAPTER 1

# PHONOLOGY

## Introduction

*Phonology* is the study of the sound systems of a language, including not only the individual phonemes (speech sounds), but also patterns of intonation, rhythm, and tone of voice (Crystal 1995). From just forty-five or so phonemes, English-speaking people have generated a dictionary of more than 600,000 words, and new words are incorporated into this dictionary every day (Lederer 1991).

By the time most English-speaking children reach six to eight years of age, they can accurately produce all of the phonemes. They also appear able to perceive them accurately, even at the rate of twelve phonemes per second. The rate of normal running speech is 200 syllables per minute (Emerick and Haynes 1986).

Children with a phonological impairment, or lack of phonological awareness, appear to have a disorder in the organization of the sound system. Although their hearing is normal, they do not accurately perceive speech. Among other factors, it could be that an average speaking rate is too rapid for these children to process accurately. Their eyes glaze over and the words simply become noise.

Phonological impairment can have an impact upon other linguistic areas. For example, in the area of morphology, a student might drop the plural marker (*-s*) or the past-tense marker (*-ed*) because he or she does not perceive those phonemes when a speaker produces them in conversation (e.g., boats sailed). More importantly, in the area of semantics, a student with a phonological impairment might completely misinterpret a piece of information. One Landmark student thought sweaters are made of *wolf* rather than wool.

Imagine the perplexity, embarrassment, and frustration of students who, in their attempts to answer questions in the classroom or converse with friends, make phonological errors. Teachers can provide the most productive remediation by listening carefully and analyzing students' responses verbatim.

## Receptive and Expressive Errors

Students often demonstrate accurate processing (hearing) of a word but make phonological errors when attempting to reproduce that word. Five types of phonological errors occur in processing, speaking, or decoding.

### Types of Phonological Errors

| What Student Said | What Student Meant | Error Type |
| --- | --- | --- |
| Sit | Slit | Omission or deletion of a phoneme |
| Slit | Sit | Addition or insertion of a phoneme |
| Slit | Silt | Transposition or reversal of phonemes |
| Stit | Slit | Assimilation or repetition of a phoneme |
| Spit | Slit | Substitution of one phoneme for another |

Most of the errors cited in the examples that follow derive from conversations with students or tests of their oral language skills.

### *Receptive (Processing) Errors*

With processing or receptive errors, students mishear a word in spite of having normal hearing in pure-tone testing. As the contextual examples below illustrate, an error of just one phoneme in a word can cause a major change in meaning. In many cases, students "hear"—or at least opt for—a more familiar word.

    **Teacher**: Use "lunge" in a sentence.
    **Student**: The students *lunged* around all afternoon.

This student probably uses "lounge" and "lunge" interchangeably without detecting the difference in the single vowel sound.

    **Teacher**: Describe a "bare head."
    **Student**: (Gestures and laughs.) Nothing up there between the ears.

    **Teacher**: Use "coax" in a sentence.
    **Student**: He put several *coats* of paint on the wall.

    **Teacher**: Did you drive through Pennsylvania on your trip?
    **Student**: Oh, no! I would never want to go to Pennsylvania!

In the third example above, the teacher learned that the student was thinking of Transylvania, with which he was probably familiar from stories about Dracula.

# Phonology

**Student**: Are you going to watch the college football playoffs? Most people think the Nebraska Corn *Huskies* are dogs, but they're not! They're really football players! (The student meant "Huskers.")

**Student**: My mom plants *bullets* in the spring. (The student meant "bulbs.")

**Teacher**: (Giving a vocabulary pretest in a literature class.) Define "rebel."

**Student**: Rebel: a little stone in a driveway or park.

**Teacher**: (Discussing harbor seals in a science class.)

**Student**: *Harvard* seals. All I hear about is Harvard. Does Harvard have to have its name on everything around here?

The table below summarizes and categorizes the contextual examples above. Letters between slashes (e.g., /ou/) are transcriptions of speech sounds.

## Examples of Receptive Errors

| What Student Heard | What Was Said | Type of Phonological Error |
| --- | --- | --- |
| Lounge | Lunge | Interior vowel substitution /ou/:/ŭ/ |
| Airhead | Bare head | Did not process initial consonant –:/b/ |
| Coats | Coax | Interior consonant substitution /t/:/k/ |
| Transylvania | Pennsylvania | Substituted most of first syllable in four-syllable word /trăn/:/pĕn/ |
| Corn Huskies | Corn Huskers | Interior phoneme substitution /ēē/:/er/ |
| Bullets | Bulbs | Addition plus substitution of interior phonemes /ĕt/:/b/ |
| Pebble | Rebel | Initial consonant substitution /p/:/r/ |
| Harvard | Harbor | Interior phoneme substitution plus addition of final phoneme /v/:/b/ + /d/:– |

## *Expressive (Production/Word Retrieval) Errors*

The table below provides examples of expressive errors in context and classifies them according to type. The last three examples in the table include a semantic component as well. Specifically, one student associated "Barnes" with "barns" to produce "stable" instead of "Noble." Another student incorrectly chose "navigator" as a synonym for "narrator." In the last example, the student's error involves place.

## Examples of Expressive Errors in Context

| What Student Said | What Student Meant to Say | Type of Phonological Error |
| --- | --- | --- |
| Remember, Jane, patience is a *virgin*. | Virtue | Substitution /jin/:/choo/ |
| That's because of the *disability* rule. | Divisibility | Omission plus substitution –/vi/ + /s/:/z/ |
| In an *error* of Roman time … | Era | Addition[1] /ər/:/ə/ |
| They didn't have that book at Barnes and *Stable*. | Noble | Substitution /stā/:/nō/ |
| He's the *navigator* of the story. | Narrator | Substitution /vig/:/r/ |
| Instead of going to Christy's, can we go to the store in *Mongolia*? | Magnolia | Transposition plus substitution /ng/:/gn/ + /ŏ/:/ă/ |

## Word-Level Examples of Expressive Errors

| What Student Said | What Student Meant to Say | Type of Phonological Error |
| --- | --- | --- |
| Shing slot | Sling shot | Transposition /sh/–/sl/:/sl/–/sh/ |
| Codorado | Colorado | Assimilation /d/, /d/:/l/, /d/ |
| Death | Deaf | Substitution /th/:/f/ |
| Servus | Versus | Transposition /s/–/v/:/v/–/s/ |

---

[1] Bostonians commonly add an *r* to most words that end in a vowel, both in spoken and written expression.

| What Student Said | What Student Meant to Say | Type of Phonological Error |
|---|---|---|
| Photograthree | Photography | Substitution plus insertion /th/:/f/ + /r/:– |
| Extercise | Exercise | Insertion /t/:/–/ |
| Pervered | Preserved | Reversals plus omission /per/:/pre/; /ver/:/erv/ + /–/:/z/ |
| Lopice station | Police station | Transposition /lop/:/pol/ |
| Tempescope | Telescope | Substitution plus insertion /mp/:/l/ |
| Lippiphines | Phillipines | Transpositions /lipif/:/filip/ |
| 'Clip | Eclipse | Omissions /–/:/ee/ /–/:/s/ |

Frequently, a student with word retrieval deficits appears to retrieve from neighboring words in phonological storage before producing the target word. For example, one student who was asked to label a scroll produced "scrab-scroble-scroll." This student had studied Egypt and, in producing "scrab," was probably combining "scarab" with the familiar "scab." In producing "scroble," he retained the *scr-* cluster, knew an *l* belonged in the word, and probably made a linkage to the board game "Scrabble." Only then did this student produce the correct word, "scroll."

The rest of this chapter presents specific goals and objectives for phonological development. The goals are idealized, inferring mastery, though most students probably will not attain mastery. The objectives, on the other hand, are largely presented in developmental order (in order of difficulty). This way, the teacher can identify an objective along the spectrum of difficulty as a realistic target for a given student. For example, one goal is for students to process and articulate multisyllabic words, and one of its objectives is to identify the accented syllable within a dictated multisyllabic word. This objective might be the realistic goal for a student who is not likely to demonstrate mastery of multisyllabic words within the school year.

# Phonological Awareness

## *Goal*

The student will demonstrate awareness of the constituent sounds of words, which can be distinguished in three ways:

- by syllables (e.g., /bŏok/)
- by onsets and rimes (e.g., /b/ and /ŏok/)
- by phonemes (e.g., /b/ and /ŏo/ and /k/)

## *Background*

An absolute prerequisite to decoding is phonological awareness, including accurate auditory perception of the forty-five or so phonemes in the English language. The assumption that children enter any reading program equipped with this ability has resulted in tragic and unnecessary failure in both teaching and learning. Countless children have entered school full of hope and excitement about reading only to fail due to lack of phonological awareness, which often goes unidentified.

Reading is not the only area affected. Oral information in the form of directions, lectures, discussion, and conversation is also severely impacted. If the receptive element is faulty, deficits in expressive language follow. When students do not accurately perceive constituent sounds, how can they accurately reproduce words?

Findings from copious research into phonological awareness in the 1980s finally reached educators in the 1990s. The objectives below were developed from Torgesen and Bryant (1994) and Rosner (1988).

## *Objectives*

The student will: ·

- identify words that rhyme
- identify two smaller words in a compound word; for example, "birth" plus "day" in "birthday"
- repeat a dictated compound word, then produce the first word only; for example, "Say 'Batman'. Now say it again without 'man.'"
- repeat a dictated compound word, then produce the second word only; for example, "Say 'Batman.' Now say it again without 'Bat.'"

*Phonology*

- repeat a dictated regular two-syllable word, then produce the first syllable only; for example, "Say 'basket.' Now say it again without /kət/"

- repeat a dictated regular two-syllable word, then produce the second syllable only

- repeat a dictated three-syllable word, then produce the last two syllables only

- blend a dictated onset plus rime (i.e., vowel plus following consonants) into a word (e.g., /k/ + /ăt/ = cat)

- identify two words that begin with the same phoneme; for example, "pet" and "pick"

- blend separate phonemes into a word (e.g., /k/ + /ă/ + /t/ = cat)

- segment a word into separate phonemes (e.g., tap = /t/ + /ă/ + /p/)

- repeat a dictated one-syllable word, then produce the rime only; for example, "Say 'boat.' Say it again, but take away /b/."

- repeat a dictated one-syllable word, then produce the word without its final phoneme; for example, for the word "lake," the correct response is /lā/

- repeat a dictated one-syllable word containing an initial consonant blend, then produce the word minus the initial consonant; for example, "Say 'stop.' Say it again, but take away /s/"; the correct response is /tŏp/

- repeat a dictated one-syllable word containing an initial consonant blend, then produce the word without the second consonant; for example, for the word "stick," the correct response is /sĭk/

- repeat two-syllable word pairs; for example, "faction" and "fraction"

- repeat three-syllable word pairs; for example, "invention" and "prevention"

# Auditory Discrimination of Phonemes

## *Goal*

The student will auditorily discriminate the English phonemes and demonstrate competence describing the kinesthetic properties of each phoneme.

## *Background*

Auditory discrimination of phonemes is an element of phonological awareness. The Lindamood® Phoneme Sequencing (LiPS) program incorporates a strong kinesthetic feedback component and proven methods for self-correcting errors (Lindamood and Lindamood 1998). In LiPS, students initially demonstrate auditory knowledge through nonorthographic representation. They use colored blocks to indicate same or different, number, and the order of phonemes they hear within a syllable. As a result, there is no "contamination" from their earlier misunderstanding of orthographic representations.

Landmark students with moderate to severe phonological deficits appear to benefit greatly from LiPS tutorials. Landmark staff have noted substantial improvement in these students' word attack skills.

While lists differ slightly, there are approximately forty-five phonemes in the English language. The table below presents transcription of speech sounds between slashes (e.g., /sh/). It also includes a few phonemic combinations (e.g., vowel plus *r*). It excludes the allophones, which are variant members of a phonemic family that depend on the phonemes surrounding them (e.g., the final /n/ in "mission" vs. the initial /n/ in "no").

The table is compiled from the International Phonetic Alphabet; however, it replaces that alphabet's symbols with diacritics from *The American Heritage Dictionary of the English Language*, 4th edition. Although these diacritics are less precise than phonetic transcription, they are adequate here. Additional resources are Crystal (1995) and Van Riper and Emerick (1984).

# Phonemes

## Consonants

| Voiceless | | Voiced | | Nasals (Voiced) | | Vowel-Like Liquids (Voiced) | |
|---|---|---|---|---|---|---|---|
| p | pit, stop | b | back, rub | m | mat, game | l | late, bill |
| t | tab, cat | d | dog, wood | n | no, any | r | rag, or |
| k | key, lock | g | go, leg | ng | ring, ankle | | |
| f | feed, beef | v | van, have | | | | |
| th | thin, bath | th | this, bathe | | | *Semi-Vowels (Glides)* | |
| s | sit, less | z | zip, buzz | | | w | way, swam |
| sh | shot, dash | zh | vision, measure | | | y | you, yelp |
| ch | chat, rich | j | just, ridge | | | | |
| h | hot, perhaps | | | | | | |
| hw | what, why | | | | | | |

## Vowels

| ē | eat, bee | ĕ | Ed | ô | awe, jaw | o͞o | boot, to, crude |
| ĭ | if | ă | at, smack | ō | rope, open | ə | about, wanted, |
| ā | ate, trait | ŭ | mug, mother | o͝o | look, put | | family, famous |
| ī | pipe, sight | ŏ | mop | | | | |

## Vowel plus R

| ür | bird, early, fur, sir | ôr | shore, born | ə + r | butter, color, solar | är | barn, far |

## Diphthongs

| ou | cow, out | oi | toy, boil | yo͞o | use, few | āĭ | May, weigh |
| ī | my, eye | ō | Joe, dough | | | | |

## Diphthongs (Vowel plus R)

| ār | wear, fair | o͞or | lure, moor | ēr | beer, weird | īr | wire, tire |
| our | flower, dour | | | | | | |

The long vowels ō, ā, and ī become diphthongs when not followed by a consonant. Also, the vowel phonemes preceding *r* and *l* are greatly distorted. Students might therefore judge the number of syllables because they hear two vowel sounds; for example, /owəl/ (owl), /owər/ (hour), and /tiər/ (tire). Students making such observations should be given credit for careful listening. The *Random House Dictionary of the English Language* (unabridged) reports "owl" as having one syllable, "hour" as having one or two syllables, and "tire" as having two syllables.

## Objectives

The student will:

- discriminate between voiceless and voiced (i.e., quiet and noisy) speech phonemes and demonstrate strategies for making such discriminations, such as placing his or her hand on the throat to feel the absence or presence of vibration in the vocal cords

- explain kinesthetic properties of target phoneme(s); for example, "For /t/, my tongue hits the ridge behind my top teeth, and I quickly pull it away. It's a quiet sound. I don't use my voice."

- use nonorthographic representation (e.g., colored blocks) to:

  - identify same or different when listening to production of phoneme pairs (e.g., /p/, /b/ vs. /b/, /b/)

  - identify the number of phonemes presented (e.g., /d/, /d/ is two phonemes and /d/, /d/, /d/ is three phonemes)

  - identify the sequence of phonemes heard in a series (e.g., /p/, /p/, /g/ and /g/, /p/, /g/)

  - discriminate between and identify initial consonant phonemes within dictated single syllables (e.g., <u>m</u>e and <u>b</u>e)

  - discriminate between and identify final consonant phonemes within dictated single syllables (e.g., e<u>p</u> and e<u>d</u>)

  - discriminate between and identify dictated short-vowel phonemes plus orthographic (letter) symbols of vowel phonemes

  - discriminate between and identify long-vowel phonemes and short-vowel phonemes (e.g., mat and mate)

  - discriminate between and identify consonant digraphs heard within dictated single syllables (e.g., <u>sh</u>in and <u>ch</u>in)

  - discriminate between and identify initial consonant blends within dictated single syllables (e.g., <u>pr</u>op and <u>pl</u>op)

  - discriminate between and identify final consonant blends within dictated single syllables (e.g., pa<u>st</u> and pa<u>nt</u>)

- describe kinesthetic properties of vowel diphthongs (e.g., "sliding" from one mouth position to another while producing single-vowel phoneme)

- associate vowel diphthong phonemes with orthographic (letter) representations (e.g., ow or ou, oi or oy, and u as in the words "use" and "fuse," and ew as in the word "few")

- discriminate between and identify three-consonant phonemic clusters (e.g., string and spring)

- identify same or different, number, and order of phonemes dictated within one syllable (real or nonsense)

# Articulation of Phonemes

## *Goal*

The student will accurately produce target phoneme(s) in a five-minute conversation with parents, a clinician, or a peer outside of the clinical setting.

## *Background*

The objectives below are included for informational purposes only. They are not intended as how-to instructions for the classroom teacher. They are intended to model micro-units for articulation therapy. Lispers will not replace "thoup" with "soup" until they gradually integrate accurate speech production through auditory training, rehearsal of nonsense words, and other strategies. These objectives are drawn from Yates and Chapin (1983).

## *Objectives*

The student will:

- discriminate between the clinician's correct and incorrect production of target phonemes

- self-monitor for correct and incorrect production of target phonemes using an audiotape recorder

- recognize and distinguish between kinesthetic properties of target phonemes and error phonemes (e.g., upper teeth on lower lip for /f/ vs. tongue between teeth for /th/)

- produce target phonemes in isolation during forty trials

- produce nonsense syllables containing target phonemes in multiple positions (e.g., initial, medial, and final) during forty trials (e.g., ŏth, thŏ, ŏthŏ)

- produce target phonemes in initial positions of words, given clinician modeling

- produce target phonemes in final position of words, given clinician modeling

- produce target phonemes in medial position of words, given clinician modeling

- produce target phonemes in consonant blends within words, given clinician modeling
- produce target phonemes while reading sentences
- produce target phonemes during a five-minute oral reading activity
- produce target phonemes while generating sentences from picture prompts
- produce target phonemes in a structured speaking situation
- produce target phonemes during a five-minute conversation with the clinician in the clinical setting
- produce target phonemes during a five-minute conversation with the clinician outside of the clinical setting
- produce target phonemes during a five-minute conversation with individuals other than the clinician in the school setting
- produce target phonemes in conversation with individuals other than the clinician outside the school setting

# Articulation of Multisyllabic Words

## *Goal*

The student will process and articulate multisyllabic words.

## *Background*

Some children do not process spoken words accurately; for example, they hear "Harvard seals" when the spoken words are "harbor seals." Other children who appear to process spoken words accurately know exactly what they want to say but cannot seem to get their mouths into motion to say it, and their speech sounds somewhat garbled. Such children might be dyspraxic. *Dyspraxia* is the "disruption of the capacity to program voluntarily the production and sequencing of speech sounds" (Van Riper and Emerick 1984). The brain signal to the articulators (tongue, jaw, and lips) is interrupted. Some expressive errors listed in the introduction to this chapter are characteristic of dyspraxic speech (e.g., "lopice station," "exterise," "Lippiphines," and "Codorado"), while others are word retrieval errors.

When conducting phonological exercises with preliterate students, it is important to be flexible with diphthongs. The rule is one vowel sound per syllable, but there are minor variations to consider.

- People actually produce schwas (ə) before /l/ and /r/.

- People produce and hear diphthongs preceding /l/ or /r/ as two vowel sounds; therefore, preliterate students often perceive certain words as two-syllable words (e.g., owl, hour, boil, Yule, tire, and tile). Further, dictionaries are not consistent. "Tire" and "hour" have one syllable in one dictionary and two syllables in another.

- People produce diphthongs preceding consonants other than /l/ and /r/ as one vowel sound. The words "out," "oink," "toy," "Ute," and "ice" have one syllable.

## *Objectives*

The student will:

- demonstrate knowledge that every syllable in English contains a single vowel sound (e.g., "eat" has two vowels and one vowel sound)

*Landmark School, Inc.*

*Phonology*

- distinguish correct from incorrect production of multisyllabic words by the instructor
- identify the number of syllables in dictated words (as the student demonstrates accuracy, the length of the dictated words should progress from one to five syllables)
- identify the sequence of syllables in dictated words
- isolate specific syllables in dictated words (e.g., the second syllable in "important")
- write separate syllables from dictated multisyllabic words
- rehearse production of multisyllabic words via forward- (e.g., fan-, fantas-, fantastic) or backward-chaining (e.g., -tic, -tastic, fantastic)
- self-monitor for correct and incorrect production of multisyllabic words using an audiotape recorder
- produce a series of multisyllabic words that contain a target phoneme in the identical position in each word (e.g., telephone, telegraph, and television)
- produce multisyllabic words in oral recitation
- write selected multisyllabic words that are within his or her decoding range
- rehearse identification of the accented syllable by placing felt squares in a row (one felt for each syllable), then moving the felt representing the accented syllable above the other felts in the row
- rehearse identification of the accented syllable by listening to the instructor's change in pitch when "humming" out the syllables (e.g., Vermont is hm-HM and Texas is HM-hm)
- identify the accented syllable within a dictated multisyllabic word
- identify the number of syllables in a dictated sentence (up to fifteen syllables)
- write dictation of sentences containing five words
- write dictation of sentences containing ten to fifteen words

# Responding to Unintelligible Speech in the Classroom

## *Goal*

The teacher will implement strategies for better understanding a student who produces unintelligible speech in the classroom.

## *Background*

Successful group discussions involve all students, including those who are difficult to understand because they mumble, talk too fast, or have speech disorders. When these students express themselves, the teacher is challenged to interpret messages that can be unintelligible. If the teacher asks them to repeat themselves too many times, these students will eventually withdraw from discussions altogether. Strategies that Landmark teachers use in the classroom are provided below. The goal is to demonstrate support for students while interpreting their messages.

## *Teaching Strategies*

The instructor will:

- ask questions for clarification, such as:
    - "If I understand correctly, you said …"
    - "Excuse me. I didn't hear it. Could you say it another way?"
    - "Could you say that more slowly?"
    - "Could you say that more loudly?"
    - "Do you mean _____ or _____?"
- paraphrase the response; for example, "So you're saying …"
- frame the request within a compliment; for example, "I want to hear what you said." or "I think what you said was really important. I want to hear it."
- say, "I'm having trouble understanding."
- model expected behavior by speaking slowly and clearly (at Landmark, the preferred oral reading rate to students is 120 words per minute; the speaking rate is somewhat faster; many professionals speak at more than 250 words per minute)

- give directions; for example, "Speak clearly and loudly, and face the listeners." or "Please slow down. I can't hear as fast as you're speaking."

- use humor; for example, "Eh?" or "Exag-ger-ate the sounds, George."

- move closer to the speaker and say, "I'm really sorry I couldn't hear you. There's too much noise in here."

- reverbalize and validate the student's ideas

- ask another student to reverbalize

- rather than provide more correction, say, "Oh, I see what you're saying."

- take the student aside later and discuss the specific difficulties in understanding his or her speech; also refer the student to the speech-language pathologist for further evaluation

- explain culturally idiosyncratic phraseology or figurative language, if appropriate; for example, an instructor said to a resident from another country, "Dry your clothes." and the resident put his hiking boots in the dryer

- provide phonemic, semantic, or gestural cues

- present an analogy between handwriting legibility and articulation

# Responding to Processing/Production Errors in the Classroom

## *Goal*

The instructor will analyze students' processing/production errors and micro-unit information as necessary to clarify students' misunderstandings.

## *Background*

Here is an actual classroom experience:

**Teacher**: Use "lunge" in a sentence.
**Student**: The students *lunged* around all afternoon.

This student did not discriminate /ou/ from /ŭ/ in medial positions of words. He had demonstrated decoding skills at an age-appropriate level and was slated for a college preparatory course (which he entered the next year) yet, at age fourteen, he continued to demonstrate deficits in phonological awareness. This persistent difficulty compromised his comprehension in conversing and reading. Had the above exchange not occurred, the error might have gone undetected.

Many students might pass pure-tone hearing screening tests but fail speech discrimination tests. Landmark has developed several strategies for handling such situations in the classroom. It is important to remember to speak slowly and clearly at all times.

## *Teaching Strategies*

The instructor will:

- provide some validation rather than the all-defeating "That's wrong."; for example, "That's very close. I may not have said it clearly."

- explore further, as by putting the word into context and repeating the question

- present sound-symbol cues:

  - write "lunge" and "lounge" on the board

  - ask, "Where do these two words differ?" (/ŭ/ vs. /ou/)

  - present other similar-sounding or -appearing words, such as "lunch" and "luge"

- clarify the miscue; for example, "What's that room where the kids hang out?"
- use gestural cues to act out the words
- use semantic cues in context; for example, "The fielder made a lunge for the ball."
- present word families and word associations for the meanings of each word
- ask for synonyms and antonyms of each, where applicable

# Bibliography of Instructional Materials

Adams, M.J., B.R. Foorman, I. Lundberg, and T. Beeler. *Phonemic Awareness in Young Children*. Baltimore: Paul H. Brooks Publishing, 1998.

Blockcolsky, V. *Book of Words –17,000 Words Selected by Vowels and Diphthongs*. Austin: PRO-ED, 1990.

———. *40,000 Selected Words Organized by Letter, Sound, and Syllable*. Austin: PRO-ED, 1990.

Bush, C. *Language Remediation and Expansion –150 Skill-Building Reference Lists*. Austin: PRO-ED, 1989.

———. *500 Thematic Lists and Activities*. Austin: PRO-ED, 1996.

Kisner, R., and B. Knowles. *Warm-Up Exercises—Calisthenics for the Brain*. Book 1. Eau Claire, WI: Thinking Publications, 1984.

———. *Warm-Up Exercises—Calisthenics for the Brain*. Book 2. Eau Claire, WI: Thinking Publications, 1985.

———. *Warm-Up Exercises—Calisthenics for the Brain*. Book 3. Eau Claire, WI: Thinking Publications, 1992.

Lazzari, A., and P. Peters. *HELP—Handbook of Exercises for Language Processing—Elementary*. Moline, IL: LinguiSystems, 1993.

Lindamood, C., and P. Lindamood. *Lindamood Auditory Conceptualization* Test (LAC). Novato, CA: Academic Therapy Publications, 1971.

Lindamood, P., and P. Lindamood. *The Lindamood Phoneme Sequencing Program for Reading, Spelling, and Speech—Teacher's Manual for the Classroom and Clinic*. Austin: PRO-ED, 1998.

Rosner, J. *Test of Auditory Analysis Skills (TAAS)*. Novato, CA: Academic Therapy Publications, 1988.

Torgesen, J.K., and B.R. Bryant. *Phonological Awareness Training for Reading—Training Manual*. Austin, TX: PRO-ED, 1994.

Wagner, R., J.K. Torgesen, and C. Rashette. *Comprehensive Test of Phonological Processing*. Austin: PRO-ED, 2000.

Yates, J., and B. Chapin. *Phonemic Context Articulation Program*. C.C. Publications, 1983.

CHAPTER 2

# MORPHOLOGY

## Introduction

A *morpheme* is the smallest meaningful unit of language. Morphemes fall into two categories: bound and free. *Bound morphemes* convey no meaning unless they are attached to nouns, verbs, or adjectives. Examples are the plural marker *-s*, the past-tense marker *-ed*, comparatives like *-er* and *-est*, prefixes like *re-* and *un-*, and suffixes like *-tion* and *-ness*. *Free morphemes* are words that cannot be further subdivided (e.g., car, man, and has).

Bound morphemes alter or enhance meaning in a very efficient way. They make distinctions in number (singular vs. plural), case (e.g., possessive), aspect (e.g., an auxiliary verb that indicates tense), and comparison (e.g., the comparative *-er* and the superlative *-est*). In the case of derivational suffixes, morphemes change the meaning of the base form as well as the grammatical role (e.g., sail/sail*or*). With prefixes, morphemes alter the meaning of the root word (e.g., enthusiastic/*un*enthusiastic).

The sequence in which morphological rules are covered in this chapter roughly follows that of normal development (Wiig and Semel 1984). By about age four, normally developing children apply their intuitive knowledge of morphological rules. One rule they discover by listening to people talk, for example, is to add *-ed* to a present-tense verb to form the past tense. Children then overgeneralize and apply the rule in every instance before they learn its numerous exceptions. A four-year-old might say, "I *heared* Ben say 'Mimi'" or "I *comed* into the house to get the train." By the age of five, most children learn ninety percent of the morphological rules they will use as adults without receiving explicit instruction (Shames, Wiig, and Secord 1994).

Children with language-based disabilities have difficulty with morphemes for several reasons.

- A child with a phonological impairment might not hear the less emphasized parts of words in conversation (e.g., can/can'_t_).

- A child with a reduced ability to process speech delivered at a normal rate might focus on the word root and lose the affix (point/_ap_point).

- If a child's short-term auditory memory is insufficient, parts of words receiving less stress are sacrificed while those receiving more stress are recalled; for example, (un)interested. The more

*Landmark School, Inc.*

complex and lengthy the utterance, the more likely the child will lose some essential part of a word.

- Some students have an overall pervasive delay in language development.
- Students for whom English is a second language, in particular, need intensive exposure to English morphology rules, which differ from the rules in their native languages.

This chapter follows the descriptive-developmental model for remediation endorsed by Paul (2000). Paul's model asks the instructor to describe the child's current level of language function in terms of form, meaning, and use. This evaluation is best made by listening carefully and recording each utterance. The best plan for remediation is to identify areas that need attention through the child's utterances in normal speech, then establish a corrective curriculum that reflects the normal pattern of development.

## Receptive and Expressive Errors

### Receptive (Processing) Errors

Even when students demonstrate pure-tone hearing within the normal range, they frequently fail to process the less audible morphemes in spontaneous speech. Evidence of these processing errors often appears in written dictation exercises. Here are three contextual examples:

**Teacher said**: The Celtics beat the Lakers.
**Student wrote**: The Celtic beat the Lakers.

**Teacher said**: He dragged his bag into the room.
**Student wrote**: He drag his bag into the room.

**Teacher said**: Harry's broom was broken.
**Student wrote**: Harry broom was broken.

The table below summarizes and categorizes the contextual examples above.

### Examples of Receptive Morphological Errors

| What Student Heard | What Was Said | Type of Morphological Error |
|---|---|---|
| Celtic | Celtics | Omission of plural marker -s |
| Drag | Dragged | Omission of past-tense marker -ed |
| Harry | Harry's | Omission of possessive marker -'s |

# Expressive (Production/Word Retrieval) Errors

## Examples of Expressive Errors in Context

| What Student Said | What Student Meant to Say | Type of Morphological Error |
|---|---|---|
| Why *is* the cookie jars broken? | Are | Did not apply noun-verb agreement |
| This is *a* easy job. | An | Used the article "a" before a word starting with a vowel |
| There are six *sheeps* in that pen. | Sheep | Used regular plural ending for irregular plural |
| I didn't *saw* him. | See | Confused irregular past tense with negative past tense |
| My niece almost *broken* that vase. | Broke | Confused irregular past tense with past participle |
| Snow is *frozed*, rain isn't. | Frozen | Combined regular and irregular past-tense verb forms |
| I *shooted* the ball into the basket. | Shot | Overgeneralized regular past tense |
| I *brang* cakes for my birthday. | Brought | Overgeneralized one irregular past-tense verb form |
| Scooter *tell* scary stories. | Tells | Did not use the third-person singular irregular verb form |
| The lamp used to *was* mine. | Be | Overgeneralized past tense |
| When I *didn't be* there . . . | Wasn't | Used incorrect auxiliary verb |
| It *doesn't* supposed to be that picture. | Isn't | Used incorrect auxiliary verb |
| I *was keep* on going. | Kept | Confused present and past participle |
| This picture has the *more* fish. | Most | Substituted the comparative for the superlative |

*Landmark School, Inc.*

| What Student Said | What Student Meant to Say | Type of Morphological Error |
| --- | --- | --- |
| He is *heaviest* than that girl. | Heavier | Substituted the superlative for the comparative |
| I *departed* the two kids who were fighting. | Separated | Inappropriate use of the prefix *de-* and word retrieval |
| That is a *containment*. | Container | Used the incorrect suffix |
| The mayor didn't *point* him to the office. | Appoint | Omitted the prefix |

The rest of this chapter presents specific goals and objectives for morphological development. The goals are idealized, inferring mastery, though most students probably will not attain mastery. The objectives, on the other hand, are largely presented in developmental order (in order of difficulty). This way, the teacher can identify an objective along the spectrum of difficulty as a realistic target for a given student. For example, the goal for "Irregular Past Tense of Verbs" is for the student to produce the irregular past tense of verbs accurately and demonstrate comprehension of the underlying rules. One of the objectives under this goal is for the student to produce the irregular past tense of verbs in sentence completion tasks. This objective might be used as a realistic goal for a student who is not likely to produce irregular past tense of verbs in spontaneous speech within the school year.

# Regular Noun Plurals

## *Goal*

The student will form regular noun plurals and demonstrate comprehension of the underlying rules.

## *Background*

Although students with language-based learning disabilities might demonstrate normal hearing in a pure-tone hearing test, they frequently falter when presented with speech-discrimination tasks. Many do not hear or process plural or past-tense word endings in conversation, decoding, or writing tasks.

## *Objectives*

The student will:

- auditorily distinguish between correct and incorrect regular noun plurals produced by the instructor while manipulating one or more objects (e.g., one card and two cards)

- auditorily discriminate voiceless /s/ from voiced /z/ phonemes (e.g., hats and cards)

- identify the presence of an extra sound (schwa /ə/, spelled *e*) in words ending in *-s*, *-ch*, or *-x* (e.g., dresses, pronounced /drĕsəz/; batches, pronounced /băchəz/; bushes, pronounced /bo͝oshəz/; and boxes, pronounced /bŏksəz/)

- auditorily discriminate voiceless /f/ from voiced /v/ when listening to singular and plural production of selected nouns (e.g., knife/knives)

- produce the singular or plural form of regular nouns, given pictures or objects

- self-monitor for accurate production of regular noun plurals using an audiotape recorder

- produce regular noun plurals in oral and written sentence completion tasks

- produce regular noun plurals within verbally formulated original sentences

- produce regular noun plurals in written exercises
- proofread for accurate production of regular noun plurals in written exercises
- produce regular noun plurals in spontaneous speaking and writing

# Noun-Verb Agreement

## *Goal*

The student will accurately produce noun-verb agreement in spontaneous speech and written expression and demonstrate comprehension of the underlying rules.

## *Background*

It is important for teachers to emphasize the auditory part of this task before asking students to produce noun-verb agreement. Even though students might have normal hearing in pure-tone auditory tests, they frequently do not identify or discriminate among plural inflections (/s/, /z/, or /əz/) in structured (classroom) or conversational speech settings.

## *Objectives*

The student will:

- auditorily distinguish between correct and incorrect production of noun-verb combinations generated by the instructor while observing action, whether in photos or with objects (e.g., otters swim/otters swims and cars race/cars races)

- formulate sentences that include regular noun plurals plus action verbs; for example, "Cats run." and "Foxes hide."

- self-monitor for correct production of noun-verb agreement using an audiotape recorder

- classify regular and irregular plural nouns in combination with correct verb forms

- produce regular and irregular plural nouns with plural verb forms (e.g., boys watch and men watch)

- include noun-verb agreement in oral or written sentence completion tasks; for example, "Let's go to the aquarium and watch the otters _____ (swim, swims)."

- include noun-verb agreement in oral or written cloze tasks; for example, "Sometimes he _____ (ride, rides) his bike to school."

- include noun-verb agreement when verbally formulating original sentences
- include noun-verb agreement when generating sentences in written exercises
- include noun-verb agreement in spontaneous speech
- include noun-verb agreement in spontaneous writing

# Definite and Indefinite Articles

## *Goal*

The student will produce definite and indefinite articles and demonstrate comprehension of the underlying rules.

## *Background*

*Articles* add subtle meaning to a noun phrase, as in "Did you feed the penguin?" vs. "Did you feed a penguin?". The *definite article* is "the," and the *indefinite articles* are "a" and "an." In rapid speech, indefinite articles might be unstressed and not easily heard, or they might be heard as part of the noun (e.g., anapple/an apple). The most common error in producing indefinite articles is substituting "a" for "an" before a word that begins with a vowel (e.g., a owl/an owl and a apple/an apple).

## *Objectives*

The student will:

- recognize that the definite article "the" refers to someone or something in particular (definite information)

- recognize that the indefinite articles "a" and "an" refer to one of a general group (indefinite information)

- discriminate between correct and incorrect use of definite and indefinite articles in familiar noun phrases dictated by the instructor (e.g., I have a uncle/I have an uncle and I have a sister/I have an sister)

- classify nouns by their beginning letters or phonemes (consonants or vowels) in terms of indefinite articles (e.g., eagle and owl vs. fox and cheetah)

- classify adjective and noun phrases by their beginning letters or phonemes (e.g., a bald eagle and an endangered species)

- select the appropriate indefinite article ("a" or "an") in phrase completion tasks (e.g., a squid and an octopus)

- select nouns to match articles in sentence completion tasks (e.g., I saw a . . .)

- verbally generate original sentences in response to visual stimuli, such as photos and drawings
- use definite and indefinite articles within oral cloze tasks; for example, "The blue whale is _____ (a, an) enormous animal." and "The orca chased _____ (a, an) seal."
- use definite and indefinite articles in oral narratives
- generate original written sentences in response to visual stimuli, such as photos and drawings
- use definite and indefinite articles in spontaneous speech
- use definite and indefinite articles in spontaneous writing

# Noun Possessives

## *Goal*

The student will produce singular and plural noun possessives and demonstrate comprehension of the underlying rules.

## *Background*

The student with language-based learning disabilities does not consistently identify the presence of the /s/ phoneme at the end of words, especially in running speech.

## *Objectives*

The student will:

- recognize auditory identity of singular and plural when listening to noun possessives generated by the instructor (e.g., boy's bat/boys' bat and boy's bats/boys' bats)
- identify the schwa sound when listening to the possessive form of nouns ending in /s/ or /z/ (e.g., "Phyllis's" sounds like /fĭlusəz/))
- identify visual differences in the spelling of possessives, depending upon his or her level of literacy (e.g., whales' tails/whale's tail and box's contents/boxes' contents)
- produce the noun possessive form in phrase and sentence completion tasks
- include the noun possessive form when verbally formulating original sentences
- produce the noun possessive form in structured writing exercises
- include the noun possessive form in spontaneous speech
- include the noun possessive form in spontaneous writing

# Irregular Noun Plurals

## Goal

The student will demonstrate competence in the use of selected irregular noun plurals. The number of irregular noun plurals the student can use should increase as the student's vocabulary increases.

## Background

It is important to ensure accurate auditory perception of plurals before expecting accurate spelling of noun plurals. Even then, the sound won't necessarily predict the spelling (e.g., woman/women). We seem to have inherited irregular plurals from Old English and Germanic languages, as well as other sources. When in doubt, teachers and students should check the dictionary.

The tables below provide examples of irregular noun plurals.

### Singular Different from Plural

| | | | |
|---|---|---|---|
| Child, children | Louse, lice | Mouse, mice | Tooth, teeth |
| Foot, feet | Man, men | Ox, oxen | Woman, women |
| Goose, geese | | | |

### Singular Same as Plural

| | | | |
|---|---|---|---|
| Balinese | Fish[2] | Reindeer | Species |
| Buffalo | Japanese | Salmon | Swiss |
| Chinese | Moose | Sheep | Trout |
| Deer | | | |

### Foreign Words[3]

| | |
|---|---|
| Alumnus (man), alumni (men) | Datum, data |
| Alumna (woman), alumnae (women) | Formula, formulas (preferred) or formulae |
| Agenda, agendas (informal) | Index, indices or indexes |
| Appendix, appendices or appendixes | |
| Crisis, crises | |

---

[2] When referring to different species, the plural is "fishes."
[3] The plural is formed as in the original language or by adding *s* or *es*.

Landmark School, Inc.

## Compound Nouns

Drive-in, drive-ins  Standby, standbys
Six-year-old, six-year-olds

## Invariable Nouns[4]

### Singular-Only Nouns[5]

| Billiards | Darts | Mathematics | Physics |
| Civics | Economics | Mumps | Skittles |

### Plural-Only Nouns

| Binoculars | Jeans | Scissors | (Swimming) trunks |
| Clothes | Pants | Shorts | Trousers |
| Glasses | Pliers | Spectacles | |

### Intrinsic Plural Nouns

| Cattle | People | Poultry | Vermin |
| Livestock | Police | | |

# Objectives

The student will:

- identify common words that undergo a major change in sound and spelling from singular to plural form (e.g., man/men and mouse/mice)

- identify the unchanging form for some nouns, whether they are singular or plural (e.g., deer, fish, sheep, reindeer, buffalo, moose, spaghetti, Chinese, and species)

- identify nouns that are plural-only (e.g., pants, which accommodate two legs, and glasses, which accommodate two eyes)

- identify nouns that are intrinsically plural (e.g., people, cattle)

- auditorily discriminate between correct and incorrect irregular noun plurals produced by the instructor

---

[4]Invariable nouns do not change in form for singular or plural. Some are always singular; the others are always plural.
[5]Singular-only nouns are misleading because they end in *s* and appear to be plural but take a singular verb.

- classify regular and irregular noun plurals in response to stimuli, such as objects and photos
- produce irregular noun plurals in phrase and sentence completion tasks
- self-monitor for correct production of irregular noun plurals using an audiotape recorder
- produce irregular noun plurals appropriate to vocabulary level in orally formulated original sentences
- produce irregular noun plurals in structured writing exercises
- produce irregular noun plurals in spontaneous speech
- proofread for accuracy of irregular noun plurals in written work
- produce irregular noun plurals in spontaneous writing

# Present Progressive Tense of Verbs

## *Goal*

The student will produce the present progressive tense of verbs (for example, "Superman is flying.") and demonstrate comprehension of the underlying rules.

## *Background*

The present progressive verb form is one of the earliest verb forms used by young children (Cazden and Bellugi 1970). Watch for older children who use the present progressive tense instead of the appropriate past tense when retelling a story (e.g., he is going/he went).

## *Objectives*

The student will:

- imitate correct present progressive-tense verb inflection produced by the instructor
- produce present progressive-tense verb inflection in response to such stimuli as gestures, manipulation of objects, and action photos (e.g., hopping and writing)
- self-monitor for correct production of the present progressive tense using an audiotape recorder
- produce the present progressive tense in original sentences in response to stimuli
- produce the present progressive tense while narrating a picture story
- formulate sentences containing the present progressive tense in structured exercises without stimuli
- produce the present progressive tense in structured writing exercises
- produce the present progressive tense in spontaneous speech
- produce the present progressive tense in spontaneous writing

# Third-Person-Singular, Present-Tense Verbs

## Goal

The student will produce third-person-singular, regular present-tense verb forms (e.g., he walks, he runs, and he marches) and demonstrate comprehension of the underlying rules.

## Background

Landmark students do not consistently identify the /s/, /z/, or /əz/ phonemes at the end of words, especially in running speech. Some students omit this third-person-singular marker in conversation.

## Objectives

The student will:

- imitate correct third-person-singular, present-tense verb inflection produced by the instructor

- distinguish between correct and incorrect production of a third-person-singular, present-tense verb form describing an action by the instructor (e.g., he run/he runs)

- produce a third-person-singular, present-tense verb inflection given such cues as gestures, manipulation of objects, and viewing action photos (e.g., marches and scoots)

- self-monitor for correct production of the third-person-singular present tense using an audiotape recorder

- produce the third-person-singular present tense in original sentences in response to stimuli

- produce the third-person-singular, present-tense verb inflection while narrating a picture story

- formulate sentences containing the third-person-singular, present-tense verb inflection in structured exercises without stimuli

- produce the third-person-singular, present-tense verb inflection in structured writing exercises

*Landmark School, Inc.*

- produce the third-person-singular, present-tense verb inflection in spontaneous speech
- produce the third-person-singular, present-tense verb inflection in spontaneous writing

# Past Tense of Verbs

## Goal

The student will accurately produce the regular past tense of verbs (e.g., sanded and walked) and demonstrate comprehension of the underlying rules.

## Background

Landmark students do not consistently identify the presence of the /t/ or /d/ phoneme as a morphological marker of past tense at the end of a verb. It is important to incorporate auditory discrimination tasks into introductory lessons to ensure students' awareness of these morphemes.

As new words enter the lexicon, such as "fax," the conventional *-ed* ending is used to form the past tense; for example, "I faxed the document to the office."

## Objectives

The student will:

- distinguish between correct and incorrect production of past-tense verb forms by the instructor
- discriminate between a voiceless phoneme /t/ (e.g., kicked, pronounced /kĭkt/) and a voiced phoneme /d/ (e.g., lined, pronounced /līnd/) when listening to the instructor produce past-tense verb forms
- identify the addition of a phoneme (schwa), /ə/, when converting one-syllable verbs that end in /t/ or /d/ (e.g., wanted, rated, sanded, and raided)
- produce the past tense of verbs when verbally describing actions associated with stimuli (e.g., bodily motion, manipulation of objects, and action photos)
- self-monitor for correct production of past tense of verbs using an audiotape recorder
- produce the past tense of verbs in sentence completion tasks
- produce the past tense of verbs while narrating sequential picture stories

- produce the past tense of verbs while relating an experience in a structured assignment
- produce the past tense of verbs in structured writing exercises
- produce the past tense of verbs in spontaneous speech
- produce the past tense of verbs in spontaneous writing

# Irregular Past Tense of Verbs

## *Goal*

The student will accurately produce the irregular past tense of verbs (e.g., rode and broke) and demonstrate comprehension of the underlying rules.

## *Background*

Irregular verb forms should be taught in small, manageable groups. The focus should be upon verbs that students use most frequently in their speaking vocabulary, followed by verbs that frequently occur in literature the student can comprehend when read aloud. For the teacher's convenience, the irregular verbs below are divided into nine tables that reflect general categories (Crystal 1995).

The past participle requires a helping or auxiliary verb, such as "is," "are," "was," "were," "have," "has," "had," and "have been." If students practice past participles aloud, they should also recite the helping verbs (e.g., have swung).

### Vowel Remains and Word Ending Changes for Past Tense and Past Participle

| Infinitive | Past Tense | Past Participle |
|---|---|---|
| Bend | Bent | Bent |
| Build | Built | Built |
| Have | Had | Had |
| Lend | Lent | Lent |
| Make | Made | Made |
| Send | Sent | Sent |
| Spend | Spent | Spent |

### Regular Past Tense; Add *n* for Past Participle

| Infinitive | Past Tense | Past Participle |
|---|---|---|
| Swell | Swelled | Swollen |

*Landmark School, Inc.*

## Vowel and Word Ending Change for Past Tense and Past Participle

| Infinitive | Past Tense | Past Participle |
|---|---|---|
| Bring | Brought | Brought |
| Catch | Caught | Caught |
| Creep | Crept | Crept |
| Feel | Felt | Felt |
| Hear | Heard | Heard |
| Keep | Kept | Kept |
| Kneel | Knelt | Knelt |
| Leave | Left | Left |
| Lose | Lost | Lost |
| Mean | Meant | Meant |
| Say | Said | Said |
| Sell | Sold | Sold |
| Sleep | Slept | Slept |
| Sweep | Swept | Swept |
| Teach | Taught | Taught |
| Tell | Told | Told |
| Think | Thought | Thought |
| Weep | Wept | Wept |

## Vowel Changes; Add *n* for Past Participle

| Infinitive | Past Tense | Past Participle |
|---|---|---|
| Bite | Bit | Bitten |
| Break | Broke | Broken |
| Choose | Chose | Chosen |
| Forget | Forgot | Forgotten |
| Freeze | Froze | Frozen |
| Get | Got | Gotten |
| Hide | Hid | Hidden |
| Lie | Lay | Lain |
| Speak | Spoke | Spoken |
| Steal | Stole | Stolen |
| Swear | Swore | Sworn |
| Tear | Tore | Torn |
| Wear | Wore | Worn |
| Weave | Wove | Woven |

*Landmark School, Inc.*

## Vowel Changes; Add *n* to Present Tense for Past Participle

| Infinitive | Past Tense | Past Participle |
|---|---|---|
| Blow | Blew | Blown |
| Draw | Drew | Drawn |
| Eat | Ate | Eaten |
| Fall | Fell | Fallen |
| Give | Gave | Given |
| Grow | Grew | Grown |
| Know | Knew | Known |
| See | Saw | Seen |
| Shake | Shook | Shaken |
| Take | Took | Taken |
| Throw | Threw | Thrown |

## Word Remains in All Forms

| Infinitive | Past Tense | Past Participle |
|---|---|---|
| Beat | Beat | Beat (or beaten) |
| Bet | Bet | Bet |
| Burst | Burst | Burst |
| Cost | Cost | Cost |
| Cut | Cut | Cut |
| Hurt | Hurt | Hurt |
| Let | Let | Let |
| Put | Put | Put |
| Set | Set | Set |
| Shut | Shut | Shut |
| Split | Split | Split |
| Spread | Spread | Spread |
| Sweat | Sweat | Sweat |
| Wet | Wet | Wet |

## Vowel Sound Changes and Word Ending Remains for Past Tense and Past Participle

| Infinitive | Past Tense | Past Participle |
|---|---|---|
| Dig | Dug | Dug |
| Feed | Fed | Fed |
| Find | Found | Found |
| Fight | Fought | Fought |
| Fling | Flung | Flung |

Landmark School, Inc.

*Morphology*

| Infinitive | Past Tense | Past Participle |
|---|---|---|
| Grind | Ground | Ground |
| Lead | Led | Led |
| Light | Lit | Lit |
| Read | Read | Read |
| Sit | Sat | Sat |
| Shine | Shone | Shone |
| Shoot | Shot | Shot |
| Slide | Slid | Slid |
| Spin | Spun | Spun |
| Stand | Stood | Stood |
| Sting | Stung | Stung |
| String | Strung | Strung |
| Swing | Swung | Swung |
| Understand | Understood | Understood |
| Win | Won | Won |
| Wind | Wound | Wound |

## Past Tense and Past Participle Differ

| Infinitive | Past Tense | Past Participle |
|---|---|---|
| Begin | Began | Begun |
| Do | Did | Done |
| Drink | Drank | Drunk |
| Drive | Drove | Driven |
| Fly | Flew | Flown |
| Go | Went | Gone |
| Ride | Rode | Ridden |
| Ring | Rang | Rung |
| Rise | Rose | Risen |
| Shrink | Shrank | Shrunk |
| Sing | Sang | Sung |
| Sink | Sank | Sunk |
| Spring | Sprang | Sprung |
| Swim | Swam | Swum |
| Write | Wrote | Written |

## Exceptions

| Infinitive | Past Tense | Past Participle |
|---|---|---|
| Come | Came | Come |
| Dive | Dived (or dove) | Dived |
| Run | Ran | Run |

*Landmark School, Inc.*

## Objectives

The student will:

- distinguish between correct and incorrect irregular past-tense forms in sentences beginning with time cues produced by the instructor; for example, "Yesterday I eated/ate lunch at school."

- distinguish between correct and incorrect irregular past-tense verb forms in sentences ending with time cues produced by the instructor; for example, "I swimmed/swam last summer."

- distinguish between correct and incorrect irregular past-tense verb forms in sentences without time cues produced by the instructor; for example, "I drived/drove to school."

- produce the irregular past tense of verbs when verbally describing actions in association with stimuli, such as gestures, manipulation of objects, and action photos; for example, "I sat.", "She stood.", "We rode.", and "They drove."

- self-monitor for correct production of irregular past tense of verbs using an audiotape recorder

- produce the irregular past tense of verbs in sentence completion tasks

- produce the irregular past tense of verbs while narrating sequential picture stories

- produce the irregular past tense of verbs while relating an experience in a structured assignment

- produce the irregular past tense of verbs in structured writing exercises

- produce the irregular past tense of verbs in spontaneous speech

- produce the irregular past tense of verbs in spontaneous writing

*Morphology*

# The Irregular Present-Tense Linking Verb "Be"

## *Goal*

The student will produce "be" verb forms and demonstrate comprehension of the rules for changing the verb forms in the second- and third-person singular (e.g., you are and he is).

## *Background*

"Be," "have," and "do" are the only verbs that play dual roles as primary (main) verbs or auxiliary verbs (Crystal 1995). The goal and objectives here pertain to linking verb forms for "be." Goals and objectives relating to "be," "have," and "do" as auxiliary verbs are provided later in this chapter.

In standard English, "be" is irregular in that the linking verb form changes in the second- and third-person singular voices: "I am," "you are," and "he is." In nonstandard English, the second- and third-person singular verb forms might remain the same: "I be," "you be," and "he be." The classroom model for Landmark students is standard English. The conjugation for "be" in standard English is provided below.

### The Present Tense of "Be"

| | |
|---|---|
| I am | We are |
| You are | You are |
| She, he, it is | They are |

In linguistic texts, "be" is also identified as a *copula*, a word used to link a subject noun with its complement. The complement identifies or describes the subject.

### "Be" Linked to Complements That Refer to Subject

| <u>Singular</u> | <u>Plural</u> |
|---|---|
| I am the queen. | We are royalty. |
| You are a knight. | You are subjects. |
| He is the prince. | They are enemies. |

*Landmark School, Inc.*

## "Be" Linked to Complements That Refer to Condition

<u>Singular</u>                      <u>Plural</u>

I am tired.                 We are enthusiastic.
You are fatigued.        You are interested.
She is exhausted.        They are bored.

Students encounter the contracted forms of "be" in very early stages of conversation, as well as early stages of literature. Therefore, contractions should be taught along with the original verb forms of "be." Please refer to the topic of contractions later in this chapter.

## *Objectives*

The student will:

- auditorily distinguish between correct and incorrect linking verb forms of "be" as produced by the instructor

- imitate the instructor's production of linking verb forms of "be" in response to multimodal stimuli (e.g., gestures, manipulation of objects, and photos)

- independently produce linking verb forms of "be" in response to multimodal stimuli

- self-monitor for correct production of linking verb forms of "be" using an audiotape recorder

- produce linking verb forms of "be" in original sentences that respond to stimuli

- formulate sentences containing linking verb forms of "be" in structured exercises without stimuli

- produce linking verb forms of "be" while narrating a picture story or relating an experience

- produce linking verb forms of "be" in structured writing exercises

- produce linking verb forms of "be" in spontaneous speech

- produce linking verb forms of "be" in spontaneous writing

# Present-Tense Linking Verbs

## *Goal*

The student will produce the regular linking verb forms and demonstrate comprehension of the rules for noun-verb agreement; for example, "She appears sleepy." and "They appear sleepy."

## *Background*

*Linking verbs* express a state or condition. They link the subject to a noun, pronoun, or adjective that describes or identifies it. While the most common linking verb is "be," which is covered in the previous section, other words can also act as linking verbs.

### Some Common Linking Verbs

| | | | |
|---|---|---|---|
| Appear | Look | Seem | Stay |
| Become | Prove | Smell | Taste |
| Feel | Remain | Sound | Turn |
| Grow | | | |

Some of the linking verbs listed above can also be used as *action verbs*, which are verbs without a subject complement. An example of "smell" as a linking verb is, "The whale's spume smells awful." Here, the verb "smell" links the subject with a complement that describes it. An example of "smell" as an action verb is, "The cats smelled the fish in his creel." In this case, "smelled" serves as an action verb between the subject, cats, and the object, fish.

## *Objectives*

The student will:

- auditorily distinguish between correct and incorrect noun-verb agreement in sentences produced by the instructor; for example, "Namu _____ (appear, appears) lonely."

- imitate the instructor's production of linking verbs in response to a sequential arrangement of drawings or photos; for example, "Jaws looks angry."

- produce sentences containing present, past, and future tense of linking verbs; for example, "The fish remain in the holding tank. The fish will remain in the holding tank. The fish remained in the holding tank."

- self-monitor for correct production of linking verb forms using an audiotape recorder

- produce linking verbs while narrating a picture story or relating an experience

- produce linking verbs in structured writing exercises

- produce linking verbs in spontaneous speech

- produce linking verbs in spontaneous writing

# The Irregular Present-Tense Verbs "Have" and "Do"

## Goal

The student will produce irregular present-tense primary (main) verb forms for "have" and "do" and demonstrate comprehension of the rules for changing the verb form in the third-person singular (e.g., he does and she has).

## Background

The three verbs "have," "do," and "be" are the only verbs that play dual roles as primary (main) verbs and auxiliary verbs (Crystal 1995). The goal and objectives here pertain to primary verb forms for "have" and "do." "Be" as a linking verb is covered in an earlier section. The subject of "have," "do," and "be" as auxiliary verbs is covered later in this chapter.

In standard English, "have" and "do" are irregular in that the verb form changes in the third-person singular. According to deVilliers and deVilliers (1978), children rarely make errors in the first- or second-person voice during conversational speech (e.g., I have and you have). Most errors occur in the third-person irregular voice (e.g., he have/he has and he do/he does). In nonstandard English, the third-person-singular verb form might remain the same (e.g., I do, you do, and he do). The Landmark classroom model, however, is standard English.

The first table below conjugates the verb "have" as a main verb. As a main verb, "have" is transitive and therefore must be followed by an object. Examples for the singular and plural forms are provided in the second table below.

### Conjugation of "Have"

| | |
|---|---|
| I have | We have |
| You have | You have |
| She or he has | They have |

### Example of "Have" as a Transitive Verb

| | |
|---|---|
| I have a kayak | We have kayaks |
| You have a kayak | You have kayaks |
| She or he has a kayak | They have kayaks |

The next table conjugates the verb "do" as a main verb. As a main verb, "do" can be transitive or intransitive. Examples for the singular and plural forms are provided below.

## Conjugation of "Do"

| | |
|---|---|
| I do | We do |
| You do | You do |
| She or he does | They do |

## Example of "Do" as a Transitive Verb

| | |
|---|---|
| I do underwater flips | We do underwater flips |
| You do underwater flips | You do underwater flips |
| She or he does underwater flips | They do underwater flips |

## Example of "Do" as an Intransitive Verb

| | |
|---|---|
| I do well in swim meets | We do well in swim meets |
| You do well in swim meets | You do well in swim meets |
| She or he does well in swim meets | They do well in swim meets |

## *Objectives*

The student will:

- imitate third-person present-tense verb forms for "have" and "do" produced by the instructor; for example, "The whale has a scarred tail." and "The dolphin does tricks."

- distinguish between correct and incorrect production of verb forms for "have" and "do" in response to such stimuli as gestures, manipulation of objects, and photos; for example, "She have/has a painting of dolphins." and "He does/do exercises."

- produce verb forms for "have" and "do" in response to stimuli; for example, "She has the money." and "He does the yard work."

- self-monitor for correct production of verb forms for "have" and "do" using an audiotape recorder

- generate original sentences containing verb forms for "have" and "do" in response to stimuli

- produce the verb forms for "have" and "do" while narrating a picture story

- formulate sentences containing verb forms for "have" and "do" in structured exercises without stimuli

*Morphology*

- produce the verb forms for "have" and "do" in structured writing exercises (note that "does" should be included on a spelling list of frequently used words)
- produce the verb forms for "have" and "do" in spontaneous speech
- produce the verb forms for "have" and "do" in spontaneous writing

# Modals

## Goal

The student will produce modals and demonstrate comprehension of the underlying rules.

## Background

A *modal* is an auxiliary verb that communicates shades of meaning when attached to a verb; for example, "I may go." and "He should run in the race." Modals only function as auxiliary verbs. Contractions for modals are addressed later in this chapter.

**Modals**

| Can | Might | Shall | Will |
|---|---|---|---|
| Could | Must | Should | Would |
| May | | | |

## Objectives

The student will:

- produce the modal "can" when describing people and actions; for example, "Sue can skip."

- generate sentences containing the modals "could" and "might" in response to instructor prompts

- include the modal "may" in role-playing a request for permission to engage in an activity

- include the modal "would" in verbal responses to instructor questions

- verbally generate sentences containing the modal "will" (meaning "with strong intent") to describe future actions; for example, "You will clean your room before we go to the movie!"

- include the modal "should" in verbal responses to instructor prompts

- include the modal "must" in verbal responses to instructor questions

*Morphology*

- include modals in oral narratives, accompanied by series of pictures
- produce modals in structured writing tasks, with templates
- produce modals in spontaneous speech
- produce modals in spontaneous writing tasks, without templates

# Auxiliary (Helping) Verbs and Modals

## *Goal*

The student will produce the auxiliary (helping) verb form with and without contractions (e.g., "He is playing for the Red Sox. He might play for the Red Sox. He's playing for the Red Sox.") and demonstrate comprehension of the underlying rules.

## *Background*

An *auxiliary verb* is a verb that precedes another verb to express time (past, present, or future), aspect (a continuing vs. a completed activity), mood (attitude or intent), or voice (active or passive). Forms of "be," "have," and "do," as well as modals, serve as auxiliary verbs.

### Conjugation of the Auxiliary Verb "Be"

I am reading
You are reading
He (she) is reading
We (you, they) are reading

I was reading
You were reading
He was reading
We (you, they) were reading

I (you, he, she) will (shall) be reading
We (you, they) will (shall) be reading

### Conjugation of the Auxiliary Verb "Have"

I (you) have read
He (she) has read
We (you, they) have read

I (you) have been reading
He (she) has been reading
We (you, they) have been reading

I (you, he, she, we, they) had read
I (you, he, she, we, they) will (shall) have read

*Morphology*

## Conjugation of the Auxiliary Verb "Do"

I (you, we, they) do read
He (she) does read

I (you, he, we, they) did read

With modals, all pronouns (I, you, he, she, we, and they) use the same modal auxiliary verb form. The list below uses "I" by way of example; "I" can be replaced with any other pronoun.

## Modals

I can (may) read
I might read
I must read
I could (should, would) read
I ought to read

I can (may) read
I might have read
I must have read
I could (should, would) have read
I ought to have read

I can (may) be reading
I might be reading
I must be reading
I could (should, would) be reading
I ought to be reading

I might have been reading
I must have been reading
I could (should, would) have been reading
I ought to have been reading

## *Objectives*

The student will:

- auditorily distinguish between correct and incorrect auxiliary verb forms produced by the instructor (e.g., I reading/I am reading)

- imitate the instructor's production of auxiliary verb forms in response to stimuli (e.g., gestures, manipulation of objects, and photos)

*Landmark School, Inc.*

- independently produce auxiliary verb forms in response to stimuli

- self-monitor for correct production of auxiliary verb forms using an audiotape recorder

- generate original sentences that include auxiliary verb forms in response to stimuli; for example, "You are reading a book."

- identify similarities and differences in meaning in sentences with modals; for example, "I might go to the game." and "I am sure I will go to the game."

- formulate sentences containing auxiliary verb forms in structured exercises; for example, when asked to paraphrase "I have to return this book.", the student might offer "I might return this book." or "I must return this book."

- produce auxiliary verb forms while narrating a picture story or relating an experience

- produce auxiliary verb forms in structured writing exercises

- produce auxiliary verb forms in spontaneous speech

- produce auxiliary verb forms in spontaneous writing

# Contractions

## *Goal*

The student will auditorily process and verbally produce contractions in spontaneous speech and written text (e.g., I can't, you don't, and he doesn't).

## *Background*

Teachers should teach contractions along with the original verb forms. Although Landmark students use contractions in conversation, most have difficulty decoding them in reading. Contractions are also confusing to students for whom English is a second language. Since contractions appear early in students' reading experience, teachers should pay particular attention to their decoding and spelling, as well as to the origins of contracted forms.

A *contraction* abbreviates a written or spoken expression by omitting one or more letters or sounds. Contractions are widely used in informal speech and writing. In written expression, an apostrophe marks where letters are omitted; for example, in "I'd," the apostrophe replaces either "woul-," as in "I would," or "ha-," as in "I had." Contractions are not used in formal writing.

Why do students have difficulty with contractions?

- Students with phonological impairment might not "hear" the less emphasized parts of words in a conversation, For example, a student might hear "He isn't picking you up at 6:00." as "He is picking you up at 6:00." Missing the less emphasized part of a contraction can greatly reduce comprehension.

- Even though they use contractions in conversation, students with decoding deficits often hesitate and appear puzzled when they encounter a contraction in literature, especially if the spelling is irregular (e.g., doesn't and won't).

### Examples of Contractions of "Be"

| Regular "Be" as a Linking/Auxiliary Verb | Contraction as a Linking Verb | Contraction as an Auxiliary Verb |
|---|---|---|
| I am | I'm the president | I'm talking |
| You are | You're the boss | You're talking |
| He is | He's the boss | He's talking |

| Regular "Be" as a Linking/Auxiliary Verb | Contraction as a Linking Verb | Contraction as an Auxiliary Verb |
|---|---|---|
| It is | It's Superman | It's broken |
| What is | What's his name? | What's broken |
| That is | That's Mars | That's broken |
| Who is | Who's there | Who's talking |
| There is | There's the bear | — |
| Here is | Here's the bear | — |
| Where is | Where's the bear | — |
| We are | We're friends | We're talking |
| They are | They're buddies | They're walking |

| Future-Tense "Be" as a Linking/Auxiliary Verb | Contraction as a Linking Verb | Contraction as an Auxiliary Verb |
|---|---|---|
| I will | I'll be president | I'll go |
| You will | You'll be happy | You'll go |
| He will | He'll be quiet | He'll go |
| She will | She'll be a star | She'll go |
| They will | They'll be late | They'll go |

## Examples of Contractions of "Have"

| Regular "Have" as an Auxiliary Verb | Contraction |
|---|---|
| I have | I've seen |
| You have | You've lost |
| He has | He's disappeared |
| She has | She's disappeared |
| We have | We've hidden |
| They have | They've left |
| It has | It's rained |
| What has | What's he done? |
| That has | That's been broken |
| Who has | Who's won the race? |
| There has | There's been trouble |
| Where has | Where's the cat gone? |

| Past-Perfect "Have" as an Auxiliary Verb | Contraction |
|---|---|
| I had | I'd left already |
| You had | You'd left already |
| He had | He'd left already |

Landmark School, Inc.

| Past-Perfect "Have" as an Auxiliary Verb | Contraction |
|---|---|
| She had | She'd left already |
| We had | We'd left already |
| They had | They'd left already |

## Examples of Contractions of "Would"

| Modal | Contraction with Linking Verb "Be" | Contraction as an Auxiliary Verb |
|---|---|---|
| I would | I'd be the boss | I'd go, but I can't |
| You would | You'd be the boss | You'd go |
| He would | He'd be the boss | He'd go |
| She would | She'd be the boss | She'd go |
| We would | We'd be the best | We'd go |
| They would | They'd be ready | They'd go |

## Examples of Contractions of Negatives

| Linking/Auxiliary Verb | Contraction as a Linking Verb | Contraction as an Auxiliary Verb |
|---|---|---|
| I cannot | I can't be president | I can't go there |
| I do not | — | I don't drive a BMW |
| He does not | — | He doesn't drive |
| I should not | I shouldn't be president | I shouldn't drive |
| I would not | I wouldn't be president | I wouldn't drive |
| I could not | I couldn't be president | I couldn't drive |
| We are not | We aren't guilty. | We aren't going |
| He wasn't | He wasn't guilty | He wasn't going |
| They weren't | They weren't there | They weren't going |
| He hasn't | He hasn't a penny | He hasn't left |
| We haven't | We haven't any oars | We haven't left |
| We hadn't | We hadn't any money | We hadn't left |
| Mustn't | — | We mustn't leave |
| Didn't | — | We didn't lie |

## Examples of Miscellaneous Contractions

| Uncontracted Form | Contraction |
|---|---|
| Let us | Let's go |
| Madam | Ma'am |
| Of the clock | O'clock |
| Class of 2002 | Class of '02 |

Landmark School, Inc.

## Objectives

The student will:

- auditorily discriminate between a linking or auxiliary verb and its contracted form (e.g., is/isn't, I would/I'd)

- imitate the instructor's production of regular and contracted forms of linking or auxiliary verbs

- point to an image that corresponds to a sentence dictated by the instructor; for example, "This boy isn't wearing a red shirt." and "This girl has finished her ice cream."

- produce the negative contracted verb form in response to the instructor's production of the positive verb form (e.g., has/hasn't)

- produce contracted verb forms in oral sentence completion tasks

- read word lists containing contracted verb forms

- read words containing contracted verb forms in context

- verbalize contracted verb forms in original sentences

- write contracted forms of verb phrases (e.g., he will/he'll)

- produce contractions in spontaneous speaking and writing

# Future Tense of Verbs

## *Goal*

The student will identify and generate sentences containing the future tense of verbs and demonstrate comprehension of the underlying rules.

## *Background*

The English language marks future tense with auxiliary verbs like "will" and "shall" and adverbs like "tomorrow." Students need to learn to perceive, recall, and apply the rules for specifying the future.

Sometimes, students assume that the first event in a sentence precedes the second event in "real time." One question, then, is whether these students have mastered the meanings of prepositions that denote time. If they have, they should be encouraged to use their knowledge to interpret such sentences. It is likely they need practice transposing the information in these sentences.

## *Objectives*

The student will:

- identify the future auxiliary verbs "shall" and "will" as marking tense in sentences that begin with these words; for example, "Will you be driving into Boston tonight?"

- identify the future auxiliary verbs "shall" and "will" as marking tense in sentences that have these words within them; for example, "After supper, we will go to the movies."

- identify the sequence of events regardless of word position in the sentence; for example, "Before supper, we will go to the movies." and "After supper, we will go to the movies."

- transpose future-tense sentences containing phrases and clauses; for example, "Before supper we will go to the movies." becomes "We will go to the movies before supper."

- identify sentences that indicate future tense but do not include the auxiliary verbs "will" or "shall"; for example, "Are you driving into Boston tonight?"

- formulate sentences containing the future tense, given a template

- formulate sentences containing the future tense without a template
- produce the future tense in structured oral narratives
- formulate sentences containing the future tense in structured writing tasks, given a template
- include the future tense in spontaneous speech
- formulate sentences containing the future tense in structured writing tasks without a template

# The Six Verb Tenses

## *Goal*

The student will identify and explain uses for the present, past, future, present perfect, past perfect, and future perfect tenses in the context of age-appropriate literature.

## *Background*

English verbs have various forms to show time of action (tense). Because some markers that indicate tense occur at the end of the verb and are less easily heard, students might not identify them; for example, Landmark students often do not notice the markers for present tense, third-person singular (e.g., she walk<u>s</u>), or past tense (they walk<u>ed</u>).

Although most of us have little difficulty expressing present, past, and future tenses, we might spend a lifetime struggling with the perfect tenses. When students encounter "had had" in a literary passage, they usually assume it is a typographical error.

Within the six verb tenses are progressive forms, which indicate continuous action. The progressive forms contain *–ing*. The present progressive verb form is one of the earliest verb forms used by young children (Cazden and Bellugi 1970). Because the sequence of this chapter roughly parallels language development, the present progressive tense is covered earlier. Accurate production of progressive forms in the other verb tenses occur later in language development.

The verb "walk" is conjugated below for all six verb tenses.

### Principal Parts of the Verb "Walk"

| Present Infinitive | Perfect Infinitive | Present Participle | Past | Past Participle |
|---|---|---|---|---|
| To walk | To have walked | Walking | Walked | Walked |

### Present Tense of "Walk"

| Singular | Plural |
|---|---|
| I walk | We walk |
| You walk | You walk |
| He, she, it walks | They walk |

### Present Progressive Verb Form

| Singular | Plural |
|---|---|
| I am walking | We are walking |
| You are walking | You are walking |
| He, she, it is walking | They are walking |

## Past Tense of "Walk"

| Singular | Plural |
|---|---|
| I walked | We walked |
| You walked | You walked |
| He, she, it walked | They walked |

### Past Progressive Verb Form

| Singular | Plural |
|---|---|
| I was walking | We were walking |
| You were walking | You were walking |
| He, she, it was walking | They were walking |

## Future Tense of "Walk"

| Singular | Plural |
|---|---|
| I will (shall) walk | We will (shall) walk |
| You will (shall) walk | You will (shall) walk |
| He, she, it will (shall) walk | They will (shall) walk |

### Future Progressive Verb Form

| Singular | Plural |
|---|---|
| I will (shall) be walking | We will (shall) be walking |
| You will (shall) be walking | You will (shall) be walking |
| He, she, it will (shall) be walking | They will (shall) be walking |

## Present Perfect Tense of "Walk"

| Singular | Plural |
|---|---|
| I have walked | We have walked |
| You have walked | You have walked |
| He, she, it has walked | They have walked |

*Landmark School, Inc.*

## Present Perfect Progressive Verb Form

<u>Singular</u>

I have been walking
You have been walking
He, she, it has been walking

<u>Plural</u>

We have been walking
You have been walking
They have been walking

## Past Perfect Tense of "Walk"

<u>Singular</u>

I had walked
You had walked
He, she, it had walked

<u>Plural</u>

We had walked
You had walked
They had walked

### Past Perfect Progressive Verb Form

<u>Singular</u>

I had been walking
You had been walking
He, she, it had been walking

<u>Plural</u>

We had been walking
You had been walking
They had been walking

## Future Perfect Tense of "Walk"

<u>Singular</u>

I will (shall) have walked
You will (shall) have walked
He, she, it will (shall) have walked

<u>Plural</u>

We will (shall) have walked
You will (shall) have walked
They will (shall) have walked

### Future Perfect Progressive Verb Form

<u>Singular</u>

I will (shall) have been walking
You will (shall) have been walking
He, she, it will (shall) have been walking

<u>Plural</u>

We will (shall) have been walking
You will (shall) have been walking
They will (shall) have been walking

## *Objectives*

The student will:

- distinguish between correct and incorrect grammar in terms of present, past, and future verb tenses in sentences with time references dictated by the instructor

*Landmark School, Inc.*

- explain that the present tense is used to describe action that is occurring now

- explain that the past tense is used to describe action that occurred in the past but did not continue into the present

- explain that the future tense is used to describe action occurring sometime in the future

- classify present, past, and future verb forms by time of action in the context of "yesterday," "now," and "tomorrow"

- use the correct verb tense (present, past, or future) in sentence completion tasks

- reformulate sentences in the verb tense dictated by a time referent (e.g., now, tomorrow, and usually)

- become aware of the function of the perfect tenses

- comprehend the function of the present perfect tense – namely, to express action that occurred at no definite time in the past – and that it is formed with "have" or "has"

- explain the difference in meaning between a sentence that contains the past tense and one that contains the present perfect tense; for example, "John attended Landmark for two years." and "John has attended Landmark for two years."

- use the present perfect tense in sentence completion tasks

- verbally formulate sentences containing the present perfect tense

- formulate sentences containing the present perfect tense in writing tasks using a template

- formulate sentences containing the present perfect tense in writing tasks without a template

- include the present perfect tense verb form in spontaneous speech

- formulate sentences containing the present perfect tense in spontaneous writing

- comprehend and explain the function of the past perfect tense – namely, to express action completed in the past before another past action or event – and that it is formed with "had"

- identify the order of events in sentences containing the past perfect tense
- include the past perfect tense in sentence completion tasks
- verbally formulate sentences containing the past perfect tense
- formulate sentences containing the past perfect tense in writing tasks using a template
- formulate sentences containing the past perfect tense in writing tasks without a template
- include the past perfect tense verb form in spontaneous speech
- formulate sentences containing the past perfect tense in spontaneous writing
- comprehend the function of the future perfect tense – namely, to express action that will be completed in the future before another future action or event – and that it is formed with "will have" or "shall have"; for example, "I shall have left for Canada before you return from New York."
- identify the future perfect tense in sentences dictated by the instructor
- use the future perfect tense in sentence completion tasks
- verbally formulate sentences containing the future perfect tense
- formulate sentences containing the future perfect tense in writing tasks using a template
- formulate sentences containing the future perfect tense in writing tasks without a template
- include the future perfect tense verb form in spontaneous speech
- formulate sentences containing the future perfect tense in spontaneous writing
- differentiate the six verb tenses in oral and written exercises

# Comparative and Superlative Forms of Adjectives and Adverbs (Regular and Irregular)

## *Goal*

The student will use comparative and superlative forms of adjectives and demonstrate comprehension of the underlying rules.

## *Background*

Some common speaking errors include using:

- the superlative rather than the comparative form; for example, "I am *biggest* than him."

- *-er* and *-est* for irregular comparisons; for example, "Aliens are *badder* than the Penguin, but Darth Vader is the *baddest* of all."

- double comparisons, such as "more better"

The rules below are helpful in correcting such errors.

- Use comparative degree when comparing two things; use superlative degree when comparing more than two.

- Include the word "other" or "else" when comparing one thing with a group of which it is a part; for example, "The blue whale is bigger than any other animal." and "Lia is faster than anyone else on the track team."

- For irregular comparisons, memorize the comparative and superlative forms as separate lexical items; for example, "I play basketball better than he does."

The tables below offer examples of comparative and superlative forms of adjectives and adverbs.

### One-Syllable Adjectives

| Positive | Comparative | Superlative |
| --- | --- | --- |
| Tall | Taller | Tallest |
| Short | Shorter | Shortest |

## Two-Syllable Adjectives

| Positive | Comparative | Superlative |
|---|---|---|
| Easy | Easier | Easiest |
| Careful | More careful | Most careful |

## Three-Syllable (or More) Adjectives and Adverbs Ending in –*ly*

| Positive | Comparative | Superlative |
|---|---|---|
| Possible | More possible | Most possible |
| Dangerously | More dangerously | Most dangerously |

## Indicating Less or Least

| Positive | Comparative | Superlative |
|---|---|---|
| Willing | Less willing | Least willing |
| Happy | Less happy | Least happy |

## Irregular Comparisons

| Positive | Comparative | Superlative |
|---|---|---|
| Bad | Worse | Worst |
| Good, well | Better | Best |
| Many, much | More | Most |

## *Objectives*

The student will:

- answer questions that ask for a comparison of two or three objects that differ in only one dimension (e.g., length, width, depth, size as a whole, and texture)

- distinguish between correct and incorrect regular comparative and superlative forms in one-syllable adjectives requiring *-er* and *-est* produced by the instructor; for example, "This ball is *bigger* than that ball." vs. "This ball is *biggest* than that ball."

- produce regular comparative and superlative forms of adjectives in oral or written sentence completion tasks; for example, "Of all the animals in the world, the blue whale is the _____ (biggest, more bigger)."

*Landmark School, Inc.*

- produce regular comparative and superlative forms of adjectives in oral or written cloze tasks; for example, "I would like to see the blue whale, the _____ (most biggest, biggest) animal in the world."
- self-monitor for correct production of regular comparative and superlative adjective forms using an audiotape recorder
- produce regular comparatives and superlatives in verbally generated original sentences
- verbally compare objects that differ in a variety of dimensions using regular comparative and superlative forms; for example, "This chair is larger and harder than the red one, but Papa's chair is the largest and hardest of all." and "Ben is shorter but heavier than Sharif."
- generate regular comparatives and superlatives in structured writing exercises
- produce regular comparatives and superlatives in spontaneous speech
- produce regular comparatives and superlatives in spontaneous writing and adverbs ending in -*ly*
- demonstrate recognition of irregular comparisons, such as "bad," "good," and "many"
- produce comparatives and superlatives for two-syllable adjectives, adverbs ending in -*ly*, and irregular adjectives
- recognize comparisons that indicate less or the least amount of a quality

# Suffixes

## *Goal*

The student will form derivations from root words by adding the appropriate suffixes and demonstrate comprehension of the underlying rules.

## *Background*

It is logical to teach suffixes before prefixes because students can more easily identify the root word when it is consistently positioned at the beginning of the derived word (e.g., teacher). Some key definitions follow, focusing upon derivational suffixes.

- An *affix* is a meaningful form (morpheme) that is attached to a base or root word to make a new word (e.g., *un-* plus avail plus *-able*).

- A *suffix* is an affix that is added to the end of a word (e.g., whale plus *-s* yields "whales"). A suffix can change a word's meaning (e.g., sail plus *-or* yields "sailor"). English, having borrowed from other languages, contains suffixes that have meanings in their original languages; for example, *-ee* is from French. It means recipient of an action, as in "grantee." Other suffixes have been retained from Old English; for example, *-dom* means state, rank, or condition, as in "freedom." In these examples and many others, the original meanings of the suffixes are probably unknown to most speakers of English.

- *Inflectional suffixes* are grammatical in nature. They include the plural marker *-s*, the possessive marker *-'s*, the regular past-tense marker *-ed*, the regular comparative marker *-er*, and the regular superlative marker *-est*. Inflectional suffixes are addressed elsewhere in this chapter.

- *Derivational suffixes* are lexical. Their primary function is to create a new word from the base or root form. The part of speech might change as well, as from a verb to a noun (e.g., sail plus *-or* yields "sailor").

- *Combining form suffixes* are used with combining form prefixes to create compound-like words (e.g., *bio-* means life; *-logy* means study of; *bio-* plus *-logy* yields "biology," meaning study of life). Over time, such words have been created to name discoveries or inventions. Each part has equal value in determining the meaning of the word.

Being able to recognize suffixes and prefixes greatly facilitates students' ability to decode multisyllabic words. To reinforce such recognition, Landmark students study word lists. Many students decode more accurately when they use a highlighter to denote the affix. When students are working on both prefixes and suffixes, they can use one color for the prefix and another for the suffix. In three-syllable words, the remaining syllable (root) stands out, which makes decoding less daunting.

Although the tables of derivational suffixes below are not all-inclusive, they include more than enough for most middle-school students' needs. Sources for additional word lists include Bush (1989); Crystal (1995); Dale and O'Rourke (1971); Fry, Kress, and Fountoukidis (2000); and Wiig and Semel (1984). Teachers should begin with the most frequently used suffixes and teach only those the student is likely to encounter at his or her level of reading or listening. Photos and objects are helpful when teaching the combining form suffixes, such as telescope/microscope and barometer/thermometer.

## Derivational Suffixes That Create Personal Nouns

| Suffix | Example |
|---|---|
| -ant | Servant |
| -ar | Beggar |
| -ee | Employee |
| -ent | Student |
| -er | Banker |
| -ess | Waitress |
| -ier | Carrier |
| -ior | Warrior |
| -ist | Tourist |
| -or | Inspector |

## Derivational Suffixes That Create Abstract Nouns (States)

| Suffix | Example |
|---|---|
| -age | Bondage |
| -dom | Freedom |
| -ery | Slavery |
| -hood | Brotherhood |
| -ism | Idealism |

# Morphology

| Suffix | Example |
|---|---|
| -ocracy | Democracy |
| -ship | Friendship |
| -ty | Liberty |

## Derivational Suffixes That Create Nouns (Varied)

| Suffix | Meaning | Example |
|---|---|---|
| -age | Result of | Leakage |
| -al | Action | Approval |
| -ance | Action | Attendance |
| -ance | State of or quality | Importance |
| -ation | Action | Exploration |
| -ence | Quality | Difference |
| -ing | From verb | Building |
| -ity | State of | Velocity |
| -ment | State of | Amusement |
| -ness | State of or quality | Gentleness |
| -tion | Action | Protection |
| -sion | State of | Confusion |

## Derivational Suffixes That Create Nouns: Combining Forms

| Suffix | Meaning | Example |
|---|---|---|
| -itis | Disease | Arthritis |
| -meter | Device for measuring | Barometer |
| -logy | Study of | Biology |
| -scope | Instrument for seeing | Telescope |
| -graphy | Denotes process or form | Photography |

## Derivational Suffixes That Create Adjectives

| Suffix | Meaning | Example |
|---|---|---|
| -able | Can be done | Restorable |
| -ible | Inclined to | Terrible |
| -al | Relating to | Natural |
| -ant | State of | Resistant |
| -ent | Quality of | Different |
| -er | Comparative | Harder |
| -est | Superlative | Hardest |
| -ful | Full of | Cupful |

*Landmark School, Inc.*

| Suffix | Meaning | Example |
|---|---|---|
| -ful | Characterized by | Wishful |
| -ial | Characterized by | Territorial |
| -ic | Characterized by | Historic |
| -ish | Characterized by | Childish |
| -ive | Tending to | Active |
| -less | Beyond range of | Countless |
| -less | Without | Careless |
| -ly | Like | Manly |
| -some | Like | Quarrelsome |
| -ous | Having qualities of | Dangerous |
| -y | Characterized by | Sleepy |

## Derivational Suffixes That Create Verbs

| Suffix | Meaning | Example |
|---|---|---|
| -ate | To make | Activate |
| -en | To induce | Frighten |
| -ify | To make | Falsify |
| -ize | To make | Terrorize |

## Derivational Suffixes That Create Adverbs

| Suffix | Meaning | Example |
|---|---|---|
| -ly | In the manner of | Desperately |
| -ly | Degree | Extremely |
| -ward | Direction | Forward |
| -wise | Way, manner | Clockwise |

## *Objectives*

The student will:

- identify root words when presented with derived words appropriate to his or her vocabulary level (e.g., <u>dark</u>ness)
- segment the derived word into its two meaningful units: the root word and the suffix
- define the derived word by analyzing the root word and its suffix (e.g., hope + *-less* = without hope)

Landmark School, Inc.

*Morphology*

- determine the grammatical function of the derived word by analyzing the root word and its suffix (e.g., "hopeless" is an adjective)

- undertake sentence completion tasks that demonstrate the ability to think about the structure of the word, as in how adding *-er* creates a noun, such as "teacher"; for example, "Mrs. Jennings teaches. She is a _____ (teacher)."

- undertake oral cloze tasks that demonstrate the ability to think about the structure of the word; for example, "Forest fires are sometimes started by _____ (careless) people who don't put out campfires."

- distinguish between the same and a different meaning when presented with two sentences, one of which contains the derived word; for example, the meaning is the same in "John worked at a slow pace." and "John worked slowly."

- verbally generate original sentences containing selected derived words that are nouns

- verbally generate original sentences containing targeted derived words that are adverbs

- generate sentences containing new words derived by adding a suffix using a template

- generate sentences containing new words derived by adding a suffix without using a template

- for decoding purposes, highlight the single suffix shared by a list of derived words (e.g., na<u>tion</u>, sta<u>tion</u>, and celebra<u>tion</u>)

- for decoding purposes, highlight a variety of suffixes in a list of derived words (e.g., care<u>ful</u>, care<u>less</u>, and car<u>ing</u>)

*Landmark School, Inc.*

# Prefixes

## *Goal*

The student will form derivations from root words by adding appropriate prefixes and demonstrate comprehension of the underlying rules.

## *Background*

Thousands of new words in English are created from adding prefixes to existing words. It is logical to introduce prefixes after suffixes because prefixes appear before the root word and create a more complex decoding task. Of course, students encounter prefixes and suffixes simultaneously in literature; therefore, it is important to observe students' miscues carefully as they attempt to interpret them.

- An *affix* is a meaningful form that is attached to another meaningful form to make a more complex word (e.g., *un-* plus avail plus *-able*).

- A *prefix* is an affix placed before the root of another word or another prefix (e.g., *im-* plus possible). The prefix creates a new word that modifies the meaning of the root word or forms a new meaning.

Prefixes with different meanings might be spelled identically. For example, the prefix *in-* means "not" in some words (e.g., ineffective) and "into" in others (e.g., inhaler). Also, the word "inflammable" confuses many adults as well as children. If one applies the meaning "not" to the prefix, the word appears to mean "not flammable"; however, "inflammable" derives from "inflame," which means "to set on fire." "Inflammable" therefore means "easily inflamed." To avoid confusion, the prefix *non-*, which also means "not," is frequently used, as in "nonflammable."

Being able to recognize suffixes and prefixes greatly facilitates students' ability to decode multisyllabic words. To reinforce such recognition, Landmark students study word lists. Many students decode more accurately when they use a highlighter to denote the prefix. When students are working on both prefixes and suffixes, they use one color for the prefix and another for the suffix. In three-syllable words, the remaining syllable (root) stands out, making decoding less daunting.

Although the tables of prefixes below are not all-inclusive, they should address the needs of most middle-school students. Sources for additional word lists include Bush (1989); Crystal (1995); Dale and O'Rourke (1971); Fry, Kress, and Fountoukidis (2000); Warriner (1988), and Wiig and Semel (1984). Teachers should begin with the most frequently used prefixes and focus upon those the student is likely to encounter at his or her level of reading or listening. Photos and objects are helpful when teaching the combining form prefixes (e.g., telephone/television/telescope/telegram and unicycle/ bicycle/tricycle).

## Selected Prefixes with Negative Connotations

| Prefix | Meaning | Example |
|---|---|---|
| *ab-* | Away from | Abnormal |
| *an-* | Without | Anarchy |
| *anti-* | Against | Antiwar |
| *de-* | Undo, down | Deregulate, defeat |
| *dis-* | Apart, off, away | Disability, dislike |
| *dys-* | Faulty | Dysfunction |
| *ex-* | Out of, from | Extract, ex-president |
| *im-* | Not | Impossible |
| *in-* | Not | Incredible |
| *ir-* | Not | Irresistible |
| *mis-* | Wrong | Mislead |
| *ob-* | Against | Obstruct |
| *mal-* | Bad | Malnutrition |
| *op-* | Against | Oppose |
| *sub-* | Under | Substandard |
| *un-* | Not, back | Unhappy, untie |
| *under-* | Under | Underwater |

## Selected Prefixes That Denote Number

| Prefix | Root | Meaning | Example |
|---|---|---|---|
| *mono-* | Greek | One | Monologue |
| *uni-* | Latin | One | Unicycle |
| *di-* | Greek | Two | Diagonal |
| *bi-* | Latin | Two | Bicycle |
| *tri-* | Greek, Latin | Three | Tricycle |
| *tetr-* | Greek | Four | Tetrapod |
| *quad-* | Latin | Four | Quadrangle |
| *pent-* | Greek | Five | Pentagon |

| Prefix | Root | Meaning | Example |
|---|---|---|---|
| quint- | Latin | Five | Quintuplets |
| hexa- | Greek | Six | Hexagon |
| sex- | Latin | Six | Sextet |
| hept- | Greek | Seven | Heptagon |
| sept- | Latin | Seven | Septet |
| oct- | Greek, Latin | Eight | Octagon |
| no- | Greek, Latin | Nine | Nonet |
| deca- | Greek | Ten | Decathalon |
| deci- | Latin | Ten | Decimal |
| semi- | Greek | One-half | Semicircle |
| hemi- | Latin | One-half | Hemisphere |
| cent- | Latin | One hundred | Century |
| mille- | Latin | One thousand | Millennium |
| kilo- | Latin | One thousand | Kilowatt |
| poly- | Greek | Many, much | Polygon |

## Selected Prefixes That Denote Time and Order

| Prefix | Meaning | Example |
|---|---|---|
| ex- | From | Ex-president |
| fore- | Before | Foreshadow |
| post- | After | Postwar |
| pre- | Before, in front | Preview |
| re- | Back, again | Review |

## Selected Prefixes That Denote Size and Degree

| Prefix | Meaning | Example |
|---|---|---|
| hyper- | Above | Hyperactive |
| mini- | Small | Minivan |
| out- | Extra | Outsized |
| over- | Above, beyond | Overweight |
| super- | Over, above | Superman |
| sur- | Over, above | Surpass |
| ultra- | Beyond | Ultramodern |

## Selected Prefixes (Varied)

| Prefix | Meaning | Example |
|---|---|---|
| ad- | To | Advocate |
| af- | To | Affiliate |

Landmark School, Inc.

# Morphology

| Prefix | Meaning | Example |
|---|---|---|
| *ambi-* | Both | Ambiguous |
| *ap-* | To | Approve |
| *at-* | To | Attain |
| *bene-* | Good | Benefit |
| *com-* | With | Comrade |
| *con-* | With | Convention |
| *contra-* | Against | Contradict |
| *homo-* | Common, like | Homogeneous |
| *im-* | Into, in | Imbed |
| *in-* | Into, in | Inflame |
| *inter-* | Between | Interstate highway |
| *out-* | Extra, not in | Outside |
| *pro-* | Move forward | Promote |
| *pro-* | In favor of | Proactive |
| *sub-* | Under | Submarine |
| *syn-* | Like | Synonym |
| *trans-* | Across, beyond | Transport |

## Selected Prefixes: Combining Forms

| Prefix | Meaning | Example |
|---|---|---|
| *auto-* | Self-propelling | Automobile |
| *bio-* | Life | Biography |
| *micro-* | Very small | Microscope |
| *para-* | Beside | Parallel |
| *photo-* | Light | Photography |
| *tele-* | Distant | Telescope |

## Objectives

The student will:

- identify root words when presented with derived words appropriate to his or her vocabulary level

- divide a derived word into its two meaningful units, the root word and the prefix

- define common prefixes (e.g., *un-* means "negative")

- recognize that prefixes often change the meaning of the root word

- judge the equivalence in meaning of two sentences, one with a root word and the other with the root word plus a prefix (e.g., lock the door/unlock the door); also, judge the equivalence in meaning of a root word with different prefixes (e.g., discover/recover)

- identify the difference in meaning between two sentences containing the same root word with different prefixes; for example, "Sharif <u>dis</u>covered Blackbeard's treasure in Nova Scotia." and "Sharif <u>un</u>covered the treasure chest."

- verbally generate original sentences with selected derived words that are nouns

- verbally generate original sentences with targeted derived words that are adverbs

- generate sentences with new words derived by adding a prefix, using a template

- generate sentences with new words derived by adding a prefix without using a template

- for decoding purposes, highlight the single prefix shared by a list of derived words (e.g., <u>pre</u>view, <u>pre</u>test, and <u>pre</u>dict)

- for decoding purposes, highlight a variety of prefixes in a list of derived words (e.g., <u>uni</u>cycle, <u>bi</u>cycle, and <u>tri</u>cycle)

- for decoding purposes, highlight prefixes using one color and suffixes using another color before decoding the words

# Bibliography of Instructional Materials

Adams, M.J., B.R. Foorman, I. Lundberg, and T. Beeler. *Phonemic Awareness in Young Children*. Baltimore: Paul H. Brooks Publishing, 1998.

Blockcolsky, V. *Book of Words – 17,000 Words Selected by Vowels and Diphthongs*. Austin: PRO-ED, 1990.

———. *40,000 Selected Words Organized by Letter, Sound, and Syllable*. Austin: PRO-ED, 1990.

Bush, C. *Language Remediation and Expansion – 150 Skill-Building Reference Lists*. Austin: PRO-ED, 1989.

———. *500 Thematic Lists and Activities*. Austin: PRO-ED, 1996.

Fry, E.B., J.E. Kress, and D.L. Fountoukidis. *The Reading Teacher's Book of Lists*. 4th ed. Paramus, NJ: Prentice Hall, 2000.

Johnson, K., and P. Bayrd. *Megawords – Multisyllabic Words for Reading, Spelling, and Vocabulary*. Cambridge: Educators Publishing Service, 1993.

Kisner, R., and B. Knowles. *Warm-Up Exercises – Calisthenics for the Brain*. Book 1. Eau Claire, WI: Thinking Publications, 1984.

———. *Warm-Up Exercises – Calisthenics for the Brain*. Book 2. Eau Claire, WI: Thinking Publications, 1985.

———. *Warm-Up Exercises – Calisthenics for the Brain*. Book 3. Eau Claire, WI: Thinking Publications, 1992.

Lazzari, A., and P. Peters. *HELP – Handbook of Exercises for Language Processing – Elementary*. Moline, IL: LinguiSystems, 1993.

CHAPTER 3

# SYNTAX

## Introduction

*Syntax* is the study of the way in which words are put together to form phrases, clauses, and sentences. In even the simplest of sentences, word order matters, as meaning can change when words are rearranged. Consider the difference between "The Yankees beat the Red Sox." and "The Red Sox beat the Yankees.", as well as between "Did they win?" and "They did win."

Sentences are constructs that are familiar to everyone. How did we arrive at a sense of sentence structure that seems accessible to all? It is astonishing that most children develop a "sentence sense" without formal training. The linguist Noam Chomsky argues that the human brain is wired to string words together in a systematic way. Chomsky's contribution is described well by Pinker (2000):

> In this century, the most famous argument that language is like an instinct comes from Noam Chomsky, the linguist who first unmasked the intricacy of the system and perhaps the person most responsible for the modern revolution in language and cognitive science.

Two-year-olds use short, simple sentences. Between ages three and four, children begin joining these sentences with "and." Before long, they add morphological endings, auxiliary verbs, articles, and even adverbial endings (e.g., quickly). They might produce sentences containing "because" in the early years but not understand that they are joining two clauses until later. At ages five and six, sentence embeddings begin to appear, such as relative clauses.

In the early elementary years, children expand upon the forms they know (e.g., noun plus verb plus object) as well as acquire new forms. Most eight-year-olds produce passive sentences that require them to transform the role of the noun from subject to object (Shames, Wiig, and Secord 1994).

Between first and seventh grades, students experience major development in their ability to use sentence embeddings. Students learn about embedding clauses and phrases and conjoining; that is, they begin composing compound and complex sentences.

The school-age child does not learn to use more complex sentences in a vacuum. By the third or fourth grade, reading to learn and writing to express thoughts are major activities in the school day. Students also receive direct instruction in sentence formulation.

For the educator, the biggest difference between the linguists like Chomsky, Pinker, and Crystal and the grammarians like Warriner and Schwegler is that linguists report what humans *do* with grammar (e.g., "He's the one we bought the tickets from.") and grammarians report what they *think* humans should do (e.g., "He's the one from whom we bought the tickets."). Of course, both schools of thought acknowledge the difference in standards between less formal oral language and more formal written language.

In Landmark's population of students with language-based learning disabilities, deficits in sentence formulation seem to have several causes.

- Students have limited auditory working memory. When asked to generate complex sentences aloud, they frequently forget the wording of their main clauses before composing the rest of their sentences.

- Students have rule-learning deficits or delays. In middle-school years, students lag behind normally achieving peers in their ability to acquire and apply rules for complex sentence structures (e.g., main clauses plus adverbial clauses). Many Landmark students do not interpret passive voice accurately.

- Students lack exposure to the written word, which is a situation that cannot be underestimated. Written expression differs in many respects from oral expression. Consider the disparity between the language in the average television program and the language in a well-crafted novel by Katherine Paterson. Children who hear or read fine literature are immersed in the richness of our language in both form and content.

English sentences are single or multiple. Study of syntax progresses from word strings in simple sentences to word strings in compound, complex, and compound-complex sentences. Simple sentences consist of one independent or main clause and no subordinate clauses. A compound sentence consists of two or more independent clauses, but no subordinate clauses. A complex sentence consists of one independent clause and at least one subordinate clause. A compound-complex sentence consists of two or more independent clauses and at least one subordinate clause.

Multiple sentence structures predominate in literature and other written texts. These structures are common in everyday conversation as well. Students with language-based learning disabilities face a triple challenge: first and foremost, to grasp the meanings of these sentences; second, to identify the grammatical elements of main and subordinating clauses; and third, to generate compound and complex sentences themselves.

According to Paul (2000), the course of development for children with language-based learning disorders parallels that of normal language development, but at a slower rate. Therefore, the sequence for remediation that follows generally adheres to the sequence of normal language development. By listening carefully to students' utterances, teachers can develop a descriptive-developmental curriculum. By analyzing students' receptive and expressive language behavior, teachers can identify the linguistic elements that require intervention. Teachers' knowledge of normal language development provides some guidance in determining appropriate targets for intervention.

## Receptive and Expressive Errors

Landmark students not only have difficulty formulating complete sentences, they also have difficulty processing certain sentence structures. These include sentences that contain:

- passive voice
- embedded clauses
- participial phrases
- subordinate clauses and phrases that precede main clauses

### Examples of Receptive (Processing) Errors

| What Teacher Said or Read | What Student Said | Student's Processing Error |
| --- | --- | --- |
| The Trans Am was passed by the Corvette. Which car did the passing? | The Trans Am. | Interpreted active voice; gave greater weight to the first noun in the sentence |
| The boy who spotted the whale was only four years old. | The whale was four years old? | Linked part of the embedded clause to the predicate |
| Carving knife in hand, he crept up. | Why would he carve in his hand? | Misinterpreted the participial phrase: added the words "with a" before "knife," then interpreted "carving" as a gerund |
| Before they ate breakfast, he rang the bell. Which happened first? | They ate breakfast. | Followed normal noun-plus-verb order in simple sentences, giving priority to the first clause heard |

### Examples of Expressive (Sentence Formulation) Errors

| What Student Said | What Student Meant to Say | Type of Error |
| --- | --- | --- |
| I don't know where *is it*. | I don't know where it is. | Word order |
| You don't cut a *saw* with a *cake*! | You don't cut a cake with a saw! | Word order |

*Landmark School, Inc.*

# Syntax

| What Student Said | What Student Meant to Say | Type of Error |
|---|---|---|
| They were three *bucks for twenty-five*. | They were three for twenty-five bucks. | Word order |
| You *both walk up them*. | You walk up both of them. | Word order, omitted preposition |
| *It* lost all interest *in me*. | I lost all interest in it. | Word order |
| When I didn't be there . . . | Before I was here . . . | Confused adverbs, substituted incorrect infinitive for "be" |
| It was covered sand. | It was covered with sand. | Omitted preposition |
| I *was a'knowing it*. | I already knew that. | Substituted progressive verb form for irregular past tense |
| I know a person *just looks like you*. | I know a person who looks just like you. | Omitted relative pronoun; incorrect word order |
| I don't know *what* she ate one of those. | I don't know whether she ate one of those. | Substituted pronoun for correlative conjunction |
| I haven't had one *since* about three years. | I haven't had one for about three years. | Used incorrect preposition |
| I forgot she looks like. | I forgot what she looks like. | Omitted head of noun clause |
| I forget *this one I got*. | I forget who gave me this one. | Omitted pronoun as head of clause |
| An apple is *alike from* the orange. | An apple is like the orange. | Substituted an adjective, "alike," for a preposition, "like" |
| I *broken* the dish. | I broke the dish. I have broken the dish. | Omitted auxiliary verb |
| *I was diverse to the neighborhood*. | I was in a diverse neighborhood. | Modified the subject instead of the object |

*Landmark School, Inc.*

The rest of this chapter presents specific goals and objectives for syntactical development. The goals are idealized, inferring mastery, though most students probably will not attain mastery. The objectives, on the other hand, are largely presented in developmental order (in order of difficulty). This way, the teacher can identify an objective along the spectrum of difficulty as a realistic target for a given student. For example, the goal for "Complex Sentences with Subordinate Adverbial Clauses" is for the student to use selected subordinating conjunctions to formulate complex sentences, while demonstrating comprehension of the underlying rules. One of the objectives under this goal is for the student to select the correct subordinating conjunctions to complete a sentence in a cloze task. This objective might be used as a realistic goal for a student who is not likely to master complex sentences with subordinate adverbial clauses within the school year.

# Word Order in Simple Sentences

## *Goal*

The student will formulate simple sentences and demonstrate understanding of correct word order in those sentences.

## *Background*

An engaging activity that is an important precursor for students to rearrange words mentally when looking at a printed page follows:

- The teacher selects sentences from the literature students are reading and prints each word from each sentence on its own card. To give beginners a jump-start, the teacher capitalizes the first letter of the preferred first word of the sentence and adds a period after the preferred final word.

- Students arrange the word cards to form complete sentences. In addition, the teacher can encourage students to see how many sentences they can assemble from any subset of the word cards. The teacher should foster discussion of the different meanings of different sentences, such as the difference between "Wilbur's mind was empty but his tummy was full." and "Wilbur's tummy was empty but his mind was full."

The motor activity involved in manipulating the cards is also valuable.

The Magnetic Story Board[6] is a kit for practicing sentence assembly. The kit consists of a metallic board and magnetic strips with words representing all parts of speech. Each strip contains one word. The word strips can also be used to create similes, cinquains (five-line stanzas), and haiku poems. Careful planning is necessary for productive activity; if the exercises are too open-ended, they are not an effective use of time.

## *Objectives*

The student will:

- auditorily distinguish between correct and incorrect word order in simple sentences dictated by the instructor

---

[6]Available from Toys to Grow On (800/542-8338 or www.toystogrowon.com)

- arrange a random array of word cards into logical word order for simple sentences
- arrange word cards into more than one correct simple sentence, if possible
- self-monitor for accurate production of word order using an audiotape recorder
- distinguish between the same and different meaning when the order of words or a phrase in a sentence is changed (i.e., same meaning/different form vs. different meaning/different form); for example, "Tom stood behind Jane." and "Jane stood behind Tom." (different meaning/different form) and "Jeff played basketball after supper." and "After supper, Jeff played basketball." (same meaning/different form)
- generate original simple sentences with correct word order from picture stimuli
- use correct word order in sentences while narrating a picture story
- use correct word order in spontaneous speech
- reorder words from scrambled sentences in structured writing tasks, using a template
- reorder words from scrambled sentences in structured writing tasks without template
- generate sentences containing correct word order in spontaneous writing

# Simple Sentences with a Noun Phrase and Action Verb

## *Goal*

The student will formulate simple sentences comprised of a noun phrase plus an action verb, while demonstrating comprehension of the underlying rules.

## *Background*

At Landmark, we distinguish between an "animate being" and an "inanimate object" early in students' writing experience (Jennings and Haynes 2002). It follows that students' verb choices are more appropriate, because a cliff can't walk and a mountain can't move, though poison ivy does creep.

Equally important is that teachers select a theme of interest to students as an anchor for teaching written expression. Students focus upon information related to the theme while tackling the nuts and bolts of grammar. Learning about dolphins, for example, greatly enhances the probability of students remaining engaged in the intensive training necessary to master sentence construction.

## *Objectives*

The student will:

- discriminate between animate (e.g., dog) and inanimate (e.g., cliff) nouns in photographs
- discriminate between animate and inanimate nouns without cues
- verbally generate lists of animate and inanimate nouns from a theme or subject provided by the instructor
- demonstrate comprehension of action verbs through gesture, manipulation of objects, or examination of action photos
- distinguish a noun phrase from an action verb
- produce noun phrases and action verbs in response to such visual cues as actions and photos

- discriminate between correct and incorrect action verbs when produced in conjunction with inanimate nouns
- distinguish complete from incomplete sentences generated by the instructor, given a template
- verbally formulate noun-phrase-plus-action-verb sentences, given a template
- distinguish complete from incomplete sentences generated by the instructor without a template
- verbally formulate noun-phrase-plus-action-verb sentences from theme-related vocabulary without a template
- self-monitor for accuracy of sentence production using an audiotape recorder
- formulate noun-phrase-plus-action-verb sentences in structured writing tasks

# Simple Sentences with *Where* Phrases

## *Goal*

The student will formulate simple sentences comprised of a noun phrase plus an action verb plus a *where* prepositional phrase.

## *Background*

"Noun phrase plus action verb plus *where* phrase" is a construct developed by Jennings (Jennings and Haynes 2002). It is part of a highly structured sequence of skills taught in language arts classes at Landmark. Jennings has also been instrumental in emphasizing the selection of a theme of interest to students as an anchor for teaching written expression. Students focus upon information related to the theme while tackling the nuts and bolts of grammar. Learning about dolphins, for example, greatly enhances the probability that students will remain engaged in the intensive training necessary to master sentence construction.

## *Objectives*

The student will:

- demonstrate comprehension of prepositions and adverbs denoting *where* through gesture, manipulation of objects, or examination of action photos

- discriminate between complete and incomplete noun-phrase-plus-action-verb-plus-*where*-phrase sentences

- produce noun-phrase-plus-action-verb-plus-*where*-phrase sentences in response to visual cues (e.g., actions and photos), given a template

- distinguish between complete and incomplete sentences generated by the instructor, given a template

- verbally formulate noun-phrase-plus-action-verb-plus-*where*-phrase sentences, given a template but with no visual cues

- distinguish complete from incomplete sentences generated by the instructor without a template

- verbally formulate noun-phrase-plus-action-verb-plus-*where*-phrase sentences from theme-related vocabulary without a template

- self-monitor for accuracy of sentence production using an audiotape recorder

- formulate noun-phrase-plus-action-verb-plus-*where*-phrase sentences in structured writing tasks

# Simple Sentences with *When* Phrases

## *Goal*

The student will formulate simple sentences comprised of a noun phrase plus an action verb plus a *when* prepositional phrase.

## *Background*

"Noun phrase plus action verb plus *when* phrase" is a construct developed by Jennings (Jennings and Haynes 2002). It is part of a highly structured sequence of skills taught in language arts classes at Landmark. Jennings has also been instrumental in emphasizing selection of a theme of interest to students as an anchor for teaching written expression. Students focus upon information related to the theme while tackling the nuts and bolts of grammar. Learning about dolphins, for example, greatly enhances the probability that students will remain engaged in the intensive training necessary to master sentence construction.

Jennings developed visual mnemonics to support words that denote time of day. A list of these words follows.

### Words That Denote Time of Day

| | | | |
|---|---|---|---|
| After lunch | Early afternoon | Midmorning | Late afternoon |
| Dawn | Early morning | Midafternoon | Teatime |
| Daybreak | Evening | Noon | Twilight |
| Dusk | Midday | Lunchtime | |

## *Objectives*

The student will:

- accurately produce words that denote *when* in response to visual cues (e.g., a picture of the sun and moon in relation to the horizon)

- categorize *where* and *when* phrases in response to visual prompts (e.g., photos)

- verbally formulate *when* phrases in response to topics presented by the instructor; for example, on the topic of whales, a student might say, "The whales breached on the horizon during late afternoon."

- produce noun-phrase-plus-action-verb-plus-*when*-phrase sentences in response to visual cues (e.g., actions and photos), given a template

- distinguish complete from incomplete noun-phrase-plus-action-verb-plus-*when*-phrase sentences generated by the instructor, given a template

- distinguish complete from incomplete noun-phrase-plus-action-verb-plus-*when*-phrase sentences generated by the instructor without a template

- verbally formulate sentences containing noun phrase plus action verb plus *when* phrases, given a template but without visual cues

- verbally formulate noun-phrase-plus-action-verb-plus-*when*-phrase sentences from theme-related vocabulary without a template

- self-monitor for accuracy of sentence production using an audiotape recorder

- formulate noun-phrase-plus-action-verb-plus-*when*-phrase sentences in structured writing tasks

# Simple Sentences with *Where* and *When* Phrases

## *Goal*

The student will formulate simple sentences comprised of a noun phrase plus an action verb plus *where* and *when* prepositional phrases.

## Background

"Noun phrase plus action verb plus *where* phrase plus *when* phrase" is a construct developed by Jennings (Jennings and Haynes 2002). It is part of a highly structured sequence of skills taught in language arts classes at Landmark. Jennings has also been instrumental in emphasizing selection of a theme of interest to students as an anchor for teaching written expression. Students focus upon information related to the theme while tackling the nuts and bolts of grammar. Learning about dolphins, for example, greatly enhances the probability that students will remain engaged in the intensive training necessary to master sentence construction.

## *Objectives*

The student will:

- categorize *where* and *when* phrases in response to visual prompts (e.g., photos)

- verbally formulate *where* and *when* phrases in response to topics presented by the instructor; for example, on the topic of whales, a student might say, "The whales leaped from the waves during late afternoon."

- produce noun-phrase-plus-action-verb-plus-*where*-and-*when*-phrase sentences in response to visual cues (e.g., actions and photos), given a template

- distinguish between complete and incomplete noun-phrase-plus-action-verb-plus-*where*-and-*when*-phrase sentences generated by the instructor, given a template

- distinguish complete from incomplete noun-phrase-plus-action-verb-plus-*where*-and-*when*-phrase sentences generated by the instructor without a template

- verbally formulate sentences containing a noun phrase plus an action verb plus *where* and *when* phrases, given a template but without visual cues

- verbally formulate noun-phrase-plus-action-verb-plus-*where*-and-*when*-phrase sentences from theme-related vocabulary without a template

- self-monitor for accuracy of sentence production using an audiotape recorder

- formulate noun-phrase-plus-action-verb-plus-*where*-and-*when*-phrase sentences in structured writing tasks

# Simple Sentences with Adjectives

## *Goal*

The student will formulate simple sentences containing adjectives.

## *Background*

In her quest to enable students to write simple sentences that are semantically rich, Jennings set about creating a list of adjective types that students can call upon at will (Jennings and Haynes 2002). Drawing from clinical observations by Wiig and Semel (1984) and others, Jennings selected twelve adjective types and grouped them into three manageable clusters. Landmark students have demonstrated over and over again their ability to generate these twelve adjective types from memory. The mnemonic cues – the Easy Four, Six Senses/Feelings, and Hard Three (*M-A-D*) – have proven quite powerful.

### Adjective Types

| Easy Four | Six Senses/Feelings | Hard Three (*M-A-D*) |
|---|---|---|
| Size | Sight | Made of |
| Shape | Smell/flavor | Age |
| Number | Taste | Design |
| Color | Texture | |
| | Sounds like | |
| | Inner feelings | |

## *Objectives*

The student will:

- discriminate between adjectives (e.g., words that tell *which*, *what kind of*, or *how many*) and other parts of speech, given a template that shows the position of the adjective before the noun

- discriminate between adjectives and other parts of speech without a template

- generate a list of theme-related adjectives

- include adjectives in verbally generated simple sentences containing a noun phrase plus an action verb, given a template

- include adjectives in verbally generated simple sentences containing a noun phrase plus an action verb without a template
- include adjectives in verbally generated simple sentences containing a noun phrase plus an action verb plus prepositional phrases, given a template
- include adjectives in verbally generated simple sentences containing a noun phrase plus an action verb plus prepositional phrases without a template
- include adjectives in writing tasks requiring simple sentences containing a noun phrase plus an action verb, given a template
- include adjectives in writing tasks requiring simple sentences containing a noun phrase plus an action verb without a template
- include adjectives in writing tasks requiring simple sentences containing a noun phrase plus an action verb plus prepositional phrases, given a template
- include adjectives in writing tasks requiring simple sentences containing a noun phrase plus an action verb plus prepositional phrases without a template
- include appropriately placed adjectives in spontaneous speech
- include appropriately placed adjectives in spontaneous writing

# EXPANDED KERNEL SENTENCE FRAMEWORK

**Easy 4**　　**6 Senses**　　**Hard 3**

1. _____　5. _____　1. _____
2. _____　6. _____　2. _____
3. _____　7. _____　3. _____
4. _____　8. _____
　　　　　9. _____

Name: _____
Date: _____
Day: _____

**WORD BOX for INANIMATE NOUNS**
sat　lay　stood　rested　leaned
hovered　stretched　hung　spread

**WHEN PHRASES**
parts of the day
weather
units of time

| Article | Adjective | Adjective | Noun | Action Verb-ed | Where Phrase | When Phrase |
|---|---|---|---|---|---|---|
| The | vast | blue | sky | hovered | over the plains | that sunny day. |
|  |  |  |  |  |  |  |
|  |  |  |  |  |  |  |
|  |  |  |  |  |  |  |
|  |  |  |  |  |  |  |
|  |  |  |  |  |  |  |
|  |  |  |  |  |  |  |
|  |  |  |  |  |  |  |

*[Handwritten note (pink):]* A sample sen[tence] framework devel[oped at] a college - differen[t...]

*[Handwritten note (yellow):]* Our daughter used this chart when she taught English in Ecuador. Adjective before noun

Landmark School, Inc.

# Simple Sentences with Adverbs

## *Goal*

The student will formulate simple sentences containing adverbs and explain that the role of adverbs in sentences is to tell *how*, *when*, or *where*.

## *Background*

An *adverb* modifies a verb, adjective, or another adverb. Adverbs tell *how*, *when*, or *where* and usually end in *-ly*. Familiar, high-frequency adverbs enter children's sentence structure at an early age. Four-year-olds use such adverbs appropriately; for example, "Mimi, we must go quickly!"

According to Wiig and Semel (1984) children with language-related learning disabilities often misinterpret or fail to process adverbs. These students may not hear the *-ly* marker at the end of a word or an adverb that receives less stress at the end of a sentence. Landmark students find adverb phrases that express direction and time particularly troublesome. They often visualize opposites, such as east/west of the Mississippi and before/after the game, in reverse order. One student described the scientific method of study fluently, but then asserted, "I still can't tell 'before' from 'after'!"

It is essential for the instructor to verify students' comprehension of words' meanings (in this case, words used as adverbs) before asking them to write sentences with adverbs and adverbial phrases.

## *Objectives*

The student will:

- use body movements to illustrate a command containing an adverb given by the instructor; for example, "Walk quickly to the door." and "Run fast."
- identify the *-ly* ending as a marker for most adverbs
- match pictures of actions with word cards containing adverbs
- discriminate between adverbs and other parts of speech
- choose the most appropriate adverb in sentence completion tasks; for example, "The orca pursued the seal _____ (lazily, calmly, or aggressively)."

- role play the sentence completion task for each adverb listed; for example, "Walk quickly.", "Knock loudly.", and "Knock quietly."
- generate a list of adverbs for theme-related action pictures
- include adverbs in verbally generated simple sentences containing a noun phrase plus an action verb, given a template
- include adverbs in verbally generated simple sentences containing a noun phrase plus an action verb without a template
- include adverbs in verbally generated simple sentences containing a noun phrase plus an action verb plus prepositional phrases, given a template
- include adverbs in verbally generated simple sentences containing a noun phrase plus an action verb plus prepositional phrases without a template
- include adverbs in writing tasks requiring simple sentences containing a noun phrase plus an action verb, given a template
- include adverbs in writing tasks requiring simple sentences containing a noun phrase plus an action verb without a template
- include adverbs in writing tasks requiring simple sentences containing a noun phrase plus an action verb plus prepositional phrases, given a template
- include adverbs in writing tasks requiring simple sentences containing a noun phrase plus an action verb plus prepositional phrases without a template
- include appropriately placed adverbs in spontaneous speech
- include appropriately placed adverbs in spontaneous writing

*Landmark School, Inc.*

# Simple Sentences with Negatives

## *Goal*

The student will formulate simple sentences containing the negative marker "not"; its contracted form, *-n't*; and such negative words as "no" and "without."

## *Background*

The importance of the word "not" and its contraction, *-n't*, cannot be overemphasized. When reading aloud, Landmark students frequently omit the negative form or its contraction. Their interpretation is, of course, the opposite of what the author intends. Students also frequently insert a negative into a simple positive statement in the text. It is clearly important for students to master decoding of positive and negative statements.

### Common Negatives and Contractions

| | |
|---|---|
| Cannot/can't | Shall not/shan't (less common) |
| Could not/couldn't | Should not/shouldn't |
| Could not have/couldn't have | Should not have/shouldn't have |
| Did not/didn't | Was not/wasn't |
| Do not/don't | Were not/weren't |
| Does not/doesn't | Will not/won't |
| Had not/hadn't | Would not/wouldn't |
| Have not/haven't | Would not have/wouldn't have |
| Has not/hasn't | |

## *Objectives*

The student will:

- auditorily distinguish between the same and different meaning in sentences containing positive and negative voice dictated by the instructor

- formulate positive and negative sentences in response to stimuli presented by the instructor (e.g., actions and photos)

- distinguish between the same and different meaning when listening to negative sentences containing various stress patterns;

for example, "He *shouldn't* feed the dolphins." vs. "He shouldn't feed the *dolphins*."

- generate alternative hypotheses about implied meaning in sentences containing negatives (e.g, mood vs. fact); for example, does "He will not go." mean he refuses to go or he is not going?

- transform positive statements into negative statements by inserting "no" or "without" immediately before the noun; for example, "I wore *no* socks." and "I wore shoes *without* socks."

- transform uncontracted negatives into contractions (e.g., transform "will not" to "won't")

- transform contractions into uncontracted negatives in oral and written work, given a template (e.g., transform "won't" to "will not")

- formulate sentences containing contracted and uncontracted negatives

# Passive Voice

## *Goal*

The student will formulate sentences in the passive voice and demonstrate comprehension of the underlying rules.

## *Background*

Many Landmark students misinterpret sentences written in passive voice and, as a result, fail to understand literature with such sentences. Role playing sentences using objects or gestures is an extremely effective strategy for teaching this concept. Once the concept is established, it is important to reverse roles and allow the student to "test" the instructor.

## *Objectives*

The student will:

- distinguish between the same and different meaning in dictated sentences containing active and passive voice while observing actions or manipulating objects; for example, "The Jeep was passed by the Corvette. The Corvette passed the Jeep. The Jeep passed the Corvette." and "The mouse was swallowed by the owl. The mouse swallowed the owl. The owl swallowed the mouse."

- distinguish correct from incorrect dictated sentences containing active and passive voice while observing actions

- identify the actor or agent in dictated sentences containing active and passive voice

- role play sentences dictated by the instructor; for example, "Nikki was tapped by Ben." and "The book was left on the table by Courtney."

- verbally formulate sentences with active and passive voice to describe activities demonstrated by the instructor; for example, "Ms. Heddon opened the door." and "The door was opened by Ms. Heddon."

- auditorily discriminate between same and different meaning while listening to dictated sentence pairs, without visual stimuli

- verbally transform sentences containing passive voice into sentences containing active voice
- verbally transform sentences containing active voice into sentences containing passive voice
- order a random array of word cards into sentences containing passive voice
- include passive voice in narration of picture stories
- include passive voice in structured writing tasks
- include passive voice in spontaneous speech
- include passive voice in spontaneous writing

# Yes-No Interrogatives

## *Goal*

The student will interpret and formulate yes-no interrogatives and demonstrate comprehension of the underlying rules.

## *Background*

As their language develops, children learn to process and formulate yes-no interrogatives before they process *wh-* interrogatives. Toddlers are experts in using rising intonation to ask a question long before they can assemble all the words in the right order. By the time they are four, normally achieving children accurately formulate tag questions (e.g., "I can go with you, *can't I?*").

Students whose native language is not English might need direct instruction in processing and producing yes-no interrogatives. The order of the objectives below roughly follows that suggested by Wiig and Semel (1984).

## *Objectives*

The student will:

- answer instructor-generated questions with forms of "to be" using photos as stimuli; for example, an answer to "Is she smiling?" might be "No! She is not smiling."

- answer and ask tag questions; for example, "We had fun, *didn't we?*"

- imitate word order in yes-no interrogatives modeled by the instructor; for example, "Will we go to the Boston Aquarium?"

- formulate interrogatives by adding auxiliaries to active present-tense verbs in declarative statements; for example, "I like that low-tide smell." becomes "Do you like that low-tide smell?"

- formulate interrogatives by adding auxiliaries to active past-tense verbs in declarative statements; for example, "The dolphins swam near the boat." becomes "Did the dolphins swim near the boat?"

- verbally formulate negative counterparts to interrogatives; for example, "Is the blue whale the biggest mammal?" becomes "Isn't the blue whale the biggest mammal?"

*Landmark School, Inc.*

- order a random array of word cards into interrogatives
- self-monitor for accurate word order in interrogatives using an audiotape recorder
- formulate yes-no interrogatives in structured writing exercises
- formulate yes-no interrogatives in spontaneous speech
- formulate yes-no interrogatives in spontaneous writing

# Indirect Requests

## *Goal*

The student will accurately interpret and formulate indirect requests.

## *Background*

Some questions are indirect. For example, "Can you please talk more quietly?" doesn't really mean "Are you able to talk more quietly?". Rather, it is a request made indirectly to avoid the tone of a command, as in "Be quiet!"

## *Objectives*

The student will:

- distinguish between direct and indirect requests produced by the instructor in multimodality presentations, such as demonstrations, short skits, and role-playing activities; for example, "Will you please turn down the radio?" vs. "Turn down the radio."

- analyze a speaker's intent in relation to a context or situation in role-playing activities

- describe situations in which indirect requests might occur

- verbally formulate indirect requests in structured activities

- verbally formulate indirect requests in structured writing activities

- verbally formulate indirect requests in spontaneous speech

- verbally formulate indirect requests in spontaneous writing

## *Teaching Strategies*

The instructor will:

- present affirmative indirect requests

- discuss students' responses, if in error, and determine whether students accurately interpreted contextual cues

- help students correct erroneous responses

- present negative indirect requests

*Landmark School, Inc.*

## Wh- Interrogatives

### Goal

The student will formulate questions containing *wh-* interrogatives and demonstrate comprehension of the underlying rules.

### Background

Normally developing children respond to *who*, *what*, and *where* questions at age three. They learn to answer *when* and *how* questions at a later age. Some students have great difficulty processing *how* and *which* questions. They frequently respond to a question that asks *how* as if it were asking *what*.

In addition to processing *wh-* interrogatives, students are expected to formulate them accurately. They should be able to re-position the linking verb in declarative sentences (e.g., "The whales are heading north." becomes "Are the whales heading north?"). They might also be expected to add a *wh-* word to the question (e.g., "When are the whales heading north?").

The objectives below reflect an order recommended by Wiig and Semel (1984).

### Objectives

The student will:

- answer questions that ask *what*
- use *what* plus a person, animal, place, time, reason, or way in interrogatives; for example, "What time are we leaving?" and "What do you want for dessert?"
- differentiate between human (*who*) and nonhuman (*what*) pronouns given visual stimuli
- answer questions that ask *who*
- verbally formulate questions that ask *who*, given a template
- verbally formulate questions that ask *who* without a template
- verbally formulate questions that ask *who* in structured writing tasks, given a template

- verbally formulate questions that ask *who* in structured writing tasks without a template
- generate words that tell *where*, given visual stimuli
- answer questions that ask *where*
- discriminate among information that tells *who*, *what*, and *where* in speaking and writing tasks
- verbally formulate questions that ask *where*, given visual stimuli and a template
- verbally formulate questions that ask *where* without a template
- formulate questions that ask *where* in structured writing tasks
- generate words that tell *when*, given visual stimuli
- answer questions that ask *when*
- discriminate among information that tells *who*, *what*, *where*, and *when* in speaking and writing tasks
- verbally formulate questions that ask *when*, given visual stimuli and a template
- verbally formulate questions that ask *when* without a template
- formulate questions that ask *when* in structured writing tasks
- answer questions that ask *why*
- discriminate among information that tells *who*, *what*, *where*, *when*, and *why* in speaking and writing tasks
- verbally formulate questions that ask *why*, given visual stimuli and a template
- verbally formulate questions that ask *why* without a template
- formulate questions that ask *why* in structured writing tasks
- answer questions that ask *how*
- discriminate among information that tells *who*, *what*, *where*, *when*, *why*, and *how* in speaking and writing tasks
- verbally formulate questions that ask *how*, given visual stimuli and a template
- verbally formulate questions that ask *how* without a template

- formulate questions that ask *how* in structured writing tasks, given a template
- formulate questions that ask *how* in structured writing tasks without a template
- answer questions that ask *which*
- discriminate among information that tells *who*, *what*, *where*, *when*, *why*, *how*, and *which* in speaking and writing tasks
- verbally formulate questions that ask *which*, given visual stimuli and a template
- verbally formulate questions that ask *which* without a template
- formulate questions that ask *which* in structured writing tasks, given a template
- formulate questions that ask *which* in structured writing tasks without a template
- substitute the correct *wh-* interrogative for specified information within sentences; for example, the correct interrogative for "time" is *when* and the correct interrogative for "over the moon" is *where*

# Basic Sentence Types, Classified by Purpose

## *Goal*

The student will recognize and formulate the basic sentence types, classified by purpose.

## *Background*

Students master the four basic terms for sentence types – declarative, interrogative, imperative, and exclamatory – through repeated exposure to those terms in combination with simple synonyms. For example, effective combinations are informing/declarative, asking/interrogative, command/imperative, and excited/exclamatory. In writing tasks at Landmark, students are exposed to both words until they master sentence classification (Jennings and Haynes 2002).

Instructors should exaggerate the tone of voice commonly associated with each sentence type. For example, instructors can end a question at a higher pitch or express an exclamation with increased stress and volume, as in "I *told* you not to do that!" Some students display no affect in their voices and have difficulty understanding the affect in others' voices.

## *Objectives*

The student will:

- interpret and explain that the verbal cue "informing/declarative" indicates that the sentence gives information about the noun (subject)
- verbally produce an informing/declarative sentence, given a template
- identify the correct punctuation that follows a declarative sentence, a period (.)
- interpret and explain that the verbal cue "asking/interrogative" indicates that the sentence asks a question
- verbally produce an asking/interrogative sentence, given a template
- transpose auxiliaries in asking/interrogative sentences, given a template

- identify the correct punctuation that follows an interrogative sentence, a question mark (?)
- interpret and explain that the verbal cue "command/imperative" indicates that the sentence is a command or request
- verbally produce an command/imperative sentence, given a template
- identify the correct punctuation that follows an imperative sentence, a period (.)
- interpret and explain that the verbal cue "excited/exclamatory" indicates that the sentence expresses strong feelings
- verbally produce an excited/exclamatory sentence, given a template
- identify the correct punctuation that follows an exclamatory sentence, an exclamation point (!)
- identify the four basic sentence types in sentences dictated by the instructor
- formulate any of the four basic sentence types in response to any of the four two-word verbal cues: informing/declarative, asking/interrogative, command/imperative, and excited/exclamatory

# Conjunction Deletions

## *Goal*

The student will process and formulate sentences containing conjunction deletions; for example, "I drive cars. I drive trucks." becomes "I drive cars and trucks."

## *Background*

The process of joining clauses and omitting repeated words or phrases is called *conjunction deletion*. Semel, Wiig, and Secord (1995) developed an oral language test that calls upon students to assemble sentences using conjunction deletion. Although Landmark students might accurately interpret such sentences, they have difficulty accurately assembling them from components without adding the deleted words.

For example, the teacher asks students to create sentences using only these six words: Debby, letter, did, Ellen, send, the. The sentences below are correct, grammatically speaking. They show students' understanding that the preposition "to" is implied. Students who add "to" to their sentences do not understand conjunction deletion.

### Examples of Conjunction Deletion

> Did Debby send Ellen the letter?
> Did Ellen send Debby the letter?
> Ellen did send Debby the letter.
> Debby did send Ellen the letter.

## *Objectives*

The student will:

- resolve conjunction deletions into their component propositions; for example, "Ben and Sharif play soccer." becomes "Ben plays soccer. Sharif plays soccer."

- synthesize component propositions into conjunction deletions; for example, "Eliza ate yogurt. Kimmi ate yogurt." becomes "Eliza and Kimmi ate yogurt."

- form a compound direct object from conjunctions and nouns; for example, "Nikki loves Elmo and Big Bird."

- form a compound indirect object from conjunctions, prepositions, and nouns; for example, "The girls modeled their Bali dresses for Poppa and Mimi."

- form a compound subject from conjunctions and nouns; for example, "Nadia and Courtney will enter first grade in September."

- form a compound predicate (verb) adjective; for example, "Unfortunately, those pesty crows are both healthy and wise."

- add the correct conjunctions (and, but, or) in oral cloze procedures; for example, "You may have lasagna _____ pizza for supper, _____ you cannot have both."

- include conjunction deletions in spontaneous speech

- include conjunction deletions in structured writing exercises

- include conjunction deletions in spontaneous writing exercises

# Phrases with Verbals: Participles, Gerunds, and Infinitives

## *Goal*

The student will formulate phrases containing verbals and include them in sentences.

## *Background*

A *participle* derives from a verb and is used as an adjective. The participle might appear as a verb plus *–ing* or a verb plus *-ed* (e.g., running water and devoted father). A *participial phrase* contains a participle and its complements or modifiers (e.g., *blowing his nose,* the survivor told his sad tale). A *gerund* derives from a verb and functions as a noun (e.g., sailing is fun); the suffix *–ing* is added to the verb to create the noun. A *gerund phrase* contains a gerund and its complements or modifiers (e.g., *finding a Tennessee quarter* made the young coin collector happy). An *infinitive* is a simple verb form, usually preceded by "to," that is used as a noun or a modifier. For example:

- In "to sleep is my desire," the infinitive is the subject.
- In "he wanted to drive," the infinitive is the object of the verb.
- In "my ambition is to fly," the infinitive is a predicate nominative.
- In "we lacked the will to diet," the infinitive is an adjective modifying "will."
- In "we practice to make perfect," the infinitive is an adverb modifying "practice."

The study of gerunds, participles, and infinitives begins in middle school and continues into adulthood. It is important for middle-school students to be able to interpret sentences with these phrases in literature and textbooks even if they cannot accurately formulate such sentences. One student reading *Iceberg Hermit*, by Arthur Roth, thought that the protagonist was carving his hand with a knife when he read the participial phrase "carving knife in hand."

## Objectives

The student will:

- distinguish between verbs and participial phrases containing verbals produced by the instructor; for example, "he is leaping" vs. "the leaping frog"
- identify a participle as a verb form that is used as an adjective (e.g., clearing sky)
- identify the *-ing* ending in a present participle produced by the instructor
- identify *-ed*, *-d*, *-en*, and *-n* endings in past participles produced by the instructor
- identify participial phrases in dictated sentences; for example, "Shedding his slicker, Ben cavorted in the warm spring rain."
- verbally formulate sentences containing participles and participial phrases, given a template
- formulate sentences containing participles and participial phrases in writing tasks, given a template
- identify the gerund as a verb form ending in *-ing* that is used as a noun while viewing a list of gerunds; for example, "Swimming is good exercise."
- identify a gerund phrase as a gerund plus any complements or modifiers; for example, "Working as a lifeguard can be rewarding."
- verbally formulate sentences containing gerunds and gerund phrases, given a template
- verbally formulate sentences containing gerunds and gerund phrases without a template
- formulate sentences containing gerunds and gerund phrases in writing tasks, given a template
- formulate sentences containing gerunds and gerund phrases in writing tasks without a template
- identify an infinitive as a verb form, usually preceded by "to," that is used as a noun or a modifier
- identify an infinitive phrase as an infinitive plus any complements or modifiers

- verbally formulate sentences containing infinitives and infinitive phrases, given a template
- verbally formulate sentences containing infinitives and infinitive phrases without a template
- formulate sentences containing infinitives and infinitive phrases in writing tasks, given a template
- formulate sentences containing infinitives and infinitive phrases in writing tasks without a template

# Compound Sentences with Coordinating Conjunctions

## Goal

The student will formulate compound sentences using the coordinating conjunctions "and," "but," and "or" and demonstrate comprehension of the underlying rules.

## Background

While established writers might use "or," "and," or "but" at the beginning of a sentence, students should not use such sentence construction when developing formal oral language skills.

Teachers can use pairs of logically related action photos to model compound sentences before asking students to generate their own. Searching for compound sentences in literary passages is another effective teaching strategy.

## Objectives

The student will:

- distinguish between two dictated sentences that are logically related and two that are not; for example, two related sentences are "Baleen whales eat krill." and "Orcas eat other sea animals."; two unrelated sentences are "Dolphins have lungs." and "Otters eat mussels."

- distinguish between correct and incorrect two-sentence combinations produced by the instructor, given a template

- distinguish between correct and incorrect two-sentence combinations produced by the instructor without a template

- orally combine two sentences by adding a coordinating conjunction, given a template, action photos, and theme-related vocabulary

- orally combine two sentences by adding a coordinating conjunction without a template

*Landmark School, Inc.*

- combine two sentences by adding a coordinating conjunction in structured writing tasks, given a template, visual cues, and theme-related vocabulary
- combine two sentences by adding a coordinating conjunction in structured writing tasks without a template
- form two simple sentences from one compound sentence, given visual cues
- form two simple sentences from one compound sentence in structured writing tasks without visual cues
- explain the inferred meanings of sentences containing the coordinating conjunctions "and," "but," and "or"
- formulate compound sentences in spontaneous speech
- formulate compound sentences in writing tasks, given theme-related vocabulary but without a template
- formulate compound sentences in spontaneous writing

# Compound Sentences with Conjuncts (Connectives)

## Goal

The student will process and formulate sentences comprised of two main clauses joined by a conjunct; for example, "She is a bright student; however, she doesn't study very hard."

## Background

*Conjuncts* are adverbs whose function is to relate or conjoin independent grammatical units, such as clauses, sentences, or paragraphs (Crystal 1995). They are used extensively in spoken and written language. According to Crystal, conjuncts link ideas *across* sentences while conjunctions link propositions *within* a sentence.

In written expression, American and British punctuation differ. The British allow a new sentence to start with a conjunct, as in "He successfully harpooned the whale. However, his leg was caught in the line." Warriner (1988), an American grammarian, advises that the two propositions be connected by a semicolon, as in "He successfully harpooned the whale; however, his leg was caught in the line."

The table below lists some conjuncts, categorized by usage (Crystal 1995; Paul 2000).

### Selected Conjuncts

| Addition | Contrast | Result | Choice |
|---|---|---|---|
| Also | Anway | Accordingly | Otherwise |
| Besides | Conversely | Consequently | |
| Finally | However | Hence | |
| Further | Instead | Meanwhile | |
| Furthermore | Nevertheless | Thereafter | |
| In addition | Nonetheless | Therefore | |
| Incidentally | Now | Thus | |
| Indeed | Rather | | |
| Likewise | Still | | |
| Moreover | Yet | | |
| Namely | | | |
| Next | | | |
| Similarly | | | |
| Then | | | |

*Landmark School, Inc.*

## Objectives

The student will:

- formulate sentences with specified conjuncts, given visual stimuli (e.g., photos) and a main-clause-plus-main-clause template

- discriminate between complete and incomplete sentence structures while listening to dictated word groups containing conjuncts; for example, "I pulled the shark in; however, it was dead." vs. "However, the shark was dead"

- identify a conjunct used in a sentence dictated by the instructor as belonging to the "addition" category; for example, "We will sail six miles out to sea; furthermore, we will use sonar to detect the presence of a whale." and "We will use a spyglass on our whale-watching cruise; furthermore, we will use sonar."

- identify a conjunct used in a sentence dictated by the instructor as belonging to the "contrast" category; for example, "We sailed six miles out to sea; however, we did not see a single whale."

- identify a conjunct used in a sentence dictated by the instructor as belonging to the "result" category; for example, "We sailed too far west; consequently, we missed the afternoon feeding of the whales."

- identify a conjunct used in a sentence dictated by the instructor as belonging to the "choice" category; for example, "We chose to take a harbor cruise; otherwise, we would have been stuck at the hotel."

- create compound sentences containing conjuncts from an array of word cards

- verbally formulate compound sentences containing conjuncts as connectives

- formulate complete sentences containing conjunct clauses in structured writing tasks, given a template

- formulate complete sentences containing conjuncts in structured writing tasks without a template

# Sentences with Correlative Conjunctions

## Goal

The student will formulate sentences containing correlative conjunctions and demonstrate comprehension of the underlying rules.

## Background

*Correlative conjunctions* link words, phrases, or clauses of equal importance. They are almost always used in pairs. "Whether" is sometimes used in isolation, but implies "or" (e.g., "I don't know whether [or not] he is going."). Many students do not recognize "nor" in oral language production tests, yet it often appears in excellent literature for young people. Landmark students must at least learn the meaning of "nor" when they encounter it in reading.

### Correlative Conjunctions

| | | |
|---|---|---|
| Both . . . and | Neither . . . nor | Whether . . . or |
| Either . . . or | Not only . . . but (also) | |

## Objectives

The student will:

- identify correlative conjunctions, which are almost always used in pairs (e.g., both . . . and)

- explain whether a sentence containing correlative conjunctions expresses a sum or a choice

- explain the negative connotation of "neither . . . nor"

- select the correct pair of correlative conjunctions in an oral cloze task

- verbally formulate sentences, given correlative conjunctions as stimuli

- transform declarative sentences containing correlative conjunctions into interrogatives; for example, "I will have either pie or cake." or "I will either have pie or cake." becomes "Will you have either pie or cake?"

- formulate sentences containing correlative conjunctions in spontaneous speech
- formulate sentences in structured writing exercises, given correlative conjunctions as stimuli
- formulate sentences containing correlative conjunctions in spontaneous writing

# Complex Sentences with Subordinate Adverbial Clauses

## *Goal*

The student will use selected subordinating conjunctions to formulate complex sentences, while demonstrating comprehension of the underlying rules.

## *Background*

*Complex sentences* consist of a main clause and one or more clauses of lesser rank, known as *subordinate clauses*. One kind of subordinate clause, the *adverbial clause*, works like an adverb; it modifies verbs, adjectives, or other adverbs. The adverbial clause is headed by a subordinating conjunction and usually follows the main clause, although it sometimes precedes it; for example, "We played soccer, although it was raining." and "Although it was raining, we played soccer."

Two oral language measures that evaluate students' ability to formulate sentences containing subordinate clauses are the "Formulating Sentences" subtest of *Clinical Evaluation of Language Fundamentals* (Semel, Wiig, and Secord 1995) and the "Recreating Speech Acts" subtest of the *Test of Language Competence – Expanded Edition* (Wiig and Secord 1989). Students frequently formulate subordinating clauses in isolation, without linking them to main clauses, and are penalized as a result (e.g., "Although we had the tickets.").

Children understand and begin using "because" clauses at an early age. In teaching subordinating conjunctions, Wiig and Semel therefore suggest "because" as a starting point, followed by "if," "when," "since," "as," "although," "though," and "even though."

The table below identifies and categorizes subordinating conjunctions used in adverbial clauses (Crystal 1995; Warriner 1988; Wiig and Semel 1984). Note that many of these words can be used as other parts of speech. For example:

- "After," "before," "since," and "until" may be used as prepositions.
- "How," "when," and "where" may be used as adverbs.
- "That" may be used as a relative pronoun.

*Landmark School, Inc.*

## Common Subordinating Conjunctions Used in Adverbial Clauses

| Time | Cause or Reason | Purpose or Result | Condition | Place |
|---|---|---|---|---|
| After | As | As if | Although | Where |
| As | As much as | In order that | Even though | Wherever |
| As soon as | Because | So that | If | |
| Before | In order that | That | In spite of | |
| Since | Inasmuch as | | Provided that | |
| Until | Since | | Though | |
| When | Whereas | | Unless | |
| Whenever | | | While | |
| While | | | | |

## Objectives

The student will:

- formulate sentences with specified subordinating conjunctions, given visual stimuli (e.g., photos) and a main-clause-plus-subordinate-clause template

- formulate sentences with specified subordinating conjunctions, given visual stimuli and a subordinate-clause-plus-main-clause template

- discriminate between complete and incomplete sentences while listening to dictated sentences containing subordinating conjunctions

- determine the temporal order of events in a sentence containing a subordinate clause

- determine the temporal order of events in a sentence that contains a subordinate clause and reverses the order of events; for example, "Before we ate dinner, we went to the movie."

- explain the relationship between subordinating conjunctions that denote subtle aspects of space and time and the primary clause

- interpret subtle indefinite and relative space, time, and quality relations

- retain and recall critical words or elements in a sentence containing an adverbial clause

*Landmark School, Inc.*

- select the most logical subordinating clause to go with the main clause in a multiple-choice task
- select the correct subordinating conjunction to complete a sentence in a cloze task
- analyze a series of short sentences that can be combined
- resolve a complex sentence into its two components
- normalize scrambled complex sentences using word cards
- synthesize component sentences into a complex sentence with a subordinating conjunction
- vary the position of subordinating clauses within sentences, given a template
- verbally formulate complete sentences containing subordinating clauses
- formulate complete sentences containing subordinating clauses in structured writing tasks, given a template
- formulate complete sentences containing subordinating clauses in structured writing tasks without a template

# Sentences with Right-Branched Adjective Clauses: Subordinate Clauses as Object-Related Adjectives

## *Goal*

The student will formulate sentences containing right-branched adjective clauses and demonstrate comprehension of the underlying rule.

## *Background*

*Adjective clauses* function as adjectives, providing additional information about the nouns or pronouns they modify. Adjective clauses are either embedded within a sentence or placed at the end of a sentence. Clauses at the end of a sentence are easier for students to identify and understand. These are *right-branched adjective clauses* (Wiig and Semel 1984) – "right-branched" because the clause occurs to the right of the noun it modifies. It is logical to introduce right-branched clauses before embedded clauses because the right-branched sentences follow the familiar pattern for simple, active declarative sentences (noun phrase plus verb phrase).

The *relative pronoun* that introduces the adjective clause serves three functions. It:

- modifies the preceding noun or pronoun
- connects the clause with the rest of the sentence
- serves as the subject or object of its own clause

The relative pronoun, adjective, or adverb must immediately follow the noun it represents. Consider the actual meaning of this incorrect statement: "The whales stayed with the boat which sprayed spume all over us." In some cases the relative pronoun is deleted; for example, "Nikki was excited about the prize [that] she won."

Complex sentences with subordinate adjective clauses are lengthy by nature. Students with short-term memory deficits have difficulty comprehending these sentences. By the time they reach the end of such a sentence, they might have forgotten essential parts – the main clause, the subordinate adjective clause, or parts of both. They might also have difficulty interpreting the relationships between the clauses unless they have a clear understanding of the roles played by relative pronouns.

# Relative Pronouns and Other Connectors for Right-Branched, Object-Related Adjective Clauses

| Relative Pronouns | Examples |
|---|---|
| That | There are the nets that have to be mended. |
| Which | The dolphins raced the boat, which was sailing eastward. |
| Who | Have you met the man who sailed around the world? |
| Whom | I saw Emily, the Olympic swimmer whom audiences adored. |
| [Deleted] | Kimmi bought the surfboard [that] she wanted. |

| Other Connectors | Examples |
|---|---|
| Whose (relative adjective) | The whale eyed Ahab, whose harpoon was broken. |
| When (relative adverb) | I'm looking forward to the time when the ship returns. |
| Where (relative adverb) | Do you remember the lodge where we stayed? |

## Objectives

The student will:

- discriminate between human and nonhuman nouns to select the appropriate pronoun for an adjective clause (i.e., human nouns take "who" or "that" and nonhuman nouns take "which" or "that")

- recognize that "whose" can modify both animate beings and inanimate objects, thus avoiding awkward phrases; for example, "He repaired the harpoon whose shaft was broken."

- discriminate between a correct and incorrect relative pronoun for a given noun; for example, "the boat that" or "the boat who"? "the captain which" or "the captain who"? "the anchor that" or "the anchor who"?

*Landmark School, Inc.*

- recognize that the relative pronoun is used for the noun immediately preceding it; for example, "He greeted the man who had sailed around the world."

- produce the correct relative pronoun for a given noun; for example, "the boat" (who, that) and "the captain ____" (who, which)

- produce the correct noun for a relative pronoun in a cloze task; for example, "Ahab harpooned the _____ (whale) that had haunted him."

- resolve a sentence with a right-branched adjective clause into its component propositions; for example, "Ben ate the fish that he had caught." resolves into "Ben had caught the fish." and "Ben ate the fish."

- normalize scrambled sentences; for example, the scrambled sentence, "the boat least they was bought that expensive" normalizes to "They bought the boat that was least expensive."

- synthesize component sentences into one sentence containing a right-branched adjective clause; for example, "They bought the boat. The boat was least expensive." becomes "They bought the boat that was least expensive."

- verbally formulate a sentence with a right-branched adjective clause, given a template

- verbally formulate a sentence with a right-branched adjective clause without a template

- formulate a sentence with a right-branched adjective clause in structured writing tasks, given a template

- verbally formulate a sentence with a right-branched adjective clause in spontaneous speech

- formulate a sentence with a right-branched adjective clause in spontaneous writing

# Sentences with Embedded Adjective Clauses: Subordinate Clauses as Subject-Related Adjectives

## Goal

The student will formulate sentences containing embedded, subject-related relative clauses and demonstrate comprehension of the underlying rule.

## Background

*Adjective clauses* function as adjectives, providing additional information about the nouns or pronouns they modify. Adjective clauses are either embedded within sentences or placed at the end of sentences. *Embedded adjective clauses*, which modify the subject of the sentence, are more difficult for students to identify because they occur between the subject and the verb and interrupt sentence flow. *Right-branched clauses*, which occur at the end of a sentence, are easier for students to identify and understand and should be introduced first; these are covered in the previous section.

The *relative pronoun* that introduces the adjective clause serves three functions. It:

- modifies the preceding noun or pronoun
- connects the clause with the rest of the sentence
- serves as the subject or object of its own clause

The relative pronoun, adjective, or adverb must immediately follow the noun it represents. Consider the actual meaning of this incorrect statement: "The whales stayed with the boat which sprayed spume all over us." In some cases the relative pronoun is deleted.

Complex sentences with subordinate adjective clauses are lengthy by nature. Students with short-term memory deficits have difficulty comprehending these sentences. By the time they reach the end of such a sentence, they might have forgotten essential parts — the main clause, the adjective clause, or parts of both. They might also have difficulty interpreting the relationships between the clauses unless they have a clear understanding of the roles played by relative pronouns.

Landmark School, Inc.

## Relative Pronouns and Other Connectors for Embedded, Subject-Related Adjective Clauses

| Relative Pronouns | Examples |
|---|---|
| That | The nets that have to be mended are on the dock. |
| Which | The Titanic, which hit an iceberg, still sits on the bottom of the ocean. |
| Who | The man who sailed around the world was glad to reach shore. |
| Whom | Nadia, whom audiences adored, loved to sign autographs. |
| [Deleted] | The surfboard [that] she wanted was already sold. |

| Other Connectors | Examples |
|---|---|
| Whose (relative adjective) | The whale whose tail was scarred stayed near the ship. |
| When (relative adverb) | The date when the ship should return is unknown. |
| Where (relative adverb) | The lodge where we stayed had no heat. |

## *Objectives*

The student will:

- discriminate between human and nonhuman nouns in order to select the appropriate pronoun for a relative clause (i.e., human nouns take "who" or "that" and nonhuman nouns take "which" or "that")

- discriminate between a correct and an incorrect relative pronoun for a given noun

- use "which" or "that" to modify a nonhuman noun immediately preceding it

- recognize that the relative pronoun refers to the noun immediately preceding it

- describe the noun-phrase-plus-adjective-clause-plus-verb-phrase pattern, given a template

Landmark School, Inc.

- formulate "which" and "that" adjective clauses plus verb phrases in sentence completion tasks, given a template

- formulate "which" and "that" adjective clauses plus verb phrases in sentence completion tasks without a template

- produce the correct noun for its relative pronoun in a cloze task; for example, "The whale, _____ (which, who) was wounded, swam toward the beach."

- verbally formulate a sentence containing an embedded adjective clause, given a template

- verbally formulate a sentence containing an embedded adjective clause without a template

- formulate a sentence containing an embedded adjective clause in structured writing tasks, given a template

- verbally formulate a sentence containing an embedded adjective clause in spontaneous speech

- formulate a sentence containing an embedded adjective clause in spontaneous writing

# Complex Sentences with Noun Clauses: Relative Clauses as Subjects, Objects, Predicate Nominatives, or Objects of Prepositions

## Goal

The student will interpret and formulate sentences containing noun clauses.

## Background

Grammar books categorize relative clauses as either noun clauses or adjective clauses, depending on their role in a sentence. (Adjective clauses are described in the preceding sections.) *Noun clauses,* which are subordinate, replace a noun in the main clause. *Indefinite relative pronouns* heading noun clauses do not need an antecedent (unlike relative pronouns heading adjective clauses). Noun clauses can function as the:

- subject of a sentence; for example, "Whoever rings the bell will get to eat first."

- direct object of a sentence; for example, "I know what you are doing."

- object of a preposition; for example, "He knew nothing about what I was doing."

- predicate nominative; for example, "The problem is that you overslept."

Complex sentences with subordinate relative clauses (both noun and adjective clauses) are lengthy by nature. Students with short-term memory deficits have difficulty comprehending these sentences. By the time they reach the end of such a sentence, they might have forgotten essential parts — the main clause, the relative clause, or parts of both. Noun clauses are especially hard to identify since the nouns they replace are not in the sentence.

### Indefinite Relative Pronouns for Noun Clauses

| Relative Pronouns | Examples |
| --- | --- |
| That | That you finished your homework is amazing! |
| What | The shark ate what we threw from the boat. |

Landmark School, Inc.

| Relative Pronouns | Examples |
| --- | --- |
| Whatever | The shark bit whatever we threw from the boat. |
| Who | I know who won the race. |
| Whoever | Whoever answers the phone first gets dessert first. |
| Whichever | Take two, whichever you prefer. |
| [Deleted] | She says [that] Gary Paulsen raises dogs. |

## Indefinite Relative Adjectives for Noun Clauses

| Relative Adjectives | Examples |
| --- | --- |
| Whose | I know whose boat that is. |
| Which | I know which boat belongs to him. |
| Whatever | I believed whatever he told me. |

## Indefinite Relative Adverbs for Noun Clauses

| Relative Adverbs | Examples |
| --- | --- |
| When | I don't know when he dived from the boat. |
| Where | I don't know where he found the raft. |
| How | I don't know how he escaped so fast. |
| Whether | I don't know whether he radioed the Coast Guard. |
| Why | I don't know why the huge fishing ship didn't detect the small vessel. |

## Objectives

The student will:

- distinguish between correct and incorrect grammar in sentences with noun clauses produced by the instructor; for example, "The man which sailed across the Atlantic lives in Gloucester." vs. "The man who sailed across the Atlantic lives in Gloucester."

- resolve sentences containing noun clauses into their components; for example, "The whale that sprayed us had bad breath." resolves into "The whale sprayed us." and "The whale had bad breath."

- use a random array of word cards to create sentences containing noun clauses; for example, the array "whose was dropped of hunt the man harpoon broken out the" becomes "The man whose harpoon was broken dropped out of the hunt."

- synthesize component sentences into a sentence containing a noun clause

- verbally formulate sentences containing noun clauses in structured exercises

- formulate sentences containing noun clauses in structured writing exercises

- verbally formulate sentences containing noun clauses in spontaneous speech

- formulate sentences containing noun clauses in spontaneous writing

# Statements with Quotations

## Goal

The student will recognize sentences containing quotations in literature and formulate sentences that include quotations in written expression.

## Background

One high-interest strategy for introducing quotes is orally reading literature with a lot of dialogue. The students and teacher take different roles. Once students become comfortable with the decoding, they can stop reading the clarifications outside the quotes, such as "he said" and "she replied." Students invariably improve their reading fluency, as well as their ability to read different speaker roles.

## Objectives

The student will:

- identify direct quotations in the reading by observing quotation marks

- recognize that a new paragraph marks a change in speaker

- read dialogue from literature aloud and recognize the change from one speaker to another

- read the dialogue for one character as a role-playing activity, with others reading other parts (as in a play script), eliminating the words outside the quotation marks, such as "he said"

- verbalize a formula for writing sentences with quotations, given a template (i.e., speaker plus verb plus statement)

- include proper punctuation for the quoted part of the statement

- match an appropriate "to say" verb with the type of statement quoted; for example, "He shouted, 'Get out of here!'" vs. "He said, 'Get out of here!'"

- vary the position of quotations in a statement, given a template

- vary the position of quotations in a statement without a template

- formulate sentences with quotations in writing tasks, given a template

*Landmark School, Inc.*

- formulate sentences with quotations in writing tasks without a template
- recognize punctuation that marks a quote within a quote; for example, "My mama asked, 'When are you going to learn *Concerto in F?*'"
- associate the marker "that" with an indirect quotation; for example, "He said that he would go."
- use the indirect quotation form in verbal tasks
- formulate sentences with indirect quotations in writing tasks

# Sentences with Structural Ambiguities

## Goal

The student will resolve structural ambiguities in written and oral expression.

## Background

Some sentences are ambiguous; they can be interpreted in more than one way and thus can be confusing. One kind of ambiguity arises from sentence structure; for example, "He found a book on Pike's Peak." Ambiguities are abundant in newspaper headlines – the result of trying to fit a message into a limited space. In many cases, sentences that are ambiguous for structural reasons are not well written. Fortunately, sentences with structural ambiguity almost never occur in literature.

In formal testing (Wiig and Secord 1989), Landmark students more easily identify lexical ambiguities (e.g., heel of foot, heel of shoe) than structural ambiguities (e.g., "Visiting Hollywood stars can be exciting.").

## Objectives

The student will:

- identify phrases in sentences that have multiple meanings because of structural characteristics; for example, "Celtics crash Lakers' party." vs. "Celtics crash. Lakers party."

- paraphrase a sentence with structural ambiguity; for example, "The Celtics broke the Lakers' winning streak." vs. "Celtics lose and the Lakers celebrate."

- select photos appropriate to ambiguous structure; for example, a photo of the Celtics celebrating victory vs. a photo of the Lakers celebrating victory

- analyze ambiguities in newspaper headlines

- identify ambiguous sentences embedded within a narrative; for example, "He was glad he found a book on Pike's Peak, because he would be going there soon."

- use semantic, syntactic, and pragmatic cues in spoken and written narratives to arrive at an accurate interpretation; for example, does the sentence "Breaking glass can be dangerous, so don't walk near that demolition site." mean that you shouldn't break glass yourself or that you should stay away from where glass is breaking?

## Bibliography of Instructional Materials

Bush, C. *Language Remediation and Expansion – 150 Skill-Building Reference Lists*. Austin: PRO-ED, 1989.

———. *500 Thematic Lists and Activities*. Austin: PRO-ED, 1996.

Jennings, T.M. and C.W. Haynes. 2002. From talking to writing: strategies for scaffolding expository expression. Prides Crossing, MA: Landmark Schoool.

Kisner, R., and B. Knowles. *Warm-Up Exercises – Calisthenics for the Brain*. Book 1. Eau Claire, WI: Thinking Publications, 1984.

———. *Warm-Up Exercises – Calisthenics for the Brain*. Book 2. Eau Claire, WI: Thinking Publications, 1985.

———. *Warm-Up Exercises – Calisthenics for the Brain*. Book 3. Eau Claire, WI: Thinking Publications, 1992.

Lazzari, A., and P. Peters. *HELP – Handbook of Exercises for Language Processing*. Vol. 2, *Specific Word Finding, Categorization, Wh- Questions, Grammar*. Moline, IL: LinguiSystems, 1980.

———. *HELP – Handbook of Exercises for Language Processing – Elementary*. Moline, IL: LinguiSystems, 1993.

Simon, C. *300+ Developmental Language Strategies for Clinic and Classroom*. Tempe, AZ: Communi-Cog Publications, 1993.

CHAPTER 4

# SEMANTICS

## Introduction

While the first three chapters primarily emphasized the form or structure of language, this chapter is devoted to the meaning of language. "Throw Mama from the train a kiss!" might have fractured syntax, but its meaning is not lost. In fact, the oft-quoted Yogi Berra might be the first to say, "Meaning is all!"

Gardner (1978) refers to *semantics* as "describing the relationship between the word and the world." This statement conveys the tremendous importance and scope of this linguistic area. This chapter highlights the topics that deserve special attention for teaching students with language-based learning disabilities.

Linguists refer to words as *lexemes* and to entire vocabularies as *lexicons*. According to Lederer (1991), the Oxford dictionary contains more than 600,000 words. Pinker (2000) concluded that the average high-school graduate knows 45,000 words, and reminds us that this is three times as many words as Shakespeare used in his complete works! Pinker reports that if we add proper names, numbers, foreign words, and the like, the average high-school graduate might be credited with about 60,000 words and superior students with twice that amount.

How many words does an average six-year-old know? Pinker (2000) suggests 13,000 words; other estimates range from 8,000 to 14,000 words (deVilliers and deVilliers 1978). Pinker (1999) converts these numbers into practical terms: "Children begin to learn words before their first birthday, and by their second they hoover them up at a rate of one every two hours."

Words are just one element of study in semantics; further, words cannot be learned in isolation, as dictionary definitions instill very limited understandings of words. Moats (2000) distinguishes between *denotative* meaning, the dictionary definition, and *connotative* meaning, the association of the word with other words and ideas. Crystal (1995) defines a *semantic field* as "a named area of meaning in which lexemes interrelate and define each other in specific ways." Exploration of semantic fields enriches our understanding of words.

Exposure to the written word in literature is the greatest resource for vocabulary development. Invariably, students who enter Landmark with rich vocabularies have had abundant exposure to the written word. Also, family

*Landmark School, Inc.*

discussions play an important role in vocabulary development. Precious little development of vocabulary occurs when children are watching television.

Interestingly, many Landmark students get the larger semantic picture but stumble over the one- or two-syllable function words that are often crucial to understanding. The teacher might overlook these words, assuming the average student has mastered them. They consist of words that can function as prepositions, pronouns, temporal-sequential markers, or directional adverbs.

*Prepositions* are particularly vexing. One Landmark student accurately explained the scientific method, then declared, "I still have trouble distinguishing between 'before' and 'after.'" Another student wrote, "Matt's been at Landmark *at* six years." She read her sentence aloud without self-correction. When asked "How long?", she accurately reported, "I've been here *for* two years."

Students for whom English is a second language must devote considerable study to interpreting the multiple meanings of these commonly used words. Consider the preposition "between," which can indicate location ("between here and the door") and time ("between now and Friday"). It has a different meaning in idiomatic expressions, as in "between you and me," "between a rock and a hard place," and "He's little Mr. In-Between."

Students need to master five kinds of *pronouns*: personal, reflexive, demonstrative, indefinite, and negative. On occasion, Landmark students confuse gender-specific personal pronouns (e.g., she/ he and him/her) well into their middle-school years. The larger problem for students is their tendency to use pronouns to the point of eliminating the original referents altogether, as in "One is pointed, and one is blunt."

Many Landmark students with at least average vocabularies have difficulty processing *temporal-sequential* words. Examples include prepositions (before, after, and until), nouns (Tuesday and tomorrow), adverbs (secondly and currently), and adjectives (first and last).

Certain students have great difficulty interpreting, recalling, and using *directional* words. Confusion between left and right is endemic among Landmark students. Numerous other words are also directional, including prepositions (across, through, and beyond) and the cardinal directions north, south, east, and west.

Vocabulary, prepositions, pronouns, temporal-sequential words, or directional words are not all. Meaning is all. Understanding expository text or literature requires students to synthesize comprehension skills too numerous to list and beyond the scope of this book. In addition to word study, a few areas of focus in the oral expression and literature curriculum at Landmark include categorizing and prioritizing information (main ideas and details), making analogies, making inferences, interpreting figurative language, and identifying literary elements in literature.

## *Receptive and Expressive Errors*

Classifying students' semantic errors should lead teachers to a clearer understanding of what to do to remedy them. Did the student misunderstand a word because it sounds similar to another word, as in the case of phonological processing errors? Or was the word itself the problem? The examples below are short words that seem simple enough but cause students major frustration. They include directional words like "left" and "right," ambiguous words, figurative language, and prepositions of all kinds.

### Examples of Challenging Words

| Type of Word | Examples |
| --- | --- |
| Locative (spatial) | In, on, under, over |
| Directional | Run under, run over, run to the left |
| Indefinite spatial | At the door, by the telephone |
| Temporal | Before noon, after supper |
| Instrumental | With, without |
| Idiomatic | In your face |

### Receptive (Processing) Errors

Many students find "before" and "after" as confusing as "left" and "right." These students might not understand the instruction, "Bring me your homework before lunch." The quotes below reflect receptive, or processing, errors. The student does not recall which meaning goes with which word.

### Examples of Receptive Errors

| Example | Nature of Student's Error |
| --- | --- |
| **Teacher**: When did you go fishing?<br>**Student**: I went the day *after* yesterday. | Confused "after" and "before" |
| **Teacher**: Does June come before or after February?<br>**Student**: June comes *before* February. | Confused "after" and "before" |

Landmark School, Inc.

| Example | Nature of Student's Error |
|---|---|
| **Teacher**: Show me tomorrow on the calendar.<br>**Student**: Tomorrow? I don't do that word! | Didn't know the meaning of an abstract word denoting time |
| **Teacher**: Explain "the time is ripe."<br>**Student**: The ground is *fertile*, so we have to strike now. | Added information to make sense of an ambiguous word ("ripe") |
| **Teacher**: Explain what Phillip, the blind boy, meant when he said, "Timothy's eyes had become mine."<br>**Student**: Phillip's eyes were black like Timothy's? | Confused literal and figurative |

## Expressive (Production/Word Retrieval) Errors

Out of hundreds of examples of word retrieval errors, most of the erroneous words are phonologically similar to the target words. The examples below fall into several error categories.

## Phonological Errors

| What Student Said | What Student Meant |
|---|---|
| Brian saw a *skin*, no, a *snail* in his tent. | Snake |
| They put a time *castle* in the new building. | Capsule |
| Bees *predict* honey. | Produce |
| Did you see the birthday *billboard* in the hall? | Bulletin board |
| He's playing a *banjorine*. | Banjo |
| Can I run the *protector*? | Projector |
| Have you seen the new *consufence* course? | Confidence |
| We drove through *Peninsula*. | Pennsylvania |
| In that book, there was a lot of *bangling*. | Gambling |
| He couldn't get the *pellet*, *propellet*, to turn. | Propeller |
| I'm so *ancient* to find out. | Anxious |
| Put on your *skepticals*. | Spectacles |
| We went to *Toys a Rust*! | Toys R Us |
| You have to go on the camping trip; its *majority*. | Mandatory |
| We'll have a *tycoon* and won't have school tomorrow. | Typhoon |

*Landmark School, Inc.*

## Morphological/Phonological Errors

| What Student Said | What Student Meant |
|---|---|
| The rainforest has boa *unstructors*. | Constrictors |
| It's *majority*. | Mandatory |
| My dad hasn't *unfilmed* it yet. | Developed |

## Phonological/Semantic Errors

| What Student Said | What Student Meant |
|---|---|
| Oh, I know what this is! It's the *Entire State Building*. | Eiffel Tower |
| Can I borrow a *close* pin? | Safety |
| They put a *weather permitter* on the roof! | Barometer |

## Semantic Errors

| What Student Said | What Student Meant |
|---|---|
| I saw a bird *troop*. | Flock |
| My father was born a *miscarriage*. | Prematurely |
| You *hear* like my mother. | Sound |
| Trees are supposed to be upside *up*. | Rightside up |
| We had to keep on *finding*. | Looking |
| I have Brownies on Wednesday, *skip one, Wednesday, skip one, Wednesday . . .* | I have Brownies every other Wednesday. |
| There's a fire, and I see a man coming down *from* sheets. | On sheets |
| We saw very old *coffins* in the cemetery. | Tombstones |

## Lack of Recall

| What Student Said | What Student Meant |
|---|---|
| These arrows tell which way you're goin'. | Directions |
| I took my letter to the mail thing. | Post office |
| Oh, I know that one . . . ooh, ooh! | Unknown |
| Um . . . don't tell me! I know. | Unknown |
| It's a, it's a, it's a . . . graph! (delay) | Graph |
| It's on a fishing rod . . . you wind it. (gestures) | Reel |

The rest of this chapter presents specific goals and objectives for semantic development. The goals are idealized, inferring mastery, though most students probably will not attain mastery. The objectives, on the other hand,

are largely presented in developmental order (in order of difficulty). This way, the teacher can identify an objective along the spectrum of difficulty as a realistic target for a given student. For example, the goal for "Figurative Language" is for the student to interpret figurative language correctly in literature or expository text. One of the objectives under this goal is for the student to explain both physical and psychological attributes of a multiple-meaning word. This objective might be used as a realistic goal for a student who is not likely to master figurative language within the school year.

# Vocabulary: Action Verbs

## *Goal*

The student will increase her or his repertoire of action verbs.

## *Background*

When asked to generate sentences, students tend to take a shortcut by using a simple linking verb, as in "The humpback whale *was* off the starboard side of our ship." To help students generate semantically richer sentences, teachers can insist upon action verbs instead, as in "The humpback whale *breached* off the starboard side of our ship."

Common sense dictates that teachers should progress from actions most familiar and easily observable (e.g., run and jump) to those less familiar and more subtle (e.g., etch and trace) when teaching action verbs.

## *Objectives*

The student will:

- differentiate among meanings by experiencing and labeling motor actions
- point to the picture that best depicts an action verb produced by the instructor
- name motor activities demonstrated by the instructor or performed in a video
- name action verbs denoted by pictures
- describe actions performed by him- or herself and others
- generate a list of action verbs performed by animate beings
- discriminate between action verbs that differ by only one phoneme (e.g., walk/talk and write/ride)
- distinguish between the same and different meaning given minimally paired sentences in oral commands; for example, "Ring the bell." and "Bring the bell."
- identify action verbs that are related by meaning (e.g., hit and bat)

- generate a list of action verbs around a theme that have subtle differences in meaning; for example, on the theme of whales, actions verbs might be "glide," "swirl," and "weave"

- verbally generate original sentences related to a theme that include action verbs

- verbally generate narratives that include an expanded repertory of action verbs

- generate written narratives that include an expanded repertory of action verbs

# General Vocabulary

## *Goal*

The student will accurately define a newly learned vocabulary word appropriate to his or her cognitive level and use it in a sentence.

## *Background*

There are over 600,000 entries in the Oxford English dictionary, more than for any other language in the world (Lederer 1991). By first grade, an English-speaking child may learn as many as 13,000 vocabulary words (Pinker 2000). How do we learn new words? We learn some through direct instruction, but we learn most through exposure to words in context. We try to figure out the meaning of a strange word in the context of a sentence. Mostly, we acquire new words through exposure to literature.

At Landmark, we directly teach vocabulary in all classes. In literature classes, the words selected for direct instruction meet three qualifications. They are high-frequency words that students are likely to encounter in future reading; words essential to understanding a particular piece of literature, such as the word "levee" from *A House with a Clock on the Wall*, by John Bellair; and words that engage students' curiosity, such as words associated with magic from the Harry Potter series by J.K. Rowling.

At Landmark, Susan Dillon explored how students best learn and retain new vocabulary words, and engaged them in discussion of their preferred methods of learning new words. Dillon applied Dale's stages of familiarity with words to pretest vocabulary from students' literature (Dale and O'Rourke 1971). She asked students to self-evaluate their familiarity with a word using these descriptors:

- "I never saw it before."
- "I've heard of it but I don't know what it means."
- "I can use it in a sentence."
- "I know it. I can tell you what it means."

To teach vocabulary, Dillon consistently formulated sentences to include modifiers that illustrated the definition of a word. She requested that students do the same. Students mastered the concept thanks to her richly worded examples and consistent standards.

*Landmark School, Inc.*

Moats (2000) emphasizes the importance of the connotative meaning of a word, which refers to the context surrounding the word. The word triggers a network of associations to other words and ideas. Semantic maps that foster the network of associations promote mastery of vocabulary words.

## *Objectives*

The student will:

- apply knowledge of roots, prefixes, and suffixes to newly introduced words
- verbally use contextual analysis while guessing at the meaning of a vocabulary word within a sentence
- identify the part of speech of a vocabulary word (e.g., noun and verb)
- participate in group discussions focusing on semantic elaboration of the vocabulary word
- group a vocabulary word with like subordinates in a categorization task
- describe likenesses and differences between a vocabulary word and its synonyms
- name antonyms for a vocabulary word, when appropriate
- name the correct vocabulary word in sentence completion tasks
- identify the superordinate category for a vocabulary word
- identify the salient characteristics of a vocabulary word (e.g., category, function, size, shape, and texture)
- fill in a semantic map that includes definition, synonyms, antonyms, examples, connotations, multiple meanings, and linguistic structure
- verbally formulate an elaborated sentence containing the vocabulary word plus modifiers that demonstrate comprehension of the word; for example, "The *generous* people *gave a lot of money* to Children's Hospital."
- formulate a written sentence containing a vocabulary word
- compare her or his definition of a vocabulary word with a dictionary definition, and identify missing features essential for an accurate definition

Semantics

## Vocabulary Word and Picture

Name: _____

Date: _____

Day: _____

**Vocabulary Word:** apprehensive

1. How many syllables are in this word? four
2. Definition: anxious, fearful, uneasy

3. Sample Sentence: Harriet felt apprehensive that Ole Golly knew she was a spy.

4. Use today's word in a sentence of your own: I am apprehensive about school.

5. Draw a picture that reminds you of the definition of this word:

Illustration by Charlotte Goff

# Vocabulary Word Map

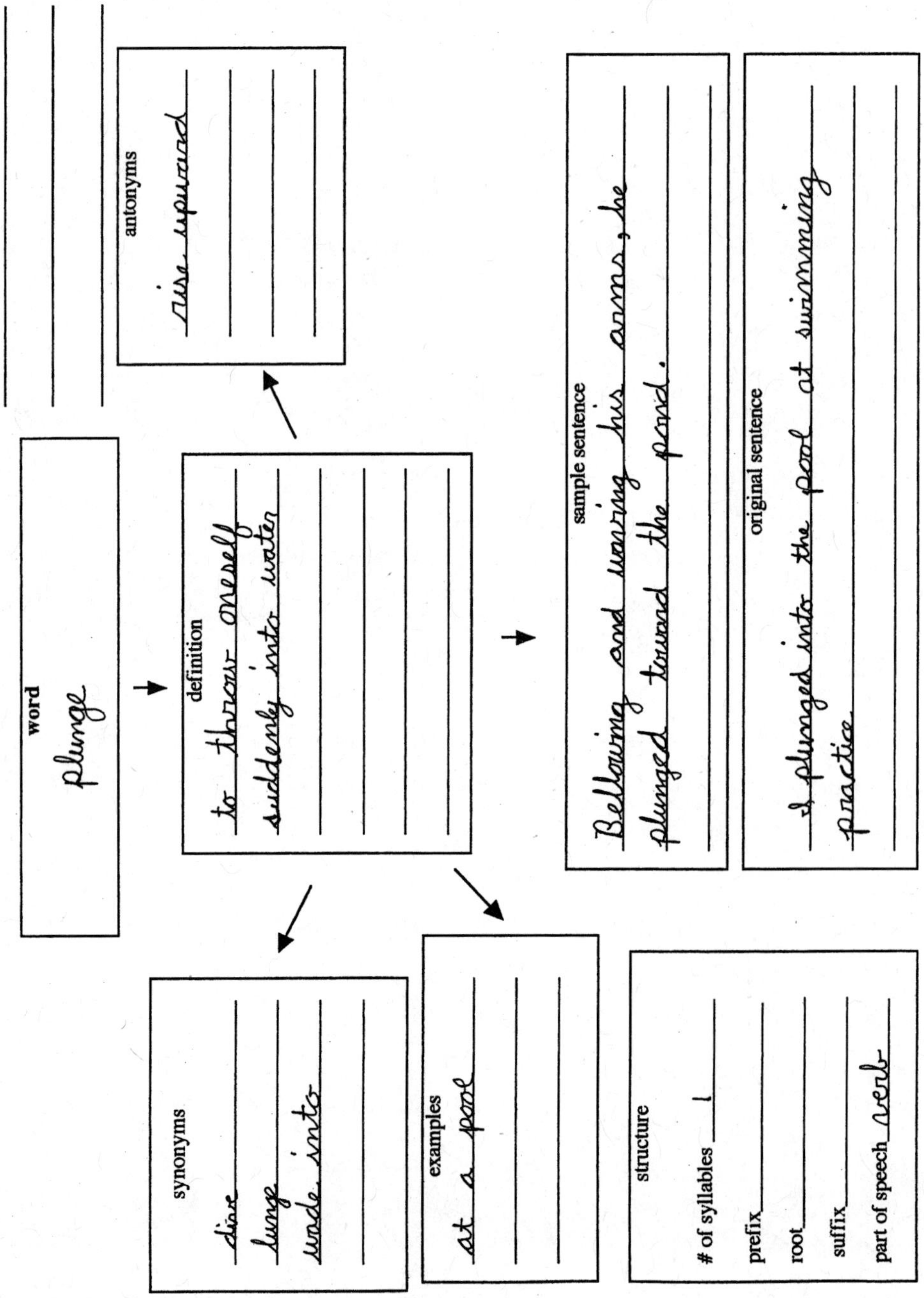

**word:** plunge

**definition:** to throw oneself suddenly into water

**antonyms:** rise upward

**synonyms:** dive, lunge, wade into

**examples:** at a pool

**sample sentence:** Bellowing and waving his arms, he plunged toward the pond.

**original sentence:** I plunged into the pool at swimming practice.

**structure:**
- # of syllables: 1
- prefix:
- root:
- suffix:
- part of speech: verb

Adapted from Moats 2000 with permission.

# Vocabulary: Adjectives That Describe Quality

## *Goal*

The student will increase her or his repertoire of adjectives that describe quality and will demonstrate comprehension of the role of adjectives in sentences.

## *Background*

Students should brainstorm specific adjectives to avoid overuse of those that are most common yet least descriptive. "Big" and "little," for example, are not very informative: "big" relative to what, an ant or a tanker?

Keeping word family charts (e.g., words for texture, age, and color) on display in the classroom is an effective tool for vocabulary expansion. When teachers display synonyms and antonyms of overused adjectives, students incorporate preferred, less common adjectives into their oral and written expository reporting.

Wiig and Semel (1984) suggested a logical order in which to introduce adjectives. The adjective tables below use that order. The words are drawn from children's literature and Landmark faculty. The first table lists adjectives that describe size. Some of these adjectives are appropriate for expressing other dimensions as well.

### Adjectives That Describe Size

| Depth | Height/Length | Width | Weight (Volume, Mass) |
|---|---|---|---|
| Deep | Big | Baggy | Chunky |
| Empty | Colossal | Broad | Crowded |
| Endless | Enormous | Bulky | Fat |
| Full | Gigantic | Fat | Feathery |
| Infinite | Great | Narrow | Heavy |
| Shallow | Huge | Slender | Lean |
| Steep | Large | Slim | Light |
|  | Little | Spacious | Lithe |
|  | Long | Thick | Plump |
|  | Mammoth | Thin | Stocky |
|  | Massive | Vast | Stout |
|  | Microscopic |  | Strong |

| Depth | Height/Length | Width | Weight (Volume, Mass) |
|---|---|---|---|
| | Mighty | Wide | Trim |
| | Miniature | | |
| | Petite | | |
| | Short | | |
| | Small | | |
| | Tall | | |
| | Tiny | | |

## Adjectives That Describe Color

| Yellows | Reds | Greens | Blues |
|---|---|---|---|
| Canary | Carmine | Apple green | Aquamarine |
| Flesh | Cherry | Avocado | Azure |
| Gold | Crimson | Chartreuse | Blue-green |
| Lemon | Fuchsia | Emerald | Cerulean |
| Ochre | Magenta | Forest green | Cobalt |
| Orange | Maroon | Jade | Ice blue |
| Peach | Pink | Kelly green | Indigo |
| Tangerine | Rose | Lime | Midnight |
| | Ruby | Olive | Navy |
| | Salmon | Sea green | Powder blue |
| | Scarlet | | Royal |
| | Vermilion | | Sky blue |
| | | | Teal |
| | | | Turquoise |

| Violets | Browns | Whites | Other |
|---|---|---|---|
| Lavender | Beige | Antique white | Black |
| Lilac | Chocolate | Bone | Carbon |
| Orchid | Cinnamon | Chalk | Charcoal |
| Periwinkle | Copper | Cream | Ebony |
| Purple | Mahogany | Ivory | Putty |
| | Rust | | Silver |
| | Sepia | | Slate gray |
| | Sienna | | |
| | Sunburn | | |
| | Tan | | |
| | Taupe | | |
| | Terra-cotta | | |

*Landmark School, Inc.*

Semantics

### Value or Degree of Hue/Shade

| | | | |
|---|---|---|---|
| Bright | Deep | Light | Translucent |
| Brilliant | Fluorescent | Pale | Transparent |
| Dark | Harsh | Soft | |

## Adjectives That Describe Shape

| | | | |
|---|---|---|---|
| Broad | Curly | Jagged | Round |
| Circular | Curved | Oval | Spiral |
| Conical, cone-shaped | Diamond-shaped | Pointed | Square |
| | | Rectangular | Triangular |
| Crooked | Flat | | Tubular |

## Adjectives That Describe Temperature

| | | | |
|---|---|---|---|
| Baking | Chilly | Heated | Scalding |
| Blistering | Cool | Hot | Scorching |
| Boiling | Feverish | Icy | Sizzling |
| Broiling | Fiery | Nippy | Sweltering |
| Burning | Frigid | Red hot | Warm |
| Cold | Frosty | | |

## Adjectives That Describe Age

### Maturational Cycle

| | | | |
|---|---|---|---|
| Adolescent | Infantile | Newborn | Senior |
| Babyish | Junior | Old | Toddling |
| Elderly | Juvenile | Senile | Young |
| Immature | | | |

### Life Cycle

| | | | |
|---|---|---|---|
| Aged | Downy | Living | Recent |
| Ancient | Dying | Modern | Remote |
| Antique | Early | Obsolete | Renovated |
| Budding | Feathering | Olden | Rotting |
| Chick-like | Fruiting | Present | Shedding |
| Decaying | Leafing | Primitive | Sprouting |
| Decrepit | | | |

*Landmark School, Inc.*

## Adjectives That Describe Flavor

| | | | |
|---|---|---|---|
| Apple | Chocolate | Lime | Pistachio |
| Banana | Chocolate chip | Marshmallow | Raspberry |
| Black cherry | Cinnamon | Mint | Root beer |
| Blueberry | Coconut | Mint chocolate | Spearmint |
| Bubble gum | Cola | chip | Strawberry |
| Butter pecan | Garlic | Onion | Vanilla |
| Butterscotch | Grape | Orange | Walnut |
| Buttery | Heavenly hash | Peanut butter | Watermelon |
| Caramel | Honey | Pecan | Winter green |
| Cherry | Lemon | Peppermint | |

## Adjectives That Describe Taste

| | | | |
|---|---|---|---|
| Acidic | Juicy | Smoked | Strong |
| Bitter | Mild | Sour | Sweet |
| Bland | Ripe | Spicy | Tangy |
| Delicious | Rotten | Spoiled | Tasteless |
| Dry | Salty | Stale | Tasty |
| Fresh | | | |

## Adjectives That Describe Odor

| | | | |
|---|---|---|---|
| Acrid | Fishy | Musty | Rotten |
| Aromatic | Floral | Oily | Smoky |
| Chemical | Fragrant | Penetrating | Sour |
| Decaying | Fresh-air | Pungent | Sweet |
| Earthy | Human | Putrid | Stale |
| Electrical | Metallic | Rancid | Woody |

### Adjectives That Use Food to Describe Odor

| | | | |
|---|---|---|---|
| Banana | Citric | Garlic | Tomato |
| Chocolate | Coconut | Peppermint | Vanilla |
| Cinnamon | Coffee | Strawberry | |

## Adjectives That Describe Appearance

| | | | |
|---|---|---|---|
| Attractive | Ghostly | Pleasing | Slender |
| Battered | Glamorous | Polished | Sluggish |
| Beautiful | Good-looking | Ramshackle | Sober |
| Broken down | Gorgeous | Repulsive | Strange |
| Charming | Handsome | Rickety-looking | Stupid |
| Cluttered | Hideous | Rotting | Swirling |
| Cracked | Lean | Rusty | Ugly |

*Landmark School, Inc.*

Semantics

| | | | |
|---|---|---|---|
| Curled | Lovely | Scowling | Unpleasant |
| Dignified | Nice | Shabby | Unsightly |
| Displeasing | Obese | Sharp | Withered |
| Fascinating | Offensive | Skinny | |

## Adjectives That Describe Time

| | | | |
|---|---|---|---|
| Ancient | First | Old | Short |
| Brief | Last | Old-fashioned | Slow |
| Current | Late | Quick | Swift |
| Early | Long | Rapid | Young |
| Fast | Modern | | |

## Adjectives That Describe Speed

| | | | |
|---|---|---|---|
| Crawling | Lagging | Rapid | Speedy |
| Dragging | Pokey | Slow | Swift |
| Fast | Quick | | |

## Adjectives That Describe Texture

| | | | |
|---|---|---|---|
| Blunt | Flaky | Prickly | Solid |
| Brittle | Flexible | Rocky | Spongy |
| Broken | Fluffy | Rough | Springy |
| Bumpy | Fuzzy | Sandy | Squishy |
| Coarse | Glossy | Scaly | Sticky |
| Crooked | Greasy | Shaggy | Stiff |
| Crumbly | Gritty | Sharp | Supple |
| Cuddly | Grubby | Silky | Thorny |
| Curly | Hard | Slimy | Tough |
| Damp | Irregular | Slippery | Uneven |
| Dense | Jagged | Slushy | Velvety |
| Dented | Loose | Smooth | Wet |
| Dry | Mushy | Soft | Wiry |
| Elastic | Notched | Soggy | Wrinkly |
| Firm | Pebbly | | |

## Adjectives That Describe Affect and Inner Feelings

| | | | |
|---|---|---|---|
| Abandoned | Curious | Grateful | Powerless |
| Adventurous | Defensive | Grouchy | Proud |
| Affectionate | Dejected | Grumpy | Puzzled |
| Afraid | Delightful | Guilty | Reassured |
| Agreeable | Despairing | Happy | Rejected |
| Alert | Desperate | Hateful | Relieved |

*Landmark School, Inc.*

| Alone | Determined | Hurt | Riled |
| Amazed | Devoted | Ignorant | Sad |
| Amused | Disappointed | Impatient | Satisfied |
| Angry | Disgruntled | Impressed | Scared |
| Annoyed | Dismayed | Indignant | Serious |
| Ashamed | Disturbed | Irritated | Sorry |
| Astonished | Dreadful | Kind | Startled |
| Blue | Dumb | Light-hearted | Stunned |
| Bored | Eager | Lonely | Suspicious |
| Bothered | Elated | Mad | Tense |
| Brave | Embarrassed | Mean | Tentative |
| Broken-hearted | Enthusiastic | Merry | Terrific |
| Calm | Exasperated | Miserable | Thankful |
| Caring | Excited | Moody | Troubled |
| Cautious | Exuberant | Mortified | Trusting |
| Certain | Fascinated | Nervous | Uncomfortable |
| Cheerful | Fearful | Nonchalant | Unhappy |
| Comfortable | Flattered | Offended | Untrusting |
| Concerned | Gentle | Overjoyed | Upset |
| Confident | Gloomy | Patient | Wary |
| Confused | Glum | Pleased | Worried |
| Contented | Good | Powerful | Worthless |

## Adjectives That Describe Distance

| Close | Faraway | Immediate | Nearby |
| Distant | Far-flung | Near-at-hand | Remote |
| Far | Far-off | | |

## *Objectives*

The student will:

- auditorily recognize and name or use adjectives that denote a specific relative size, given pictures or objects to view

- auditorily recognize and name or use adjectives that denote a specific color, given visual stimuli

- auditorily recognize and name or use adjectives that denote a specific shape, given pictures or objects to match or manipulate

- auditorily recognize and name or use adjectives that denote temperature, given pictures or objects to compare and contrast (including antonyms, such as cool/warm)

Semantics

- auditorily recognize and name or use adjectives that denote age, given pictures or objects to compare and contrast (including antonyms, such as ancient/modern and old/young)

- auditorily recognize and name or use adjectives that denote taste quality, given pictures or foods to compare and contrast (including antonyms, such as bitter/sweet and spicy/bland)

- auditorily recognize and name or use adjectives that denote odor, given pictures or scents to compare and contrast (including antonyms, such as rancid/sweet and mild/strong)

- auditorily recognize and name or use adjectives that denote appearance, given pictures or objects to compare and contrast (including antonyms, such as plain/fancy)

- auditorily recognize and name or use adjectives that denote time, given pictures or objects to compare and contrast (including antonyms, such as early/late)

- auditorily recognize and name or use adjectives that denote speed, given pictures or objects to compare and contrast (including antonyms, such as fast/slow)

- auditorily recognize and name or use adjectives that denote texture, given pictures or objects to compare and contrast (including antonyms, such as rough/smooth)

- auditorily recognize and name or use adjectives that denote affect (feelings), given photos or drawings to compare and contrast (including antonyms, such as pleased/angry)

- auditorily recognize and name or use adjectives that denote distance, given actions, maps, or illustrations to compare and contrast (including antonyms, such as near/far)

- recognize and name or use adjectives featured in literature and expository text appropriate to his or her cognitive level

- recognize and name or use strings of two or three adjectives (e.g., shaggy, friendly Rosa)

- recognize and name or use antonyms of selected adjectives in speaking and writing situations

- recognize and name or use synonyms of selected adjectives in speaking and writing situations

# Vocabulary: Adjectives That Tell *Which* or *How Many*

## Goal

The student will increase her or his repertoire of adjectives that tell *which* or *how many* and demonstrate comprehension of the role of these adjectives in sentences.

## Background

An *adjective* is a word that modifies or limits the meaning of a noun. Adjectives explain *which*, *how many* (amount), or *what kind of* (quality). They fall into four categories.

- *Descriptive adjectives* express a quality (e.g., a ghostly manta ray).
- *Limiting adjectives* specify range; they include possessives (e.g., my and our) and words that show number or amount (e.g., eight and several).
- *Demonstrative adjectives* specify which one(s) (e.g., this ship and those dolphins).
- *Interrogative adjectives* ask for specifics (e.g., what fog horn and which island).

The most commonly used adjectives are the articles "a," "an," and "the." Articles are covered in the chapter on morphology.

A word can represent more than one part of speech. The words in the tables below are all adjectives that are sometimes pronouns.

### Adjectives That Specify *Which*

| This, these | What (interrogative sentence) |
| That, those | Which (interrogative sentence) |

### Adjectives That Indicate *How Many*

| All | Each | Many | Other |
| Another | Either | Neither | Several |
| Any | Few | One, etc. (numbers) | Some |
| Both | More | | |

Landmark School, Inc.

## Objectives

The student will:

- identify the different locations of objects, animals, and people by observing spatial relationships indicated by the instructor; for example, "I am pointing to this pencil." and "I am going to pick up that book."

- carry out oral directions that include demonstrative adjectives; for example, "Pick up this pencil." and "Please give me that book."

- demonstrate the ability to take the perspective of the listener by using appropriate demonstrative adjectives; for example, would "this chair" or "that chair" be correct from the listener's position (as opposed to the speaker's position) in the room?

- distinguish between singular and plural forms of demonstrative adjectives (e.g., this pencil/these pencils and that pencil/those pencils)

- categorize adjectives using the terms "near" and "further away"; for example, "This pencil is near; that pencil is further away."

- differentiate among adjectives that indicate greater or fewer in number; for example, "Many surfers are competing on the North Shore of Oahu." and "Few surfers are competing on the North Shore of Oahu."

- generate original directions to classmates or the instructor using adjectives that tell *which* or *how many*

- generate oral narratives and include adjectives that tell *which* or *how many*

- include adjectives that tell *which* or *how many* in writing tasks, given a list of adjectives from which to choose

- include adjectives that tell *which* or *how many* in writing tasks without cues

- include adjectives that tell *which* or *how many* in spontaneous speech

- include adjectives that tell *which* or *how many* in spontaneous writing

# Vocabulary: Adverbs

## *Goal*

The student will increase her or his repertoire of adverbs and demonstrate comprehension of the role of adverbs in sentences.

## *Background*

Landmark students find adverbial phrases that express direction and time particularly troublesome. Students often visualize opposites in reverse order, such as east/west of the Mississippi and before/after the game. One student fluently described the scientific method of study, then asserted, "I still can't tell 'before' from 'after'!"

It is essential for the instructor to verify students' comprehension of words – in this case, words used as adverbs – before asking them to write sentences containing adverbs and adverbial phrases.

### Examples of Adverbs

| Statement | Explanation |
|---|---|
| The humpback whale sings *beautifully*. | Tells *how* |
| The humpback whale migrates *annually*. | Tells *how often* |
| It leaves the waters of Hawaii *early in the spring*. | Tells *when* |
| The whales can be seen *near* Maui. | Tells *where* |
| The baby whale is *almost* strong enough for the swim to Alaska. | Tells *to what extent* |
| The humpback whale is a *very* good mother. | Modifies the adjective "good" |
| The spume from the whale's blow hole is *extremely* smelly. | Modifies another adverb, "smelly" |

The tables below list various types of adverbs. The lists are drawn from various sources, including children's literature.

*Landmark School, Inc.*

Semantics

## Adverbs That Describe Location (Tell *Where*)

| Abroad | Ashore | Far | Near |
| Asea | Everywhere | Here | There |

## Adverbs That Describe Clock or Calendar Time

| Annually | Daily | Monthly | Weekly |
| Biweekly | Hourly | Semiannually | Yearly |

## Adverbs That Describe Specific Time (Tell *When*)

| Afterwards | Punctually | Soon | Today |
| Later | Quickly | Speedily | Tomorrow |
| Monday, etc. | Rapidly | Suddenly | Yesterday |
| Promptly | Slowly | | |

## Adverbs That Describe Personal Manner

### Positive

| Bravely | Gracefully | Merrily | Smoothly |
| Brightly | Happily | Neatly | Softly |
| Eagerly | Honestly | Perfectly | Successfully |
| Elegantly | Innocently | Politely | Tenderly |
| Encouragingly | Joyously | Powerfully | Thoughtfully |
| Enthusiastically | Justly | Quietly | Truthfully |
| Faithfully | Kindly | Reverently | Victoriously |
| Fondly | Longingly | Safely | Warmly |
| Gently | Magically | Sharply | Well |
| Gladly | | | |

### Negative

| Angrily | Grimly | Obnoxiously | Smugly |
| Anxiously | Guiltily | Painfully | Stealthily |
| Awkwardly | Hastily | Poorly | Sternly |
| Darkly | Lazily | Recklessly | Suspiciously |
| Evilly | Miserably | Reluctantly | Tensely |
| Fiercely | Nastily | Rudely | Violently |
| Foolishly | Nervously | Sadly | Weakly |
| Forcefully | Nimbly | Savagely | Wearily |
| Frantically | Noisily | Selfishly | Wildly |
| Greedily | | | |

*Landmark School, Inc.*

<u>Neutral</u>

| | | | |
|---|---|---|---|
| Curiously | Mysteriously | Oddly | Silently |
| Exactly | Nearly | Repeatedly | Sleepily |
| Hungrily | Obediently | Seriously | Very |

## Adverbs That Describe Frequency (Tell *How Often*)

| | | | |
|---|---|---|---|
| Always | Normally | Often | Seldom |
| Frequently | Now and then | Rarely | Sometimes |
| Never | Occasionally | Regularly | Usually |

## Adverbs That Describe Emphasis
## (Tell *to What Extent or Degree*)

| | | | |
|---|---|---|---|
| Actually | Dimly | Indeed | Really |
| Clearly | Distinctly | Mainly | Truly |
| Considerably | Exactly | | |

## Objectives

The student will:

- auditorily recognize and name or use adverbs that denote a specific location (that tell *where*), given bodily movement and scenes to view

- auditorily recognize and name or use adverbs that denote time (that tell *when*), given visual representations, such as a calendar, clock face, and drawings of the sun in different positions

- auditorily recognize and name or use adverbs that denote a specific manner (that tell *how*, such as "angrily," "sadly," and "joyously"), given actions, stances, and pictures of facial expressions

- select prepositional adverbs that denote *where* to complete sentences; for example, "I saw the dolphin _____ (in the ocean, at Sea World)."

- select prepositional adverbs that tell *when* in order to complete sentences; for example, "We went snorkeling _____ (yesterday, today)."

- select adverbs that tell *how* (manner) to complete sentences; for example, "The otter rolled over _____ (lazily, noisily)."

*Landmark School, Inc.*

- auditorily recognize and name or use adverbs that denote emphasis (that tell *to what extent or degree*); for example, "Harry saw his reflection in the mirror _____ (dimly, clearly)." and "Hagrid truly loved dragons; that is, he loved them _____ (a lot, a little)."

- auditorily recognize and name or use adverbs that describe frequency (that tell *how often*), such as "always," "occasionally," and "seldom"; for example, "The whales frequently approached our boat during the spring season."

- recognize and name or use adverbs featured in literature and expository text appropriate to his or her cognitive level

- recognize and name or use adverb strings of two or three words (e.g., hastily and carelessly)

# Word Retrieval

## Goal

The student will generalize self-cueing techniques to recall or produce words that he or she infrequently uses.

## Background

The vast majority of Landmark students exhibit word retrieval difficulties under sufficiently demanding conditions. The importance of this cannot be overestimated, and teachers need to be sensitive to it. Examples of students' struggles with word retrieval are provided throughout this book and most pointedly in the chapter introductions.

One teenage student developed severe word retrieval deficits as a result of a severe head trauma. In conversation and discourse, he would fill his word-searching time lapses with fillers like "um" and "uh," a habit that listeners found distracting and annoying. Through rehearsal, this student learned to replace the fillers with silence while he searched his memory for a word. When he listened to his follow-up narratives on tape, he agreed that silence was better than vocalizing fillers.

Veteran Landmark students will say, "Don't tell me. Give me the first sound." When these students retrieve the word from the cue, the satisfied looks on their faces reflect their success. They are then less hesitant to search for an elusive word on another occasion.

### Cueing Strategies for Word Retrieval

| Type of Cue | Strategies and Examples |
| --- | --- |
| Phonemic | Begin sound |
| | Begin syllable of a multisyllabic word |
| | Say a rhyming word |
| | Show phonemic placement; for example, position lips for /sh/ to elicit "shoe" |
| Associative-semantic | Use antonyms; for example, say "It's the opposite of 'old.'" to elicit "young" |
| | Use synonyms; for example, say "Another word for 'kid' is _____." to elicit "child" |

*Landmark School, Inc.*

| Type of Cue | Strategies and Examples |
| --- | --- |
| | Use associated words; for example, say "Bread and . . ." to elicit "butter" |
| | Refer to a conceptual category; for example, say "It's a winter snow sport." to elicit "skiing" |
| | Use serial cueing for well-established series; for example, say "October, November, _____" to elicit "December" |
| Visual | Encourage and model visual imagery; for example, say "Close your eyes and picture . . ." |
| Situational | Locate the item; for example, say, "It's in the produce section." to elicit "eggplant" |
| Gestural | Use bodily action; for example, make a typing motion to elicit "word processor" |
| Melodic-stress | Sing a well-known tune; for example, sing "*Three Blind* _____" to elicit "mice" |
| | Hum and tap out the syllabic stress pattern; for example, tap three times to elicit "Florida" |
| Multiple choice | Give multiple choices; for example, say "Is it New York or Pennsylvania?" |

Do any of these strategies bring about positive results? In hundreds of pre- and posttests that ask students to name objects pictured, the average gains exceed a year for a year (i.e., a year of academic growth for each year in school). In many cases the gains are significant. Changes in verbal behavior are the most encouraging indicators that these efforts are worthwhile. When parents report that their silent children have become chatterboxes, something good is happening.

Landmark students participated in a pilot study designed by Wolf and Segal (1992). The students underwent eight weeks of intensive intervention training aimed at increasing their breadth and depth of knowledge of a specific group of words and their ability to retrieve these and related words rapidly and accurately. The focus was on developing fluency, accuracy, and richness. Activities included rapid-naming drills, definitions, word associations, semantic-field exercises, and innovative word coining. Wolf and Segal concluded that their intervention design did improve naming accuracy for this group. They suggested that the approach might carry over to improve these students' word retrieval skills in general.

*Landmark School, Inc.*

## Objectives

The student will:

- become familiar with various kinds of cueing techniques that facilitate word retrieval
- describe similarities and differences between a target word and others in its category, given visual cues and manipulatives
- attempt to use visual imagery to aid recall with his or her eyes closed
- attempt to use visual imagery to aid recall with his or her eyes open, but fixed on a point
- verbally analyze a prefix or root, if applicable
- verbally describe the context for a target word; for example, "It's found in the produce department."
- produce the target word, given a phonemic (sound-related) cue; for example, "It starts with 'mi-.'" (microscope)
- name synonyms for the target word, when applicable
- name antonyms for the target word, when applicable
- generate word associations for the target word
- group the target word with like subordinates
- demonstrate increased knowledge of the target word by giving an accurate definition
- request cues, when appropriate
- inhibit dysfluency, perseveration, redundancy, circumlocutions, word substitution, and fillers in spontaneous speech

## Teaching Strategies

The instructor will:

- allow the student time to process the question and retrieve the target word
- refrain from providing the answer, but provide cues once it is apparent that the student would appreciate assistance

- display word charts on the wall, such as a word chart for the names of tools, until the student demonstrates recall of target words for particular subjects
- discover which word retrieval strategies are most effective for each student
- become familiar with the various cueing strategies that foster word retrieval

# Locative, Directional, Spatial, and Temporal Prepositions

## Goal

The student will incorporate locative, directional, spatial, and temporal prepositions into spoken and written language and demonstrate comprehension of the underlying rules.

## Background

*Prepositions* are small words that cause big headaches for Landmark students, as well as for those who are learning English as a second language. Consider the word "between," for example. It can be locative (between here and the door), temporal (between now and Friday), or idiomatic (between you and me, between a rock and a hard place).

Similarly, consider the choice of specific temporal prepositions:

- "at" denotes specific times of the day, such as "at lunch" and "at noon" (Wiig and Semel 1984)

- "on" denotes specific days of the week, such as "on Monday"

- "in" denotes specific months of the year or seasons, such as "in the fall"

- "during" and "in" are used interchangeably to denote seasons, such as "during the holidays" and "in summer"

Although we use just nine prepositions ninety percent of the time, those nine words carry about 250 possible meanings (Wiig and Semel 1984). They are italicized in the list of prepositions below.

### Prepositions

| | | | |
|---|---|---|---|
| Above | Beneath | *From* | Past |
| About | Beside | *In* | Since |
| Across | Besides | Inside | Through |
| After | Between | Into | *To* |
| Against | Beyond | Like | Toward |
| Along | But (except) | Near | Under |
| Among | *By* | *Of* | Until |
| Around | Concerning | Off | Up |
| *At* | Down | *On* | Upon |

*Landmark School, Inc.*

*Semantics*

| | | | |
|---|---|---|---|
| Before | During | Out | *With* |
| Behind | Except | Outside | Within |
| Below | *For* | Over | Without |

The simple visual representations below are modeled after those in Dale and O'Rourke's *Techniques of Teaching Vocabulary* (1971). They are effective in teaching locative prepositions.

## Locative Prepositions

| | | | |
|---|---|---|---|
| on top of / upon / on | onto | along | across |
| below / under / underneath | over / above | through | to / up to |
| in / inside | into | out of | out / outside |
| up / upward(s) | around | toward | away from / from |
| down / downward | between | beside / by / nearby | |

Landmark School, Inc.

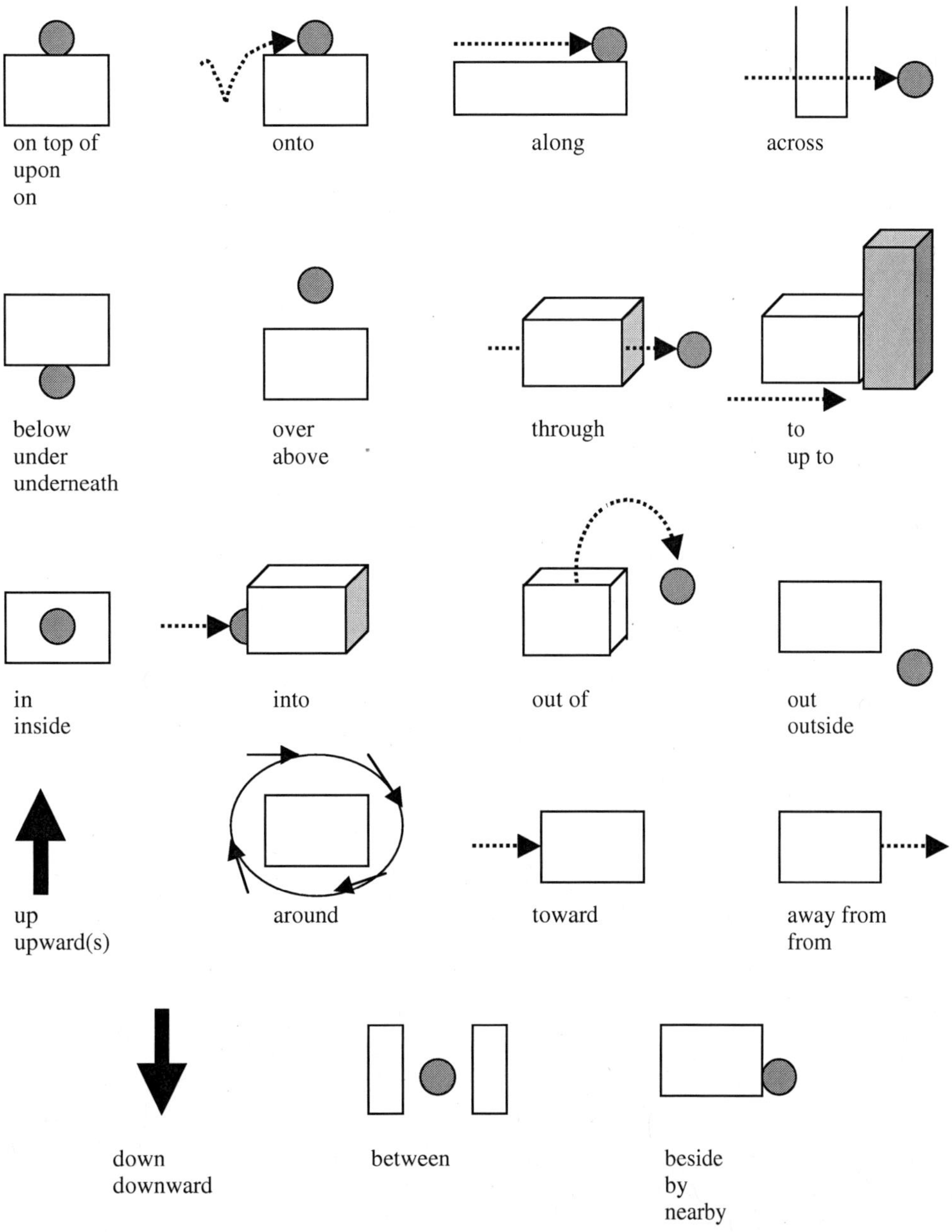

## Objectives

The student will:

- point to an object in a position described by the instructor; for example, "Which book is on top of the pile of books?"
- respond with his or her body to an oral command with locative and directional prepositions to convey understanding; for example, a locative command might be to "Sit on the table." and a directional command might be to "Walk across the room."
- manipulate objects to convey comprehension of locative and directional prepositions
- name antonyms for selected locative prepositions (e.g., in/out and over/under)
- discriminate among similar-sounding prepositions (e.g., on/in and for/from)
- verbally describe and label pictures, photos, or drawings using locative or directional prepositions
- verbally generate sentences containing locative and directional prepositions
- identify indefinite spatial prepositions (e.g., at the door)
- learn rules that determine the choice of specific temporal prepositions
- verbally generate sentences containing definite spatial prepositions (e.g., in, on, and under)
- verbally generate sentences containing indefinite spatial prepositions (e.g., at, by, and beside)
- differentiate between spatial and temporal uses of prepositions (e.g., at the door vs. at five o'clock)
- include temporal prepositions within an oral narrative
- include locative, directional, spatial, and temporal prepositions in spontaneous speech

# Instrumental and Idiomatic Prepositions

## Goal

The student will incorporate instrumental and idiomatic prepositions into spoken and written language and demonstrate familiarity with common usage.

## Background

Most common prepositions can be used as idioms, but there are no clear-cut rules. Students should understand the literal spatial representations of prepositions before they are introduced to idiomatic usage. They probably benefit from hearing examples and then contrasting familiar phrases with incorrect phrases. Here is one example of the confusion idiomatic prepositions can cause: One student said, chuckling, "That really broke me out!" Some examples of idiomatic use of prepositions follow:

- Jim's in trouble.
- In a nutshell, Sara and I made up.
- Mrs. Blanchard is counting on Laura to know the schedule.
- He's up against a lot of opposition.
- I'll be there, by golly.
- Run that by me again, will you?
- I ran into Mr. Swanson.
- Pat's really into archery.
- Mr. Kahn certainly did get his point across, didn't he?
- I voted for you.
- Quit foolin' around.
- I was beside myself.
- He was at wit's end.
- We're going to run through our lines.

## Objectives

The student will:

- verbally formulate sentences that include locative, directional, spatial, and temporal prepositions to demonstrate knowledge of these four types

- verbally formulate phrase pairs containing "with" and "without" using visual stimuli (e.g., with a suitcase/without a suitcase)

- differentiate between instrumental and noninstrumental uses of "with" and "without" (e.g., I cut the bread with a knife/I went to the circus with my dad)
- differentiate between the literal and the most common idiomatic uses of prepositions (e.g., on the table vs. on guard)
- verbally formulate sentences containing instrumental prepositions given a list of choices
- verbally formulate sentences containing instrumental prepositions without cues
- verbally formulate sentences containing selected high-frequency idiomatic prepositions given a list of choices
- verbally formulate sentences containing selected high-frequency idiomatic prepositions without cues
- include instrumental and idiomatic prepositions in spontaneous speech
- include instrumental and idiomatic prepositions in structured writing exercises
- include instrumental and idiomatic prepositions in spontaneous writing

*Landmark School, Inc.*

# Personal, Reflexive, and Intensive Pronouns

## *Goal*

The student will accurately produce personal, reflexive, and intensive pronouns and demonstrate comprehension of the underlying rules.

## *Background*

*Pronouns* are words that substitute for nouns. *Personal pronouns* refer to a person or persons; for example, "Kimmi went swimming at Waikiki. She saw surfers there."

### Personal Pronouns

| Person-Number | Subjective Case | Objective Case | Possessive Case (Adjective) | Possessive Case (Predicate Adjective) |
|---|---|---|---|---|
| First-person singular | I | Me | My | Mine |
| First-person plural | We | Us | Our | Ours |
| Second-person singular | You | You | Your | Yours |
| Second-person plural | You | You | Your | Yours |
| Third-person singular (reflects gender) | He She It | Him Her It | His Her Its | His Hers Its |
| Third-person plural | They | Them | Their | Theirs |

It is important to be alert to reflexive and intensive pronouns in literature or expository text and to ensure that students understand their meaning, as they might have difficulty identifying the antecedents for these pronouns.

*Reflexive pronouns* refer to the subject of the verb and receive the action of the subject. An example of reflexive use is "Dad bought himself a coat." A student might think that Dad bought "him" – another person – the coat. Another example is, "Ben splashed water all over himself in the tub."

*Intensive pronouns* indicate increased emphasis. An example of intensive use is "Nadia wrote the poem herself." "Herself" emphasizes "Nadia." Another example is, "Although they tipped out of the canoe, Ben himself did not get hurt."

Landmark School, Inc.

## Reflexive and Intensive Pronouns

| Myself | Yourself | Herself, himself, itself |
| Ourselves | Yourselves | Themselves |

### ESL and Pronouns

Personal and reflexive pronouns present a daunting challenge to adults whose primary language does not include pronouns in the various forms and cases that exist in English. Role playing is the most successful strategy for establishing these forms and cases. For example, teachers can have the class recite statements aloud as they hand each other objects: "I gave the pen to Thai. I gave the pen to him."

### Gender

Most Landmark students master gender references (e.g., he/she) by middle school, though a few middle-school students use incorrect gender on occasion. Teachers should run exercises that include matching or multiple-choice questions, cloze procedures, or oral narratives; for example, "Nadia walked the dog. _____ (she, he) got a leash for the dog." Teachers can also use male and female puppets as a teaching aid.

### Order and Case

In conversation, many students – as well as adults – not only substitute the objective for the subjective case, but also use incorrect order. For example, a student might say that "me and him went fishing" rather than "he and I went fishing." The first person is always last in a sequence. On August 13, 1999, George W. Bush was quoted in *The Boston Globe* as follows: "I hope you will join Laura and I . . ." The order is correct, but the case is not.

### Spelling

The word "it's" will always and forever be the contracted form of "it is." Even so, Landmark teachers remain busy deleting apostrophes from "its" in school reports, as in "a word and it's definition." The confusion is understandable, since the third-person possessive form of nouns requires an apostrophe. "It" is not a noun, however, but a pronoun.

*Landmark School, Inc.*

## Objectives

The student will:

- auditorily discriminate between correct and incorrect pronouns produced by the instructor based on semantic features; for example, "Sarah went to the play. She didn't like it." is correct, as "she" refers to Sarah and "it" refers to the play

- verbally produce the singular form of pronouns in the subjective case (I, you, he, she, and it)

- verbally produce the plural form of pronouns in the subjective case (we, you, and they)

- verbally produce singular and plural pronouns in the objective case (me, us, you, him, her, it, and them)

- verbally produce singular and plural possessive-replacive personal pronouns (mine, ours, yours, his, hers, its, and theirs); for example, "This is my book." is the same as "This is mine."

- identify antecedents of reflexive pronouns; for example, the antecedent in "Eliza looked at herself in the mirror." is "Eliza"

- identify antecedents of intensive pronouns; for example, "The boys themselves made up the rules for the game."

- categorize gender and number of reflexive pronouns

- select pronouns in multiple-choice tasks

- name correct pronouns in sentence completion and oral cloze tasks

- use the correct order when generating sentences containing pronouns; for example, "Don, Pedro, and I went to the Red Sox game. Nomar signed a baseball for Pedro and a program for me."

- self-monitor for accurate pronoun usage in narratives using an audiotape recorder

- refrain from using apostrophes when writing personal possessive pronouns (e.g., "its" not "it's")

- include accurate pronoun usage in spontaneous speech and writing

# Demonstrative, Indefinite, and Indefinite Negative Pronouns

## Goal

The student will produce demonstrative, indefinite, and indefinite negative pronouns and demonstrate comprehension of the underlying rules.

## Background

*Demonstrative pronouns* enable us to avoid wordiness and auditory overload in oral language. Teachers can place objects around the classroom, model use of demonstrative pronouns – as in "I will pick this up." – then ask students to give commands using these pronouns.

### Demonstrative Pronouns

| That  | This  |
|-------|-------|
| These | Those |

*Indefinite pronouns* do not refer to a specific antecedent. Most indefinite pronouns suggest quantity. *Indefinite negative pronouns* indicate less or the least amount. The table below lists indefinite and indefinite negative pronouns in a continuum according to quantity or amount, ranging from most to least.

### Indefinite and Indefinite Negative Pronouns

Most ——————————————————————————→ Least

| All | Most | Several | Another | Few | Any | Neither |
|-----|------|---------|---------|-----|-----|---------|
| Everybody | More | Some | Each | Fewer | Anybody | Nobody |
| Everyone | Many | Both | Either | | Anyone | No one |
| | Much | | One | | Anything | None |
| | | | Other | | | Nothing |
| | | | Somebody | | | |
| | | | Someone | | | |
| | | | Something | | | |

## Objectives

The student will:

- identify the different locations of objects, animals, and people by observing spatial relationships

*Landmark School, Inc.*

- carry out oral directions that include demonstrative pronouns; for example, "Go get that."

- demonstrate the ability to take a listener's perspective by using the appropriate demonstrative pronoun; for example, "Pick up that." and "Point to this."

- distinguish between singular and plural forms of demonstrative pronouns (e.g., this/that and that/those)

- categorize pronouns using the terms "near" and "far away" (e.g., these are near and those are far away)

- use inclusion and exclusion to differentiate between indefinite and indefinite negative pronouns (e.g., some are swimming and no one is swimming)

- define the root words "body," "one," "thing," and "where," which take indefinite and indefinite negative prefixes (e.g., somebody, nobody, everyone, and no one)

- generate original directions to classmates or the instructor using demonstrative, indefinite, and indefinite negative pronouns

- generate oral narratives that contain demonstrative, indefinite, and indefinite negative pronouns

- include demonstrative, indefinite, and indefinite negative pronouns in writing tasks, given a list of pronouns from which to choose

- include demonstrative, indefinite, and indefinite negative pronouns in writing tasks without cues

- include demonstrative, indefinite, and indefinite negative pronouns in spontaneous speech

- include demonstrative, indefinite, and indefinite negative pronouns in spontaneous writing

# Categories

## Goal

The student will classify words by selected semantic categories, appropriate to her or his cognitive level.

## Background

Discrete language skill activities, such as categorization, deliver more educational value when related to a topic or theme. Therefore, Landmark teachers use themes as vehicles for developing expressive language. They choose themes with student interests in mind, as well as their own. In oral expression and literature classes, themes relate to the literature. If students are reading Scott O'Dell's *Black Star, Bright Dawn*, for example, theme-based activities might be the study of Alaska, the Iditarod sled dog race, or the Inuit people.

Before setting priorities for teaching categorization, teachers can present students with an array of objects or photos and ask them to select those they think go together. In groups of six or seven students, everyone sits in a circle on the floor with about twenty photo cards in the center. The challenge is for each student to create a category different from those already mentioned. The category should be the most inclusive yet specific (e.g., motorized vehicles vs. white objects). Students always appear quite engaged in such activities. The exercise offers insight into each student's thinking process, as students frequently generate unique categories. Also, students begin on a successful note by independently creating a category, whether or not it is one the teacher has in mind.

## Objectives

The student will:

- match a subordinate member with a superordinate category, given visual stimuli (e.g., objects and photos) and a template
- match the superordinate category with a subordinate member, given visual stimuli and a template
- delete false subordinates, given visual stimuli and a template (i.e., identify subordinates that do not belong)
- categorize subordinates by function, given visual stimuli and a template

*Landmark School, Inc.*

- categorize subordinates by attributes (e.g., taste and size), given visual stimuli and a template
- categorize subordinates by class label (e.g., games and fruit), given visual stimuli and a template
- simultaneously apply several dimensions for classifying, given visual stimuli and a template
- verbally describe similarities and differences of subordinates (e.g., circles and squares)
- maintain consistent classification constraints through an exercise
- form subgroups within categories
- apply categorization skills when writing paragraphs; that is, adhere to one topic in each paragraph

# Antonyms

## Goal

The student will use a repertoire of antonyms appropriate to her or his vocabulary level.

## Background

The origin of the word "antonym" is Greek, from *anto*, meaning "opposite," and *nym*, meaning "name." Students often find antonyms easier to study and generate than synonyms.

Moats (2000) reminds us to consider the categories of antonyms. Context is necessary for recognizing *gradable antonyms*, which fit within a continuum, such as more/less. *Complementing antonyms* are either-or, such as dead/alive. Moats also describes *relational* or *symmetrical antonyms*, which associate two words with a reciprocal relationship, such as coach/team.

When introducing a new vocabulary word, students benefit from learning its antonym at the same time, when applicable. The contrast often clarifies the meaning for the student.

### Antonyms for Words That Identify Gender

| | |
|---|---|
| Boy | Girl |
| Brother | Sister |
| Father | Mother |
| Grandfather | Grandmother |
| He | She |
| Husband | Wife |
| King | Queen |
| Man | Woman |
| Prince | Princess |
| Son | Daughter |

### Locative and Directional Antonyms

| | |
|---|---|
| Behind | Ahead |
| Below | Above |
| Bottom | Top |
| City | Country |
| Front | Back |
| High | Low |

*Landmark School, Inc.*

| | |
|---|---|
| Left | Right |
| Near | Far |
| Out | In |
| Top | Bottom |
| Under | Over |
| Up | Down |

## Antonyms for Adjectives That Describe State

| | |
|---|---|
| Alive | Dead |
| Awake | Asleep |
| Bad | Good |
| Beautiful | Ugly |
| Best | Worst |
| Black | White |
| Closed | Open |
| Cold | Hot |
| Dark | Light |
| Dirty | Clean |
| Dry | Wet |
| Easy | Hard |
| Fast | Slow |
| Fat | Skinny |
| Happy | Sad |
| Hard | Soft |
| Healthy | Sick |
| Heavy | Light |
| Little | Big |
| Long | Short |
| New | Old |
| Noisy | Quiet |
| On | Off |
| Poor | Rich |
| Right | Wrong |
| Shallow | Deep |
| Sharp | Dull |
| Slow | Fast |
| Small | Large |
| Smart | Dumb |
| True | Falso |
| Ugly | Pretty |
| Wet | Dry |
| Young | Old |

Landmark School, Inc.

## Antonyms for Words That Describe Temporal Order

| | |
|---|---|
| Before | After |
| Day | Night |
| Early | Late |
| First | Last |
| Sunrise | Sunset |

## Antonyms for Verbs

| | |
|---|---|
| Arrive | Depart |
| Begin | End |
| Come | Go |
| Find | Lose |
| Laugh | Cry |
| Lead | Follow |
| Lock | Unlock |
| Pass | Fail |
| Push | Pull |
| Take | Give |
| Work | Play |

## Antonyms for Words That Describe Quantity or Frequency

| | |
|---|---|
| All | None |
| Many | Few |
| More | Less |
| Most | Least |
| Full | Empty |
| Always | Never |
| Often | Seldom |

## *Objectives*

The student will:

- demonstrate understanding of the relationship between high-frequency antonym pairs (e.g., yes/no, on/off, and hot/cold), then produce an accurate definition of "antonym"

- pair picture or word cards that depict highly familiar antonym pairs by imitating the instructor

- select the correct member of antonym pairs in sentence completion and oral cloze tasks

*Landmark School, Inc.*

- respond to questions designed to elicit specific antonyms
- complete analogy tasks designed to elicit antonyms
- verbally generate original sentences containing both members of an antonym pair, using the conjunction "but" to mark the contrast; for example, "Lions are wild but house cats are tame."
- identify antonyms in a selection of literature or expository text
- formulate sentences containing antonym pairs in writing tasks
- demonstrate appropriate use and comprehension of antonyms in spontaneous speech

# Synonyms

## Goal

The student will use a repertoire of synonyms appropriate to her or his vocabulary level.

## Background

*Synonyms* are words with nearly the same meaning. No synonyms share exactly the same definition. A thesaurus is the best source for finding synonyms. However, teachers should advise students that a synonym from a thesaurus might apply to one meaning of a multiple-meaning word but not to another. For example, a synonym for "little" in the context of a person might be "small," whereas a synonym for "little" in the context of time might be "brief."

Brainstorming sessions occur daily at Landmark, especially in language arts and oral expression/literature classes. Before teachers introduce unfamiliar words as synonyms, they encourage students to generate as many synonyms for a target word as they can on their own. When students are introduced to a new vocabulary word from the literature, teachers encourage them to associate the word with a synonym whenever feasible.

Bush (1989) and Fry, Kress, and Fountoukidis (2000) provide extensive synonym lists. The adjective and adverb lists in this chapter also include synonyms. The tables below offer synonyms for a few words (adjectives and verbs) overused by students.

### Synonyms for Overused Adjectives That Express Size

| Overused Word | Synonyms |
|---|---|
| Big | Large, great, enormous |
| Fat | Plump, thick, heavy |
| Great | Excellent |
| Little | Small, tiny, short, brief |
| Long | Lengthy, extensive |
| Short | Small, little, brief |
| Tall | High, soaring |
| Thin | Lean |

## Synonyms for Overused Adjectives That Express Quality

| Overused Word | Synonyms |
| --- | --- |
| Bad | Mean, unkind |
| Boring | Tiresome, monotonous |
| Dirty | Soiled |
| Easy | Not difficult |
| Funny | Amusing, humorous |
| Good | Nice, agreeable |
| Hard | Difficult |
| New | Recent, modern |
| Old | Ancient, aged |
| Strong, | Mighty, powerful, tough |
| Very | Exceptionally |
| Weak | Faint, feeble |

## Synonyms for Overused Adjectives That Express Degree

| Overused Word | Synonyms |
| --- | --- |
| Fast | Rapid, speedy, swift, quick |
| Slow | Lagging |

## Synonyms for Overused Adjectives That Express Feeling

| Overused Word | Synonyms |
| --- | --- |
| Glad | Happy, delighted, pleased |
| Mad | Angry, furious |
| Sad | Unhappy, gloomy, depressed |
| Scared | Frightened, fearful |
| Tired | Fatigued, run down |

## Synonyms for Overused Verbs

| Overused Word | Synonyms |
| --- | --- |
| Answer | Respond |
| Beat | Defeat, best, win |
| Break | Smash, split, ignore, fracture |
| Build | Construct, assemble, develop |
| Catch | Seize, capture |
| Choose | Select |
| Come | Arrive, appear |
| Cut | Trim |

*Landmark School, Inc.*

| Overused Word | Synonyms |
|---|---|
| Do | Perform, act |
| Find | Locate, discover |
| Fool | Cheat, mislead, trick, deceive |
| Free | Release, liberate |
| Get | Acquire, obtain |
| Give | Donate, contribute |
| Go | Move, walk, run |
| Grab | Grasp |
| Hate | Dislike, detest, despise |
| Have | Hold, own, possess |
| Help | Assist, aid |
| Hit | Strike, slap |
| Hurt | Harm, damage, injure |
| Know | Understand, recognize, realize |
| Leave | Depart |
| Like | Enjoy |
| Make | Build, create, invent |
| Move | Stir |
| Plan | Arrange, prepare, organize |
| Push | Shove, nudge, thrust, poke |
| Pull | Tug, yank |
| Put | Set, place, lay |
| Run | Move with haste, go quickly |
| Say | Mention, state, declare |
| See | Notice, watch, examine |
| Send | Deliver, mail, ship |
| Shut | Close, suspend |
| Take | Obtain, carry, catch, choose |
| Tell | Explain, say, speak, inform |
| Think | Imagine, plan, consider |
| Throw | Toss, catch, pitch, fling, hurl |
| Try | Attempt |
| Use | Operate, employ |
| Want | Desire |

## *Objectives*

The student will:

- demonstrate understanding of antonyms as a foundation for synonyms

*Landmark School, Inc.*

- demonstrate understanding of the similarities between high-frequency synonym pairs (e.g., nice/good)
- describe similarities in appearance using photos of synonymous objects (e.g., jeans, slacks, and trousers)
- define "synonym" and contrast its meaning with "antonym"
- describe both underlying similarities and slight differences within a group when shown pictures representing synonyms
- respond to questions designed to elicit specific synonyms; for example, "What is a synonym for 'push'?" should produce words like "start," "shove," and "jump"
- complete analogy tasks designed to elicit synonyms; for example, "Laugh is to giggle as sob is to _____ (cry, wail, pout)."
- identify synonyms as they occur in literature or expository text
- formulate sentences containing synonyms in writing tasks
- demonstrate appropriate use and comprehension of synonyms in spontaneous speech

# Homonyms: Multiple-Meaning Words

## *Goal*

The student will correctly identify and define homonyms appropriate to her or his vocabulary level.

## *Background*

*Homonyms* are words with multiple meanings. The two types are *homophones*, which are pronounced the same but spelled differently (e.g., mail/male), and *homographs*, which are spelled alike and usually pronounced the same (e.g., bark/bark). Homographs that are pronounced differently are *heteronyms*. The change in pronunciation might be due to an accent shift, as in the two-syllable word "conduct"; it might also be due to a change in meaning, as in "tear" as a noun vs. as a verb.

Teachers should not assume that students recognize homonyms. One complicating factor in the study of homonyms is faulty phonological processing. For example:

- When asked to generate two or more meanings or contexts for the dictated word "fair" (fare), the student defined "fear."

- When asked to generate two or more meanings or contexts for the dictated word "steel" (steal), the student defined "stale."

- When asked to generate two or more meanings or contexts for the dictated word "soar" (sore), the student defined "sure."

- When asked to generate two or more meanings or contexts for the dictated word "heel" (heal), the student defined "hail."

- When asked to generate two or more meanings or contexts for the dictated word "air" (heir), the student defined "ear."

Testing of oral language skills at Landmark shows that most students benefit from training that follows an orderly progression from simple, concrete homonyms to those that are more difficult or subtle. Landmark students in the elementary program receive extensive exposure to homonyms. For example, they make art booklets with drawings that show two meanings shared by a word (e.g., watch/watch).

A list of high-frequency homonyms follows. Many of these words were generated by Landmark students in classroom activities. Extensive homonym lists appear in Bush (1989) and Fry, Kress, and Fountoukidis (2000).

Semantics

## Homophones

| | | | |
|---|---|---|---|
| Ate, eight | Do, due, dew | Knot, not | Read, red |
| Buy, by | Eye, I | Main, mane | Real, reel |
| Beat, beet | Fair, fare | Mail, male | Right, write |
| Bear, bare | Flea, flee | Maid, made | Sail, sale |
| Board, bored | Flower, flour | Night, knight | Son, sun |
| Break, brake | Hear, here | No, know | Threw, through |
| Course, coarse | High, hi | Nose, knows | Tide, tied |
| Cells, sells | Horse, hoarse | Piece, peace | To, too, two |
| Cent, sent | Heard, herd | Plane, plain | Weight, wait |
| Cents, sense | Heel, heal | Pail, pale | Way, weigh |
| Clothes, close | Hall, haul | Pair, pear, pare | Week, weak |
| Dear, deer | Hair, hare | Read, red | Waist, waste |

## Homographs

| | | | |
|---|---|---|---|
| Act | Flat | Lot | Saw |
| Arms | Fly | Mark | School |
| Bank | Free | Miss | Serve |
| Bark | Fresh | Note | Sharp |
| Bill | Game | Park | Sign |
| Box | Glasses | Plant | Stand |
| Catch | Group | Play | Store |
| Change | Hand | Player | Story |
| Check | Hard | Point | Strike |
| Cross | Head | Press | Table |
| Deal | Hold | Ring | Top |
| Draw | Last | Rock | Track |
| Ear | Leaves | Row | Train |
| Fast | Left | Ruler | Watch |
| Feet | Letter | Run | Wave |
| Fire | Light | | |

## One-Syllable Heteronyms (Two Pronunciations)

Rēad (present-tense verb)/   Teār (verb)/tēar (noun)   Wīnd (verb)/wĭnd
   rĕad (past-tense verb)    Lēad (verb)/lĕad (noun)      (noun)

## Two-Syllable Heteronyms (Accent Changes)

Cón duct/con dúct          Ób ject/ob ject          Prés ent/pre sent

Landmark School, Inc.

## Objectives

The student will:

- auditorily discriminate between similar-sounding words that are not homonyms (e.g., soar and sewer)
- identify and name picture pairs that represent homonyms
- draw pictures representing homonym pairs
- use contextual cues to distinguish between same and different meaning in sentence pairs containing homonyms
- generate two or more meanings for homonyms featured in literature or expository text
- verbally formulate sentence pairs containing homonyms given visual cues
- generate two or more interpretations of sentences from literature or expository text containing homonyms
- include homonyms when formulating sentences in written expression given visual cues
- include homonyms when formulating sentences in written expression without cues

# Analogies

## Goal

The student will determine logical relationships in selected analogies and supply the missing words in the formal construction format.

## Background

According to Gardner (1978), being able to make analogies is an important precursor to interpreting figurative language. One must be able to identify a trait common to two subjects in a metaphor; for example, one must relate "see the light" to "hope" and "walk in darkness" to "despair."

Many Landmark students demonstrate relative strength in analogies. The spare wording in the conventional analogy format may appeal to them once they learn how to use it.

Teachers should introduce analogies in active declarative sentences ("A superintendent leads a school system and a president runs a corporation.") before introducing the formal construction format ("Superintendent is to school system as president is to corporation."). Teachers should also allow students to learn one analogical class, or frame of reference, before introducing exercises with a variety of classes. Teachers can add classes gradually until students can shift among several classes within a single exercise.

## Objectives

The student will:

- complete an instructor-produced analogy given visual cues; for example, "A hippo is large, and a mouse is _____. Small or gray? Choose the opposite of 'large.'"
- judge the consistency of an expressed relationship in a right-or-wrong task; for example, a horse has a hoof and a dog has a collar (wrong)
- complete analogies describing whole-to-part relationships
- complete analogies describing part-to-whole relationships
- complete analogies describing agent-to-action relationships
- complete analogies describing action-to-agent relationships

- complete analogies describing object-to-action relationships
- complete analogies describing action-to-object relationships
- complete analogies describing class or synonym relationships
- complete analogies describing opposite relationships
- complete analogies describing spatial relationships
- complete analogies describing temporal or sequential relationships in correct order
- complete analogies describing temporal or sequential relationships out of correct order
- complete analogies describing familial relationships
- complete analogies describing grammatical relationships
- complete analogies within a single exercise that describe an assortment of relationships

# Temporal-Sequential Relationships

## *Goal*

The student will correctly express temporal-sequential relationships and demonstrate comprehension of the underlying rules.

## *Background*

Instant feedback during individual tutorials is the most efficient route for students to master concepts related to time and space. One fifteen-year-old Landmark student, for example, had no concept of temporal-sequential relationships. He wore a digital watch, and when anyone asked him the time, he simply read the numbers. They meant nothing to him. He also struggled with severe word retrieval and memory deficits. When asked how he made it through each day, he said:

> I follow all the other kids from class to class. Then after school I watch to see when they leave for our soccer practice. I missed it one day, because I lost track of where everyone was.

We began a step-by-step process in which part of each tutorial was devoted to temporal-sequential relationships. (We met once a week throughout the school year for a total of about twenty-five hours.) When we began to study telling time, we asked the student's parents to buy him an analog watch. After the summer, the student's mother reported that, for the first time, the student was able to estimate when he should leave for work on his bicycle in order to arrive on time. She further reported that he wore his watch throughout the summer and attained a new independence.

## *Objectives*

The student will:

- demonstrate comprehension of words associated with time, including "before," "after," "last," "first," "later," "next," "between," and "in a while"
- identify calendar words given a calendar to view; for example:
  - a day, and names of days of the week
  - a week, and which week of the month
  - the twelve months of the year

- yesterday, day before yesterday, tomorrow, day after tomorrow, last week, next week, and next month
- associate words with pictures that show each of the four seasons (e.g., photos and paintings)
- name the four seasons of the year in order, given a picture of the earth's continuous oval path around the sun
- arrange cards labeled with days of the week in order
- identify calendar words in conjunction with temporal modifiers while looking at a calendar (e.g., point to last Thursday or show the next month)
- answer questions relating to temporal relationships; for example, "What is the name of the day before yesterday?"
- identify words that refer to parts of the day given visual mnemonic cues (e.g., pictures of the sun rising from the horizon, sitting high in the sky, and descending into the horizon)
- demonstrate comprehension of how the twenty-four-hour day divides into hours, minutes, and seconds
- write numbers on a conventional clock face (i.e., analog)
- identify any hour on an analog clock face
- manipulate the hands on a clock face to indicate a specific hour dictated by the instructor
- identify half-hour times on a clock face
- manipulate the hands on a clock face to indicate half-hour times dictated by the instructor
- identify quarter-hour times on a clock face
- manipulate the hands on a clock face to indicate quarter-hour times dictated by the instructor
- manipulate the hands on a clock face to indicate any time the instructor requests
- explain the modifiers associated with telling time, such as "past," "after," "before," and "until"
- demonstrate flexible usage of terms in reporting the time (e.g., 5:40 is the same as twenty minutes to six)

*Landmark School, Inc.*

- identify the time on any conventional clock or watch face
- estimate the time remaining in an activity (e.g., class ends in twenty minutes)

# Directional Words

## Goal

The student will include accurate directional words and explain the strategies he or she uses for recall.

## Background

Many students have extreme difficulty mastering directional words or concepts. Some never do. Micro-uniting and frequent rehearsal are the most effective ways of helping these students.

## Objectives

The student will:

- imitate the instructor's modeling of left-hand and right-hand actions; for example, "I am picking up the card on the left, the coin on the right."

- discuss or evaluate mnemonic cues for distinguishing left from right with the instructor; for example, "I write with my right hand and I wear my watch on my left hand."

- follow directions in motor activities by distinguishing left from right given visual cues

- follow directions in paper-and-pencil activities by distinguishing left from right given visual cues

- follow directions in motor activities by distinguishing left from right without visual cues

- follow directions in paper-and-pencil activities by distinguishing left from right without visual cues

- imitate visual cues and gestures for indicating directions modeled by the instructor

- name directions, given a globe and a compass rose

- label directional arrows drawn on paper given a compass rose

- make designs on paper grids given directional terms and a compass rose

*Landmark School, Inc.*

- use mnemonic cues, if needed, to recite the cardinal directions "north," "east," "south," and "west" (e.g., <u>n</u>ever <u>e</u>at <u>s</u>tringy <u>w</u>orms)
- accurately draw a compass rose containing the cardinal directions to use as a guide for drawing designs
- follow instructions for designs that include midpoint directionals given a compass rose; for example, "Move your pencil northeast one space."
- deliver oral instructions for designs that include midpoint directionals given a compass rose
- accurately draw a compass rose containing cardinal and midpoint directions to use as a guide for drawing designs
- draw a compass rose to use as a guide for completing orienteering tasks on a map
- deliver oral directions to others for orienteering on a map
- complete orienteering tasks in space using a compass as a guide
- deliver oral directions to others for orienteering in space using a compass as a guide

# Figurative Language

## *Goal*

The student will correctly interpret figurative language in literature or expository text.

## *Background*

> Figurative language tells it like it isn't to show the way it really is.
>
> Richard Lederer, *The Miracle of Language*

Fine literature – both prose and poetry – frequently owes its richness to figurative language. A *figure of speech* is an expressive use of language to create an image that enriches the message. Words are used not in their literal sense but creatively and nonliterally. "The long black snake wound around the mountain, hissing steam along the way," for example, conjures the image of a train.

Figures of speech fall into several categories, several of which are described below.

### **Figurative Expressions**

Elementary and middle-school students are likely to encounter the higher frequency figurative expressions defined below. It is important to note that these definitions are included as a resource for the instructor, not as a lesson for the student. At Landmark, emphasis is on understanding and appreciating the richness of figurative language in literature, not on terminology.

- *Hyperbole* is extreme exaggeration for effect and is not to be taken literally; for example, "Pecos Bill lassoed that tornado and brought it down."

- *Idioms* are figurative expressions whose meanings cannot be discerned from the individual words. These expressions must be learned as a whole, like new vocabulary words. While idioms often disappear from popular usage, new ones emerge, such as "pushing the envelope," which means taking a risk or going to the edge of technology or propriety.

- *Metaphor* is a figure of speech that equates two elements from different domains of experience (Gardner 1978); for example, "Calvin was certainly a tiger today."

- *Onomatopoeia* refers to words that, when spoken, sound like the sound they describe, such as "clanging, crashing cymbals."

- *Personification* is application of human or personal qualities to inanimate things or ideas; for example, "The once-powerful wind moaned and sighed, then, after fading to a whisper, finally died."

- *Similes* are figurative expressions that compare two different subjects. Such expressions are usually introduced by "like" or "as"; for example, "It was as dark as midnight in the cave."

- *Slang* is a very informal use of vocabulary that might be more colorful or playful than a literal expression; for example, "Take a hike." means "Go away." and "Don't go there." means "Don't talk to me about that."

Figures of speech that are more complex appear in more advanced literature.

- *Allegory* is a story in which abstract or spiritual meaning is portrayed by way of concrete or material forms. The underlying meaning might not be mentioned. Longfellow wrote a memorable poem, "The Ship of State," to mourn Lincoln's death, but also to express faith in this country (the Ship of State) to carry on.

- *Irony* appears in single sentences, short passages in stories, and even in entire books. Winner (1988) provides an excellent explanation of irony and a child's unfolding comprehension of it. In her words, "Understanding irony involves substituting one meaning for another, although the meaning that is substituted is not simply the opposite of what was said. The meaning that is substituted in irony includes the speaker's belief about his utterance as well as his attitude toward those who would espouse such a view." Irony allows us not a peek at the real world, but a peek into the speaker's inner world.

- *Litotes* is an understatement in which, for example, a compliment is expressed in the form of a negative; for example, "To beat Harlem in the Little League playoffs was no small feat!"

- *Euphemisms* are indirect expressions of unpleasant facts; for example, "passed away" is a euphemism for "died" in the sentence "Mr. Brown passed away yesterday."

- *Metonymy* is an expression in which one name is used for another to which it relates. In the newspaper, for example, one reads, "The White House announced today that . . ." Here, "The White House" refers to the president or presidential staff.

- *Sarcasm* is a form of irony intended to hurt; for example, a spectator at a chess tournament might say "Oh, brilliant move!" after seeing a player set him- or herself up for defeat.

- *Synecdoche* is an expression in which the reader must add information the author leaves unsaid; for example, the reader must supply the word "sailors" in the sentence "All hands on deck!"

## **Analyzing Emerging Figurative Language**

Gardner and Winner extensively researched children's emerging ability to understand figurative language. They also – singly and in collaboration – wrote very accessible articles and books on the topic (Gardner 1974, 1978, 1983; Gardner et al. 1975; Gardner and Winner 1976; Gardner et al. 1978; Winner 1988; Winner, McCarthy, and Gardner 1978; Winner, Rosenstiel, and Gardner 1976). This research leads to three important conclusions. Educators must:

- appreciate figurative language and understand its role in fine literature

- be aware of the developmental stages for comprehending figurative language

- consider the developmental steps before they lead students toward comprehension and appreciation of figurative language in fine literature

The phrase "figurative language" makes many people think of idioms, those tired figures of speech. It's unfortunate, because the finest and most prevalent representation of figurative language in children's literature is *metaphor*. In fact, metaphor and irony are the two chief forms of nonliteral language (Winner 1988). The origin of the word "metaphor" is from the Greek word "pherin"; *meta* means "over" and *phor* means "carry."

> Consider appreciation of a figure of speech like a metaphor, which equates two elements from different domains of experience.
>
> Howard Gardner, *Developmental Psychology – An Introduction*

> Metaphor has traditionally been viewed in both fields (linguistics or philosophy) as a matter of peripheral interest. We shared the intuition that it

is, instead, a matter of central concern, perhaps the key to giving an adequate account of understanding.

George Lakoff and Mark Johnson, *Metaphors We Live By*

## Stages of Development

Diagnostic teaching of metaphor calls for teachers to understand where breakdowns occur in students' interpretation of literature. The stages described here are designed to help teachers understand that students' capacity to process figurative language reflects their stage of development. The explanation uses the metaphor "Emily is the sunshine in our lives."

- The *magical stage* corresponds to the chronological age of six or younger. The child might interpret the metaphor as "Emily turned herself into the sun. They are the same."

- The *metonymic stage* corresponds to the chronological age of seven or eight. The student knows that the statement describes an impossibility and adds information so it "makes sense." The student's understanding of the metaphor is "Emily is standing outside in the sun."

- The *primitive/incorrect stage* corresponds to the chronological age of eight or nine. The student seizes upon a property related to the metaphor, but not the correct one. For example, the student's understanding of the metaphor might be "Emily is bright (smart) or shines, like the sun."

By age ten or eleven, students interpret the metaphor correctly. They might express their understanding as "Emily is always cheerful, like we feel on a sunny day. She makes us feel good or happy."

## Student Capacity

Students must have certain knowledge and skills to understand metaphoric language. They need to be able to perceive similarity between two dissimiliar domains – here, between a child and sunshine. In the sample metaphor above, the student must be able to understand that Emily's demeanor has a quality resembling sunshine. The student must:

- know the precise meaning of the words, both actual and implied – in this case, "human" and "brightness or radiance"

- be able to think of words and language in other than literal terms – in this case, to know that the word "sunshine" is borrowed for the metaphor because it has certain traits
- bring certain logical capacities to the situation and apply prior experience (e.g., that Emily has a sunny smile) – in this case, to know that Emily and sunshine are alike in some respects, but not all

In addition, students must accurately process speech sounds, sentence structure, and ambiguous words. The following errors of interpretation were noticed in classroom discussions of literature. These interpretations illustrate earlier stages of development or incorrect processing in phonology (speech sounds), syntax (sentence structure), or semantics (ambiguous words, vocabulary).

## Errors of Interpretation (Receptive)

| Metaphor | Student's Inaccurate Interpretation or Question | Stage/Type |
|---|---|---|
| He was a man of many faces. | They took pictures of him from different angles. | Metonymic |
| The golden lilies that Ramon picked for me have faded, but I'll keep them alive in my diary. | She smashed them and kept them in her diary. | Metonymic |
| A blind boy said, "His eyes had become mine." | My eyes became black like his. | Metonymic |
| She's two-faced. | She has a double memory. | Metonymic |
| Stevie Wonder said, "Being blind has helped me see clearly." | In his head he can see anything he wants to see. | Primitive |
| He read him the riot act. | He read his mind. | Primitive |
| He's taking poetic license. | He's using no punctuation. | Primitive |
| Let a smile be your umbrella. | Be happy under the rain. | Primitive |
| Let's take the law into our own hands. | Let's carry out the law. | Primitive |
| His voice was hollow. | His voice was low. | Phonological |

Landmark School, Inc.

| Metaphor | Student's Inaccurate Interpretation or Question | Stage/Type |
| --- | --- | --- |
| He was the odd man out. | He's an old guy. | Phonological |
| She is easily crushed. | She likes him. | Syntactical |
| It smarts (i.e., it hurts). | Everyone knew about it. | Ambiguity |
| It stretched for 4,000 unbroken miles. | What does "unbroken" mean? | Ambiguity |
| He'll zero in on his ideas. | He has no ideas. | Ambiguity |
| She sure casts a spell over me. | She told him "no." She was mean. | Ambiguity |
| He kept his word. | He didn't say anything. | Ambiguity |
| She's superstitious. | She can see into the future. | Vocabulary |

## **Training and Remediation**

Several sections in this chapter are springboards for comprehending figurative language. As stated, the best vehicle for studying figurative language is literature, both prose and poetry. Other media formats – advertising, newspaper headlines, and articles, especially in the sports section – are useful to a degree. It is important to note that worksheets are best used to reinforce concepts, not teach them. And here's a reminder to us all:

> Studying metaphor should be less like learning the periodic table of elements and more like learning how to model clay. Style is like a frog – you can dissect the thing, but it somehow dies in the process.
>
> Arthur Quinn, *Figures of Speech – 60 Ways to Turn a Phrase*

## *Objectives*

The student will:

- study advertisements in magazines or on television, which are great sources of multiple-meaning words, implied meanings, puns, and the like

- produce two or more meanings for target multiple-meaning words dictated by the instructor (e.g., bark and sign)

- identify two elements in a simile; for example, in "the train looked like a snake," the two elements are "train" and "snake"

- describe the shared physical characteristics of the two elements in a simile, using an example from poetry or literature
- identify the connectives used in similes (e.g., like, as, than, and so)
- provide key words in recall of the word "simile" (e.g., similar and same)
- distinguish between a factual statement and one that creates an image, using an example from poetry or literature
- describe cross-sensory metaphors (i.e., implied comparisons, such as bright smell), using an example from poetry or literature
- select the picture that best depicts a target metaphor from a choice of several pictures
- select the correct metaphor in a multiple-choice exercise
- translate a physical attribute of a target word into an explanation of psychological attributes
- explain both physical and psychological attributes of a multiple-meaning word
- identify the shared attributes of something being compared by implication in a metaphor, using an example from poetry or literature
- identify the connotative meaning conveyed by one concept in a metaphor, using an example from poetry or literature
- identify and explain personification (i.e., attributing human qualities to an inanimate object), using an example from poetry or literature
- verbally generate metaphoric expressions
- include figurative language in written expression
- explain contemporary idioms (e.g., chill out)
- identify hyperbole (e.g., he hit the ball a mile), using an example from literature
- match a common contemporary proverb with its abstract interpretation, given two or three choices
- match proverbs to short stories or fables

- identify proverbs in the curriculum or literature
- improve his or her ability to identify figurative language used on television and in advertising and propaganda
- explain selected puns and riddles

# Making Inferences

## *Goal*

The student will express plausible inferences from spoken or read passages in which information is implied, but not stated.

## *Background*

Making an *inference* requires students to draw upon outside knowledge to reach an understanding of information provided in a reading passage. Making an inference is not the same as drawing a conclusion, as the latter only requires students to work with information provided in the text.

The *Test of Language Competence – Expanded Edition* (Wiig and Secord 1989) has a subtest called "Making Inferences" that uses multiple-choice questions to probe general cognitive ability as well as linguistic ability. Landmark students demonstrate, on average, at least an average ability to make inferences based on this test.

## *Objectives*

The student will, within a literature or expository test passage:

- interpret a variety of events and predict their possible outcomes
- rearrange comic strips from a random array into a proper sequence of panels
- predict an outcome by examining panels from a comic strip in which the final panel is missing
- guess what precedes the middle and final panels in a three-frame comic strip in which the first panel is missing
- make an inference from single-frame comics, such as Dennis the Menace (e.g., preceding events, intentions, and outcomes)
- anticipate the outcome of an event in a short story
- identify the missing link in a chain of events in which one link has been deleted
- verbally test her or his chosen inference in a multiple-choice task against information provided in the reading

- supply supporting evidence for the inference selected in the multiple-choice task
- explain why the incorrect options in the multiple-choice task are not probable or possible
- specify a plausible intervening event that is implied but not stated
- provide reasons for making an inference based on the topic, content, or other information

# Literature

## Goal

The student will comprehend and evaluate literature that he or she has heard or read.

## Background

Most of the goals and objectives in this book apply, in one way or another, to the comprehension, discussion, and appreciation of literature. In this chapter alone, these topics directly relate to literature:

- ambiguities
- homonyms
- analogies
- vocabulary
- word retrieval
- figurative language
- making inferences

The guidelines below are valuable for starting discussions of literature in the classroom. They are modeled after the discussion group ideas of Fitzgerald and Wollman-Bonilla (Cullinan 1993). Also helpful are McCarthy's very accessible guides for teaching literary elements (1997, 2000).

- The teacher should sit among the students as a participant.
- The teacher should pose questions that invite students to draw from personal experience; for example:
  - "Are there events in this book very similar to any of your experiences?"
  - "Are there events that contrast sharply with your own experiences?"
  - "Is there a character very much like you or perhaps one who is most different from you?"
  - "What do you think was the most interesting scene in this book?"
- The teacher should share his or her own previous misunderstandings of the text and pose questions that reflect genuine puzzlement, if applicable.

*Semantics*

- The teacher should model appropriate behavior for a discussion by thinking aloud, listening with interest, responding to students' contributions, respecting others' ideas, and challenging students intellectually, not personally.

- The teacher should respect the different perspectives students bring and make clear that it is fine if everyone is not of one opinion.

## Objectives

The student will:

- recognize and sequence ideas and events
- determine and recall main ideas and details
- deliver oral summaries that contain relevant information
- make inferences
- describe contextual cues when inferring the meaning of a newly introduced vocabulary word
- copy the dictionary definition of a new vocabulary word
- write a new vocabulary word in an original sentence
- define a new vocabulary word
- complete exercises designed to stimulate retention of a new vocabulary word (multiple-choice tasks, sentence completion tasks, art projects, and creative writing projects, such as cinquain, haiku, and word pictures)
- generate two or more meanings for multiple-meaning words
- interpret figurative language in the literature (e.g., similes, metaphors, personification, hyperbole, idioms, proverbs, and puns)
- resolve sentence ambiguity in context, where applicable; for example, "They were proud of their race."
- generate character analysis (e.g., physical characteristics, personality, and feelings) using oral and written expression
- describe character development
- describe plot development using oral and written expression

*Landmark School, Inc.*

- describe the setting using oral and written expression
- describe the theme using oral and written expression (e.g., friendship, survival, and coming of age)
- describe the mood using oral and written expression
- describe the author's point of view using oral and written expression (e.g., first-person or "I" voice vs. omniscient or "every character's" voice)
- coherently express comparisons and contrasts between characters, plots, and authors within one selection or between two different selections
- participate in group discussion about the literature
- consider other students' opinions
- provide data that supports her or his position when expressing an opinion
- write chapter summaries that include relevant information
- interpret complex sentence structure in literature
- include complex sentence structure in written or oral summaries, where applicable
- resolve sentence ambiguity from its context, where applicable
- apply oral reading skills like intonation, phrasing, and fluency

## Character Analysis

**Book Title:** Bandit's Moon  **Author:** Sid Fleischman

**Name of Character:** Annie Rose

**Physical Characteristics:**

thin and pretean
short boy's hair
wears overalls and boys boots

| Personality: | Actions in story that give you clues about character's personality: |
|---|---|
| kind | putting up with O.O. Mary |
| tomboy | the way she dressed and she lied about being a boy |
| strong | she kept up with the group on a horse |

| Feelings: | Clues from story about character's feelings: |
|---|---|
| unhappy | she said her parents died |
| scared | Wakeen scared her |
| hungry | O.O. Mary didn't feed her |

**Does the character change during the story?**

Yes, Annie Rose changes.

**If so, how does the character change?**

She has gotten more used to Wakeen and the group of bandits.

# Bibliography of Instructional Materials

Bush, C. *Language Remediation and Expansion – 150 Skill-Building Reference Lists*. Austin: PRO-ED, 1989.

———. *500 Thematic Lists and Activities*. Austin: PRO-ED, 1996.

Dale, E., and J. O'Rourke. *Techniques of Teaching Vocabulary*. Menlo Park, CA: Benjamin Cummings Publishing, 1971.

———. *Vocabulary Building – A Process Approach*. Columbus, OH: Zaner-Bloser, 1986.

Gorman-Gard, K.A. *Figurative Language – A Comprehensive Program*. Eau Claire, WI: Thinking Publications, 1992.

Johnson, K., and P. Bayrd. *Megawords – Multisyllabic Words for Reading, Spelling, and Vocabulary*. Cambridge: Educators Publishing Service, 1993.

Kisner, R., and B. Knowles. *Warm-Up Exercises – Calisthenics for the Brain*. Book 1. Eau Claire, WI: Thinking Publications, 1984.

———. *Warm-Up Exercises – Calisthenics for the Brain*. Book 2. Eau Claire, WI: Thinking Publications, 1985.

———. *Warm-Up Exercises – Calisthenics for the Brain*. Book 3. Eau Claire, WI: Thinking Publications, 1992.

Lazzari, A., and P. Peters. *HELP – Handbook of Exercises for Language Processing*. Vol. 2, *Specific Word Finding, Categorization, Wh- Questions, Grammar*. Moline, IL: LinguiSystems, 1980.

McCarthy, T. *Teaching Literary Elements*. New York: Scholastic, 1997.

———. *Teaching Literary Elements with Short Stories*. New York: Scholastic, 2000.

Zachman, L., C. Jorgensen, M. Barrett, R. Huisingh, and M. Snedden. *Manual of Exercises for Expressive Reasoning*. Moline, IL: LinguiSystems, 1982.

CHAPTER 5

# PRAGMATICS

## Introduction

*Pragmatics* is "the study of how language is used in the context of communication" (Paul 2000). Paul goes on to state that beyond learning speech sounds, words, and sentence structure, children must learn how to get things done in the real world with those sounds, words, and sentences. In addition to words and sentences, language in the pragmatic sense includes nonverbal forms of communication – facial expression, eye contact, gestures, intonation, and volume, to name a few. Effective communicators use language as a tool to achieve their purposes, whether engaging in conversation, participating in group discussion, or speaking before an audience.

Students' lives include many contexts for communication: at home, in the neighborhood, at school, and in the larger community. A child is expected to learn the communication skills to be a family member, friend, learner, and positive member of the community, among other roles. The contexts are endless, and the rules for each can seem bewildering. Let's examine "no." Crystal (1995) listed fifty-seven ways to say "no," each conveying a slightly different meaning, including "any other time," "no chance!", "are you serious?", and "sorry."

According to Wiig and Semel (1984), children with normal language development become fairly effective communicators by the third or fourth grade. They perform appropriate verbal rituals with peers and adults in a variety of contexts, such as introducing two people, maintaining a conversation, and using the telephone. Wiig and Semel also report that third- and fourth-graders can use language to inform (e.g., to ask for and offer help, give directions, summarize, explain their values, and ask for reasons). In addition, they have begun to use language to control, as in expressing agreement or disagreement, taking the viewpoint of others, or persuading. Furthermore, children in this age group can use language to convey feelings, such as affection, approval, dissatisfaction, and difference of opinion. Finally, third- and fourth-grade children use language to imagine, such as in role playing and creating group games.

Children with language learning disabilities might be compromised in one or all of these pragmatic areas. By middle school, pragmatic deficits begin to take their toll, and these children become social misfits in their classrooms and communities.

One Landmark student's vocabulary, both receptive and expressive, was above average. His ability to formulate grammatically correct single sentences was at least average. However, when this student attempted to converse, summarize, explain a process, or express an opinion, he became completely disfluent. His disfluency was marked by repetitions, pauses, and on-line repairs. He had the knowledge, but could not share it in a concise, coherent manner.

The interaction below quotes another Landmark student. In addition to extreme difficulty formulating his thoughts, this student had severe deficits in his ability to recall single words in picture-naming tasks.

> **Teacher**: (Showing photos of a candle and a light bulb [Simon 1994].) Tell me how these two items are alike and how they are different.
> **Student**: One has wax and it has this li'l string goin' right through and one is wires and, and . . . um . . . the wire goes up and hooks it to the light bulb and that's how it gets its light and how the candle gets its light is that you light a match and put it near the . . . um . . . string, and it . . . uh . . . melts the wax.

Both students greatly benefited from organizational frameworks that facilitate delivery of information.

Delayed development in phonology, morphology, syntax, and semantics is often the cause of a communication breakdown. Consider the faulty sentence structure in "I quit reading that book. It lost all interest in me." Word retrieval errors can result in misunderstanding or ridicule. For example:

- "You have to go on the camping trip. It's *majority*." (meaning "mandatory")

- "This object is made of *plaster*." (meaning "plastic")

- "I need to be excused from class to *ease* myself." (meaning "relieve")

In addition, these students might be delayed in moving from self-oriented to other-oriented forms of communication. They might have difficulty understanding another point of view and be unable to conduct a conversation without alienating the listener, who feels misunderstood. Also, as students progress through middle school, the importance of group discussion increases. Students who process information more slowly or labor to formulate their thoughts might withdraw from discussion for fear of being considered stupid. Students who feel extreme frustration with being unable to express themselves might resort to physical demonstration of their feelings, such as slamming a door, punching the wall, or stomping out of a room.

*Pragmatics*

Some nonverbal forms of communication vary from one culture to another. Children from some cultures are taught to avoid direct eye contact with authority figures, but are then instructed to use direct eye contact in the typical American classroom. Americans tend to stand about two feet apart when talking with one another. Students from other countries might violate the personal space observed by most Americans and get chastised – even by teachers who are probably unaware of the student's cultural training.

Pragmatic disability strikes both ends of the verbal spectrum, as some children have nonverbal learning disabilities. They have relatively strong verbal skills – excellent vocabularies and the ability to produce long, complex sentence structures – yet are unable to read nonverbal cues in conversation or discussion. They become social misfits as well.

Normally achieving children gain pragmatic skills through exposure and observation. They test their hypotheses about pragmatics by trial and error. Since students with language learning disabilities failed to develop pragmatic skills through exposure, observation, and intuition, it is appropriate to introduce skills directly and in isolation, with the intention of integrating the skills into real-life situations as quickly as possible.

The pragmatics curriculum at Landmark has two goals: first, to improve the students' ability to present, understand, and respond to information, and second, to improve the students' social communication skills. All students take oral expression/literature classes, in which they use organizational templates to retell or summarize, describe, explain a process, identify comparisons and contrasts, express and justify opinions, explain cause and effect, and make predictions based upon logical reasoning. Students also study literary elements, such as setting, plot, character, theme, and mood. Students then integrate pragmatic skills into discussions about literature and related themes. During discussions, students are expected to agree or disagree in a constructive manner and to demonstrate understanding of the viewpoints of others.

In the area of social communication skills (using language to express feelings), Landmark counselors meet with all oral expression/literature classes biweekly. They follow a curriculum designed to foster self-esteem and a desire to become responsible members of the classroom community. Students are introduced to creative conflict resolution as well. Kreidler (1984) has created an excellent workbook for middle-school students.

In conclusion, a warm, supportive environment prevails when every member of the school community is involved in fostering communication skills. At Landmark, students who are not ready for full engagement with peers find comfort and reassurance in the administrative assistants' offices, library, or kitchen during breaks in the school day. These compassionate

adults are not only serving as sympathetic and supportive listeners, but are also willing to give advice. They are developing students' pragmatic skills without students realizing it.

The sections in this chapter are grouped into three major categories – discourse (sharing information of an academic nature), social communication, and paralinguistic communication – and each section title includes its category, as in "Discourse: Presenting a Topic." It is important to note, however, that students can experience difficulties from the three categories simultaneously and that teachers can address them simultaneously.

Further, the goals in this chapter are idealized, inferring mastery, though most students probably will not attain mastery. The objectives, on the other hand, are largely presented in developmental order (in order of difficulty). This way, the teacher can identify an objective along the spectrum of difficulty as a realistic target for a given student. For example, the goal for "Discourse: Expressing Comparisons and Contrasts" is for the student to organize and describe comparisons and contrasts systematically. One of the objectives under this goal is for the student to deliver an oral summary of comparisons and contrasts, given a visual framework as a guide. This objective might be used as a realistic goal for a student who is not likely to master comparisons and contrasts within the school year.

# Discourse: Presenting a Topic

## Goal

The student will select a topic and maintain it during discourse.

## Background

A student's ability to remain on topic is an everyday issue in the classroom. Teachers apply various strategies to stem the overflow from students who tend to be stream-of-consciousness talkers. Strategies include saying:

- "I like that idea. Hold onto it until we finish this exercise."
- "That's an interesting question. Could you stay a minute after class, and we'll discuss it?"
- "Let's check our agenda. Is that subject on the schedule for today?"

During discussion, teachers can employ and teach certain phrases as signals for subject change. Landmark's Susan Dillon works with her classes to develop phrases like these:

- "Speaking of unsolved crimes, have you read . . . ?"
- "Your experience reminded me of the time . . ."
- "If we've finished that topic, may I please bring up . . . ?"

Weinrich, Glaser, and Johnston (1986) provide excellent exercises for enhancing students' ability to maintain a topic. Because Landmark combines oral expression classes with literature, topic maintenance is usually addressed by discussing topics related to the literature.

## Objectives

The student will:

- establish a topic and make appropriate comments
- remain on topic for an appropriate length of time and number of sentences
- use discourse connectors if the topic is lengthy (e.g., first, second, and third)

- appropriately terminate the topic
- transition to another topic using appropriate transitional phrases, such as "By the way . . ." and "This changes the topic, but . . ."

# Discourse: Summarizing an Event or a Selection from Literature

## *Goal*

The student will orally summarize an event or a selection from literature.

## *Background*

By delivering oral summaries of events, students develop proficiency in their ability to report personal experiences in sequential order. By delivering oral summaries of news events or literature, students develop proficiency in recall and interpretation of factual, sequential, and inferential information.

## *Objectives*

The student will:

- write the discourse connectors "first," "next," "then," "after that," and "finally" on a piece of paper and draw an image for each to use as cues while reporting a personal experience

- use discourse connectors in sequential delivery of a personal experience or an event

- identify the main idea and details of a reading passage read aloud by the instructor

- provide a sequential oral summary of a reading passage, including main idea, relevant details, and transitional words

## Summary of an Event, Story or Chapter

Name: _____
Date: _____
Day: _____

Topic sentence: David was asleep when the storm hit.

First, he was awakened by waves moving the boat.

Then, he went top side and looked at the sky but it was pitch black.

Next, the wind picked up and the boat was going up and down.

After that, he was on top of a sandbar.

In conclusion, David is in trouble.

*Landmark School, Inc.*

# Discourse: Sharing Descriptive Information

## *Goal*

The student will clearly and coherently describe an object, animal, person, scene, or concept.

## *Background*

The object description framework follows this section. Students who extensively practice using this framework demonstrate excellent recall of recommended priorities (i.e., label, category, and function). Two examples of object descriptions follow:

> A tic®tac box is a container that holds candy. It is transparent and multicolored. The shape is rectangular. It is made of plastic and paper. A tic®tac box is smooth. I bought it at the convenience store. It's smaller than my hand. It has a flip-top cover. I have many of them around my house. In conclusion, tic®tac boxes are handy.

> My object is a skateboard. It's a piece of sport equipment that people use to ride on the street. The colors of my skateboard are red, white, and black. My skateboard shape is like an oval. It is the size of a desk. The skateboard has four wheels. The grip tape is very rough. The skateboard is made of wood, metal, and rubber. It is plain, with no design. I got my skateboard because I did well in school. I can do some tricks, like an "ollie" and a kick flip. In conclusion, I love skateboarding.

## *Objectives*

The student will:

- recognize and identify the first three priorities in an object description – label (what), category, and function (used for) – given a template

- use a cue chart for generic category terms that can be substituted for "thing" or "stuff" when describing objects, such as utensil, device, item, tool, appliance, object, implement, accessory, gadget, instrument, and equipment

- generate object description statements that contain the label, category, and function of objects without a template

*Landmark School, Inc.*

- include characteristics that add information about the object being described, given cue words; for example, size, what it's made of, shape, texture, color, and condition

- prioritize details in an object description; for example, color is more relevant in some descriptions than in others

- generate a complete but concise object description that contains feature and subordinate details without a template

- describe an animal – including a label, species, and subgroup, if known – given photographs and a word chart for the five main species (mammal, reptile, bird, fish, and insect); for example, "A lion is a mammal. It is a member of the cat family."

- report salient facts about the animal, such as its physical appearance, habitat, food, reproduction, and behavior

- describe essential or interesting information about a setting or location (e.g., time, place, action, details)

- define a concept and provide a context, including a contrast (e.g., free speech vs. censorship in newspaper editorials)

- analyze the need for description within a specified context, including essential details; for example, a description of a shoplifter should include what he or she looked like, was wearing, and was doing

- provide other meanings for a word, if applicable; for example, a hammer is a mechanism that strikes the firing pin or cap in a firearm, a felted mallet that strikes the strings of a piano, or a bone in the middle ear

- recognize that a single word might serve as more than one part of speech; for example, "hammer" as a verb means to strike repeatedly, while "to hammer out" is a figurative expression that means to develop by careful thought or repeated effort

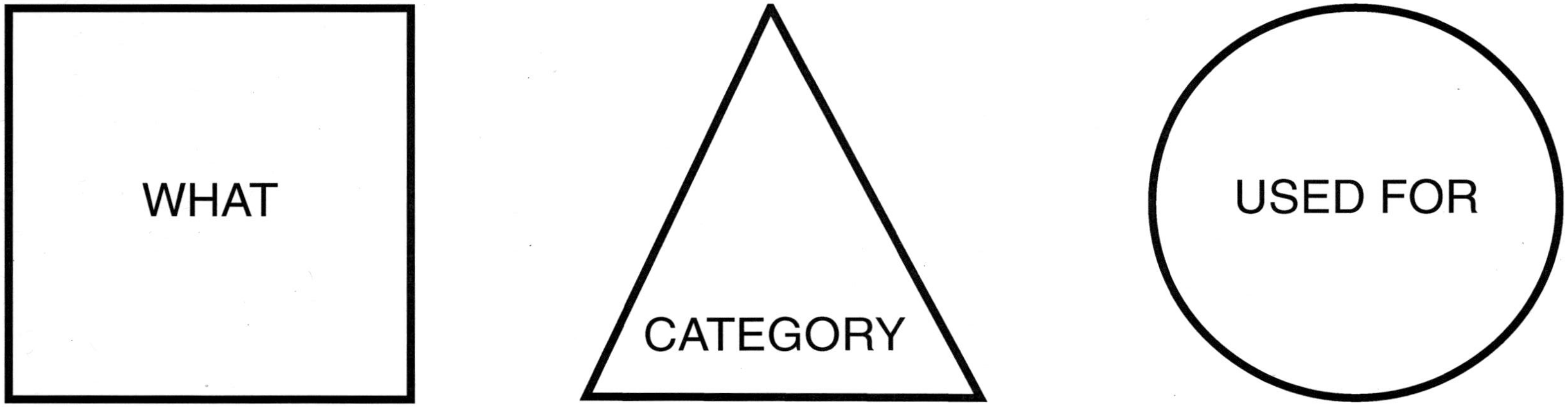

*Pragmatics*

◯ USED FOR

△ CATEGORY

▢ WHAT

I am describing a _____. It is a/an _____ that _____.

Size
Shape
Color
Made of
Texture
Other

*Landmark School, Inc.*

# ANIMAL DESCRIPTION

**MAMMAL**

**NAME**
Leopards

**CATEGORY/SPECIES**
big cat
carnivores

**HABITAT**
parts of Africa,
Middle East,
and Asia

**FOOD**
antelopes, deer,
rodents, and
fish

## APPEARANCE

Colors: yellow with black rosetts

Looks something like?
jaguar

Size
length 3 1/2 to 5 1/2 ft.
height
weight 66 to 176 lbs.

Shape cat

Features/Senses
eyes/eyesight great eyesight

ears/hearing good hearing

nose/sense of smell excellent smell

mouth/teeth
sharp teeth

legs, feet, claws
pads on paws
sharp claws

## LIFESTYLE

How it survives
their colors
hide them
can climb trees

Natural enemies?
hyenas

Family groupings
mother, cubs

Social community
live alone

Unusual/Quirky behaviors?
laughing don't
mean

## REPRODUCTION

Length of pregnancy

How many babies
usually 2 cubs

Babies' appearance
dull gray fur
spots hard to
see

Caring for babies
teach them
to hunt

How long until offspring are independent?
about a year

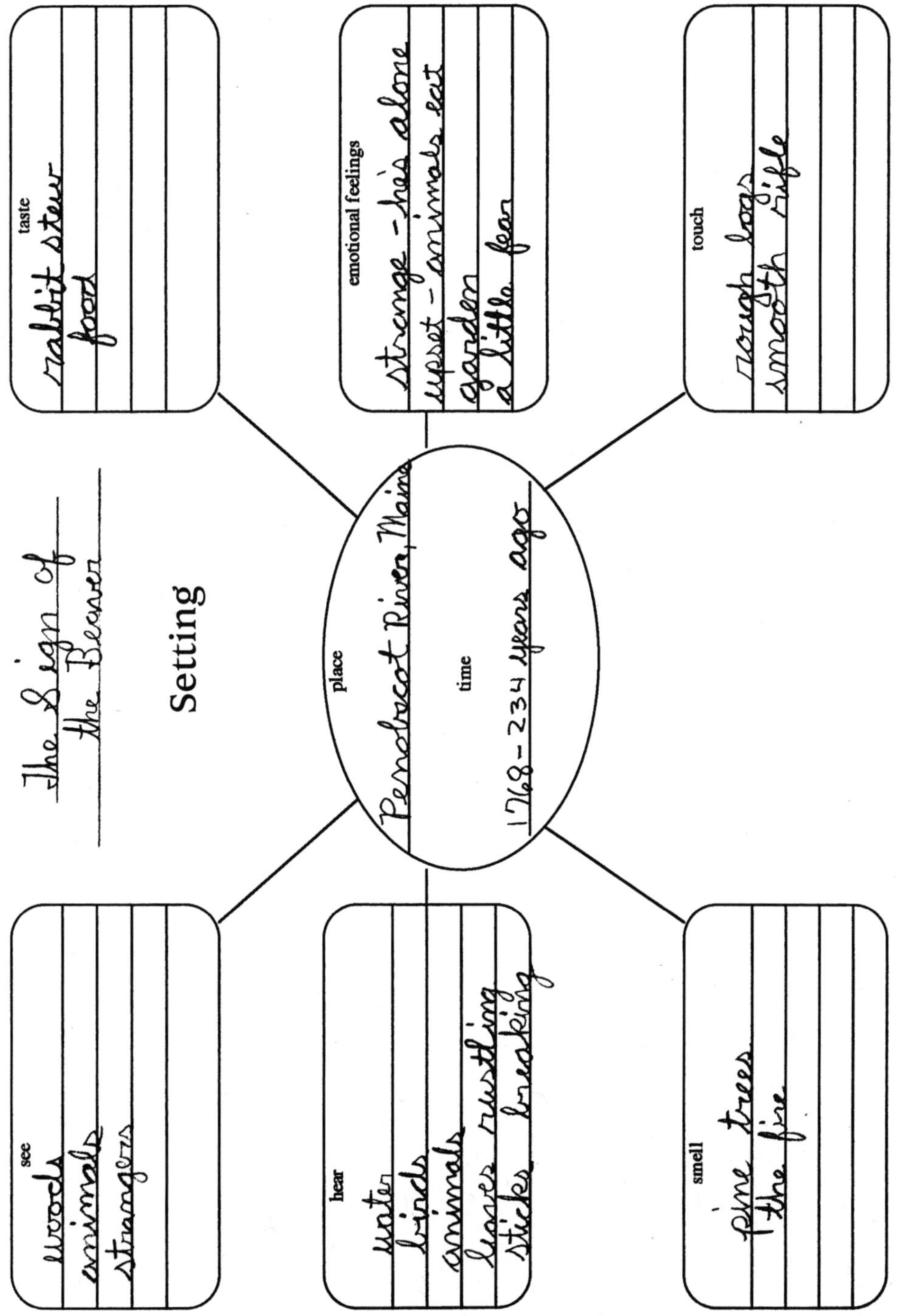

*Pragmatics*

The Sign of the Beaver

## Setting

**place:** Penobscot River, Maine
**time:** 1768 — 234 years ago

**taste**
rabbit stew
food

**emotional feelings**
strange — he's alone
upset — animals eat garden
a little fear

**touch**
rough logs
smooth rifle

**see**
woods
animals
strangers

**hear**
water
birds
animals
leaves rustling
sticks breaking

**smell**
pine trees
the fire

Worksheet courtesy of M. Heddon (2000)

Landmark School, Inc.

# Discourse: Expressing Comparisons and Contrasts

## *Goal*

The student will systematically organize and coherently describe comparisons and contrasts.

## *Background*

Expressing comparisons and contrasts is a skill we call upon throughout our academic and adult lives. The comparison-contrast essay format appears in the Massachusetts Comprehensive Assessment System (MCAS) tests, as well as numerous other tests containing essay questions. For example, in the spring 1998 MCAS tests, fourth-grade students were asked to read a Greek myth and a Native American legend and explain similarities and differences between the two stories.

At Landmark, we have informally pretested hundreds of students for their ability to verbalize comparisons and contrasts. This experience has consistently proven the need for a framework. The Landmark framework helps students develop parallel contrasts. For example, if a student is describing the habitat of the eagle, then he or she should describe the contrasting habitat of the owl, not the color of the owl.

Students have two formatting options for reporting comparisons and contrasts. First is the teeter-totter approach; for example:

> The eagle is a diurnal raptor; the owl is a nocturnal raptor. The eagle lives on cliff edges or in high treetops. The owl lives in trees that are located in wooded areas.

Second is the one-subject-at-a-time approach, still keeping the details parallel; for example:

> The eagle is a diurnal raptor and lives on cliff edges or in high treetops. The great horned owl is a nocturnal raptor. It lives in trees that are located in wooded areas.

In *Evaluating Communicative Competence,* Simon (1994) shares students' pretest responses to illustrate a range in ability. In one example, students were shown a picture of a stapler and a picture of a paper clip and asked to compare and contrast them. A ten-year-old whose performance Simon cites as impressive said:

> They both hold things together, but the paper clip, you can just stick it on and pull it off easily and the staple, you have to rip it off.

*Landmark School, Inc.*

*Pragmatics*

A ten-year-old who gave a less impressive but still partially good performance said:

> A stapler and a paper clip are alike because they can both hold together something and they're different because a stapler's bigger.

In a second example from Simon, students were shown a picture of a candle and a picture of a light bulb. A ten-year-old whose performance Simon cites as impressive said:

> They both light up a room, but the uh candle melts and the light bulb doesn't melt.

A ten-year-old who gave a less impressive but still partially good performance said:

> They're alike because they can both shine light and different because one of them – the candle – is green and the light bulb isn't.

## *Objectives*

The student will:

- identify the category shared by two objects or beings in a comparison, given visual stimuli (e.g., photos and objects); for example, "Owls and eagles are birds."

- identify salient characteristics shared by the two items or beings in the comparison

- verbally compare the salient characteristics of the two items or beings in the comparison, given a framework; the comparison should include a topic sentence, the superordinate category of the subordinate members, characteristics the subordinate members share, and prioritized characteristics the subordinate members share (e.g., color is less important than function)

- identify the ways in which the two items or beings differ (i.e., contrast them)

- express the contrasts in a parallel manner, given a framework and topics as guidance; for example:

| Eagle | Topic | Great Horned Owl |
|---|---|---|
| Diurnal raptor | Behavior | Nocturnal raptor |
| Cliff edges, tree tops | Habitat | In trees, wooded areas |

- avoid random descriptions (e.g., explaining two similarities, one difference, then more similarities)
- prioritize among types of contrasts (e.g., should behavior rank above color, size, or longevity?)
- prepare a verbal summary that includes a topic sentence; the category shared by both items or beings; major similarities; transitional words, phrases, or sentences to signal the change from comparisons to contrasts; contrasts; and a concluding sentence
- deliver an oral summary of comparisons and contrasts, given a visual framework as a guide
- deliver an oral summary of comparisons and contrasts without a visual framework

Pragmatics 233

Oral Expression/Literature
Comparison / Contrast Graphic Organizer
_Emperor_ and _Adelie_

Name: _____
Date: _____
Day: _____

Topic sentence: _____

**SIMILARITIES**

Category: penguins which nest in Antarctica (flightless bird)
- can't fly, can swim
- similar diet of krill and fish
- male incubate the eggs first
- when not nesting, live in the ocean

both
also
same
like
each
similarly
have in common

→ transition sentence

**DIFFERENCES**

① nesting time
② nesting + eggs
③ hatching
④ size

_Emperor_
- March until October
- no legs, no nest
- male hatch egg, it sits on them for 2 months
- 3½ ft, 66 pounds

_Adelie_
- October until March
- made of rocks, two eggs
- parents switch off sitting on eggs, 30 days
- 2 ft, 11 pounds

but
while
although
however
yet
whereas
on the
other
hand

Concluding sentence: _____

Landmark School, Inc.

Worksheet courtesy of R. Stacey, M. Heddon, B. Miller, and T. Jennings (1999)

# Discourse: Explaining a Process

## Goal

The student will order each step in a process so that a listener can complete or visualize the task.

## Background

The biggest challenge in delivering a how-to speech is putting oneself in the naïve role of the listener. The speaker must be careful not to assume background knowledge on the part of the audience. He or she must plan ahead and order the steps so the listener can complete the task. This fourteen-year-old's response to being asked how to use a pay telephone illustrates the need for explicit instruction when explaining a process:

> How you use a phone is you talk to your friends on the phone and you pick up the phone and you just . . . there's a place where you put it on your ear and there's a place where there's a mouthpiece and that's how you use a phone.

An exemplar of a how-to speech is in *Charlotte's Web*, by E.B. White. Charlotte, the spider, explains to Wilbur, the pig, her intricate process of capturing and storing her victims for later consumption.

An organizational template with transitional words, like the one at the end of this section, reminds students of the sequence for explaining a process.

## Objectives

The student will:

- select the most important items needed to execute a task from an array of picture cards; for example, cards for making a hand puppet would illustrate a pattern, felt, chalk, scissors, needle, thread, plastic eyes, and glue
- order the steps to execute a task from an array of picture cards; for example, first trace the pattern onto the felt, then cut out the shape, next thread the needle, and so on
- select a familiar process topic for purposes of demonstrating to others
- use visual aids in a process speech

Landmark School, Inc.

- develop a topic sentence
- label the objects
- describe their function
- use an organizational template with sequential transitional words (first, then, next, after that, and finally) to mark steps in the process
- explain *why* or *how* at each step of the process; for example, "Next, sauté the chicken. You sauté chicken by . . ."
- demonstrate the ability to take another person's perspective – that is, to realize that the listener might not possess background knowledge related to the topic
- develop a concluding sentence using an introductory phrase (in conclusion, in summary, to conclude)
- answer questions from the audience
- observe and critique videotapes of demonstrations by peers
- observe and critique a videotape of his or her demonstration

**PROCESS SPEECH (how to...)**

(student's oral report)

Name: _____
Date: _____
Day: _____

Introduction: *I'm going to explain fly fishing.* _____

First of all, *you need waders and a #6 fly rod.* _____

(Why?/How?) *Waders are water-proof and have material on the bottom that sticks to rocks. Just any old shoe won't do. A #6 rod is good if you're just starting out.*

Then, *put a fly on your line, and 1 to 2 feet from the end, put on an orange floater.*

(Why?/How?) *You need the floater so you can see where your line is. The fly sinks.*

Next, *hold the rod with one hand and pull line out of the reel with the other hand.*

(Why?/How?) *You keep one hand on the line as a guide.*

After that, *position the line between the slow and fast river currents, and flick the line.*

(Why?/How?) *The fish hang out between the currents. You flick the line to make the fly lure look alive.*

Finally, *when you catch a fish, let the fish pull the line out a bit, but keep tension on the line.*

(Why?/How?) *You want the hook to sink in, and if you pull on the line too fast, the hook might slip out.*

In conclusion, *I find fly fishing very peaceful and relaxing.*

T. Jennings and C. Haynes (2002)

# Discourse: Describing Cause and Effect

## *Goal*

The student will explain the cause-and-effect relationship between two items, actions, or events.

## *Background*

Understanding cause-and-effect relationships is essential to all academic pursuits, including literature. A *cause* is a fact that explains the occurrence of something else, which is the *effect*. Determining cause and effect requires inferential thinking. Given a relationship between two items, such as ice skates and skate guards, one should be able to explain what would happen if one didn't have guards on the skates. Students should also be able to think through the cause-and-effect relationship between two actions (e.g., arguing after being told to be quiet results in being sent to the supervisor's office).

If children can think of several possible causes of an event, they might avoid the pitfall of jumping to the wrong conclusion. For example, if a child's rollerblade is missing, it is helpful if he or she realizes that it may have been misplaced before accusing someone of taking it. Conversely, children should be able to explain causes for their own actions that might otherwise be misinterpreted.

The *Manual of Exercises for Expressive Reasoning* (Zachman et al. 1982) and *RAPP! Resource of Activities for Peer Pragmatics* (McConnell and Blagden 1986) provide numerous cause-and-effect questions.

## *Objectives*

The student will:

- explain the cause-and-effect relationship between photos of two items provided by the instructor, such as a bicycle and a lock

- answer questions about familiar topics that ask *why*; for example, "Why are there yellow lines in the middle of the road?"

- answer questions about personal opinions that ask *why*; for example, "Why do you wear jeans as soon as you get home from school?"

- answer negative questions that ask *why*; for example, "Why wouldn't you feed your dog turkey bones?"

- identify possible causes of an event; for example, causes of a bicycle's flat tire
- explain plausible consequences of actions; for example, the consequences of going to the mall without permission
- explain an event from a literature selection; for example, "Why did Little Willy have a black eye?"

# Discourse: Expressing Opinions

## *Goal*

The student will express an opinion and justify it with logical, relevant data or reasons.

## *Background*

Numerous Landmark students are intimidated by requests for their opinions, while others feel free to express their opinions (solicited or not!). More than anything else, students need validation for their opinions. Many students do not realize that their opinions are valid as long as they support their opinions with reasons.

The objectives below have two purposes: to give reticent students confidence in expressing opinions without fear of being wrong and to channel those who freely express opinions without justification to provide supporting evidence. The objectives progress from the least personally threatening to the more challenging.

Landmark's Jenny Hanchett places particular emphasis on developing students' ability to express opinions. She introduced a framework that requires at least two reasons for each opinion. The requirement is to put the reasoning in writing, in her framework. This strategy, repeated over and over again, has been extremely effective. A copy of the framework is provided at the end of this section.

## *Objectives*

The student will:

- express a preference between two food choices and provide at least one reason for that preference; for example:

    **Teacher**: Which food do you prefer, spaghetti or pizza?
    **Student**: Pizza.
    **Teacher**: Why?
    **Student**: You can eat it with your hands.

- discriminate fact from opinion

- begin an opinion statement with a phrase marker, such as "I think," "I feel," and "I believe"

- express a preference between two magazine ads (not the products) that differ in visual appearance and provide at least one specific reason for the preference; for example, "I prefer this ad because I like the colors."

- distinguish between a reason that adds information and a reason that does not add information; for example, "Dark chocolate tastes too bitter to me." rather than "Dark chocolate is yucky."

- express an opinion about liking or disliking an activity, such as a sport or hobby, using at least one bit of supporting information

- express an opinion about preferring group or individual activities and provide at least one reason to support the opinion

- express an opinion about a contemporary issue of interest and provide at least one fact or reason to support the opinion; for example, "Should students be required to wear school uniforms?"

- express an opinion about the actions of a character in a literary selection and provide one or two facts or reasons to support the opinion; for example, "Do you think Karana should have jumped out of the boat and swum back to the island to search for her brother?"

- express an opinion and state a position on articles or speeches by people with opposing views (e.g., editorials, newspaper columnists, and political candidates)

- respond in a constructive manner to opposing opinions

- provide two facts or reasons that would support an opposing opinion

## Teaching Strategies

The instructor will:

- acknowledge opposing opinions, while encouraging data or logical reasons that support each opinion

- act as an objective referee during a debate about issues, authors, or writing styles

- ensure that opposing proponents of an argument enjoy equal opportunity to support their opinions

*Pragmatics*

**OPINION - EMOTIONS**

**How would you feel?**

Name: _____

Date: _____

Day: _____

Topic Sentence: If I were in his posishon I would be mad, sad, lonnly, scard.

First of all, Mad

(Why?/How?) because it might have ban my only chance to be recued.

Secondly, sad

(Why?/How?) because the people on the oil rig didn't see me.

Thirdly, lonnly

(Why?/How?) because I haven't seen any one in days and I had the chance to be recued by people.

Finally, scard

(Why?/How?) because I might die, and I all most hit the oil rig.

In conclusion, I would be sorry that I didn't lison to my mom or dad or tell someone.

*Landmark School, Inc.*

# Discourse: Eliciting Comments from Students Who Give No Response

## Goal

The teacher will create an environment that maximizes opportunities for student responses.

## Background

In the following exchange, a teacher's question gets no response from a student.

> **Teacher**: What do you think will happen next?
> **Student**: I dunno.

"I dunno" can mask a variety of problems: lack of comprehension, word retrieval deficits, lack of confidence, or the need for scaffolding to formulate a response.

Through classroom experience and careful observation, it is possible to detect the real issue underlying the response, "I dunno." The goal is to create an environment that maximizes opportunities for each student to develop expressive language skills. The strategies listed below (in no particular order) are tried and true.

## Teaching Strategies

- Change the wording of the question; for example, "What will happen next?" suggests a single possible answer, while "What could happen next?" sounds less threatening.

- Rephrase the question to put the student into the story personally; for example, "What do you think you would do in this situation?"

- Retrace what has already happened, such as by making a timeline, referring to events that foreshadow upcoming events, asking each student to report a plot element in sequence, and acting out earlier scenes.

- Reduce the open-ended nature of the question, such as by referring to a specific character.

*Landmark School, Inc.*

- Offer the student a multiple-choice format to limit the possible responses.

- Provide a preface lesson; for example, present a thematic unit on predictions that includes the term "betting" and address such topics as the scientific method, weather, horoscopes, gambling, and a crystal ball.

- Allow wait time before intervening.

- Give an absurd example to get a reaction.

- Cue the student; for example, to elicit the word "sprinkler," give a semantic cue ("a garden hose attachment"), a phonemic cue ("It begins with sp-."), a gestural cue (pretending to sprinkle a lawn), or a situational cue ("You find it in yards, and children might run through it with their bathing suits on.").

- Ask the student questions that will get him or her started.

# Discourse: Encouraging Students to Expand on Minimal or Incomplete Responses

## *Goal*

The teacher will implement strategies that elicit expanded responses from hesitant students.

## *Background*

Many students are afraid of venturing into dangerous (i.e., "wrong") territory by attempting to say more than the minimum, especially in situations that call for them to express an opinion. Here is an example of a teacher soliciting an opinion and a student providing only a minimal response:

**Teacher**: What do you think of hitchhiking?
**Student**: It's good.

## *Teaching Strategies*

The Landmark faculty has developed numerous strategies to elicit elaboration following a minimal response. The first is to conduct a preparatory lesson to familiarize students with the concept of pros and cons. The content of this lesson might include:

- explaining that all issues have pros and cons
- showcasing ten issues
- sharing stories
- defining and sharing ideas
- citing real-life examples
- bringing in visuals to tap students' background knowledge
- reading a related story, showing a related movie, or inviting a guest speaker
- relating an issue to current events
- asking a safe, neutral question before asking for an opinion on a controversial issue

Another strategy is for the teacher to offer the student choices related to the subject scenario. Using the hitchhiking example above, the teacher might ask, "'Good' as in you get where you're going or 'good' as in you meet lots of people?" Similarly, the teacher can lead the student to define "good" by asking, "Do you mean morally good or good because it's free?" Additional strategies for encouraging a student follow.

- Rephrase the question; for example, "What are positive and negative things about hitchhiking?"
- Write the headings "pro" and "con" on the blackboard and ask the student to fill in the columns.
- Provide minimal cues like "Say more.", "Why?", and "Would you share your thoughts?"
- Ask the student for a scenario that supports his or her opinion.
- Generate guiding questions like "Have you ever hitchhiked?" and "Why would someone choose to hitchhike?"
- Ask the student to share personal experiences.
- Brainstorm different scenarios; for example, discuss specific times when it is OK and not OK to hitchhike, using cueing questions like "Who's picking you up?" and "Where are you going?"
- Role play different sides of the issue with the student.
- Present legal facts that may influence the student's opinion.
- Expand the minimal cueing question "Why?" to "Why do you think hitchhiking is good?"
- After the student expresses one opinion, have him or her express the opposite view.

Another tack for generating discussion is to initiate a class discussion.

- Ask students to write their opinions, pro or con, on slips of paper, then share them. Some students are less self-conscious about expressing their thoughts when they read something they have written rather than attempting to compose their thoughts as they speak.
- Draw a continuum on the blackboard from 1 to 100 and ask students to write a plus sign (+) on the continuum to show where they stand on the issue. Then invite two students with opposing views to debate the issue in front of the group.
- Invite the larger group to get involved, such as by saying, "Can anyone give another reason?"

# Discourse: Accommodating Students Who Exhibit Slow Processing or Delay in Formulating a Response

## Goal

The teacher will employ strategies to elicit responses from students who process information slowly or who exhibit a delay in formulating a response.

## Background

Some students have extreme difficulty competing with high-verbal, rapid-processing classmates in group discussion. The larger the group, the greater the problem. To avoid negative feedback from peers, these students frequently shut down. By fifth grade, they might become completely silent in the classroom.

Although slow processing and delay in formulating a response appear to go hand in hand, it is important to consider alternatives. Some students might be rapid processors who are quick to respond if the answers require minimal word-search activity, such as yes-no, one-word, and multiple-choice responses. The same students might exhibit notable delay if asked for an extended response, such as a summary and an opinion. Other students might be slow processors who impulsively and incorrectly answer a question without allowing themselves the extra time they need to process and deliver an accurate response.

The strategies below open the gates for many such students, allowing them to enter the group as active participants. Teachers play an important role in making sure these students get their fair chance in the classroom. In fact, the importance of the teacher's role as mediator cannot be overestimated.

## Teaching Strategies

Landmark strategies for managing student delays in formulating thoughts follow.

- Allow wait time.
- Establish class rules for turn-taking, patience, and expectations. Do not allow students to call out answers.
- Modify the overall pacing of the class, when appropriate.
- Rephrase, using fewer words.

- Prompt students with cues; for example, to generate the response "cotton candy," the teacher might give a semantic cue ("It's a sweet treat you can buy at the fair."), a phonemic cue ("It starts with /k/ or /kŏ/."), or a gestural cue (pretending to eat cotton candy).

- Use a round-robin format, giving each student a chance to pass. A student who passes may call on a classmate to provide the answer.

- Provide modeling or ask another student to provide modeling.

- Divide the class into subgroups to encourage participation.

- Set the classroom climate, such as by reducing distractions and maintaining eye contact.

- Don't always call on the first student to raise his or her hand.

- In writing assignments, give faster students a meaningful supplementary writing task.

- Ensure that everyone understands the question before calling on a student for the answer.

- Prearrange an agreement with a slow processor by privately asking him or her, "When would you like me to call on you?"

- Say a student's name to get her or his attention before asking a question that the student is likely to be able to answer.

- Design the question to fit the student.

- Implement a pattern of listening and repeating in which each student has to repeat what the previous student said before adding information.

- Talk with a highly verbal, faster processor individually, outside of class.

- Appoint a highly verbal, quick responder as the class summarizer.

# Social Communication: Ritualizing

## *Goal*

The student will engage in appropriate ritualizing speech acts.

## *Background*

The familiarity of language-based rituals gives us a feeling of security. For example, introductory rituals – "Hello. How are you?" – establish a comfort level between two people. In everyday life, students face the rituals of greeting peers and teachers, saying goodbye, and talking on the telephone.

Many Landmark parents report that their children are unwilling to answer the telephone or make calls. Landmark has developed training programs to improve students' ability to conduct conversations over the telephone.

## *Objectives*

The student will:

- respond nonverbally to greetings with a nod or smile
- respond verbally to greetings, while maintaining eye contact with the greeter
- greet people spontaneously; for example, "Hello, Sharif. How are you?"
- respond nonverbally to farewells with a gesture, such as a wave
- respond verbally to farewells; for example, "See you later, Ben."
- express farewell spontaneously
- seek another person's attention; for example, "Excuse me. Can you help me find my bus?"
- respond to a verbal introduction by another person; for example, "It's nice to meet you, too."
- introduce two people
- introduce him- or herself to others
- answer the telephone in an appropriate manner

*Landmark School, Inc.*

- provide necessary information during a telephone call (e.g., identify him- or herself and explain the purpose of the call)
- conclude a telephone call in an appropriate manner

# Social Communication: Requesting Information or Assistance

## *Goal*

The student will appropriately request information or assistance, when needed.

## *Background*

Too many students suffer silently. They might be afraid of appearing stupid if they ask for clarification. They might not realize that they have misunderstood the directions for homework. They might deny their need for extra help or extra processing time. They might not want attention drawn to their physical differences, such as impaired hearing. A great step forward for many hesitant students is to develop self-advocacy. The Landmark environment, with sensitive instructors and homogeneously grouped peers, lends itself to self-advocacy.

## *Objectives*

The student will:

- request clarification, if needed
- ask for repetition, if necessary
- make requests
- ask for directions
- explain a problem
- express desires or needs
- respond appropriately to denial of a request

## *Teaching Strategies*

The instructor will:

- ask students to reverbalize directions just assigned
- provide multimodal directions (verbal, written, and by example)

*Landmark School, Inc.*

- ensure that students can complete homework assignments independently
- double-check for students who might not speak up (e.g., look for quizzical expressions)

# Social Communication: Conversation and Discussion

## Goal

The student will appropriately initiate, maintain, and terminate conversation or discussion.

## Background

When two or more people exchange thoughts or feelings in an informal manner, they are having a conversation. For many students, carrying on a conversation is a more challenging task than delivering a book report. A conversation can be derailed in any number of ways: a misunderstood word, inaccurate interpretation of a gesture or tone of voice, an interruption that leaves the speaker unable to complete a thought, or the speaker wandering off topic. It is difficult for many of us to be as good at listening as we are at talking, and we risk turning a conversation into a monologue. Students benefit from practicing strategies that lead to more positive experiences in conversation.

## Objectives

The student will:

- use an ice-breaker to initiate a conversation or discussion; for example, "How did you like that movie last night?"
- introduce him- or herself to a stranger in a group
- volunteer to talk during pauses in a conversation
- maintain attentive listening behavior during a conversation or discussion
- take both speaker and listener roles, being careful not to monopolize a conversation
- decrease interruptive behavior
- make comments that support the speaker and maintain conversation
- ask questions to maintain a conversation or get clarification
- greet a new member of a conversational group and briefly explain the topic under discussion

*Landmark School, Inc.*

*Pragmatics*

- open and close a conversation on the telephone
- take messages for others in a telephone conversation
- provide adequate information when leaving a message on a telephone answering machine: name, time of call, nature of call, and telephone number if a return call is desired

*Landmark School, Inc.*

# Social Communication: Classroom Discussion

## Goal

Through appropriate participation in group discussion, the student will become a contributing member of the classroom community.

## Background

The most successful classrooms are those in which there is a sense of community among students. Landmark's Joni McLaughlin popularized a simple mnemonic that is now used by many Landmark teachers. The "three *R*'s" are respect, responsibility, and routine.

- *Respect* is often the most difficult challenge for many students, as their battered self-esteem causes them to display a misguided lack of respect for their peers. It is an ongoing challenge for instructors. Ground rules seem to help.

- *Responsibility* for academic work and for an atmosphere conducive to learning belongs to every student as well as every teacher.

- *Routine* has become a byword at Landmark. Each teacher's schedule is posted on the board in every classroom throughout the day. Students have come to rely upon these agendas, which often serve to establish a working atmosphere at the beginning of each class.

## Objectives

The student will:

- use appropriate language in response to criticism
- disagree with another student's point of view in a constructive manner
- express a complaint in an objective manner, using facts to support it; for example, "A lunch plate and a coffee cup were left in my room." rather than "They left a mess in my room."
- suggest a course of action in response to a problem
- listen to others in an attentive manner

Landmark School, Inc.

- support others' opinions, if he or she is in agreement with them
- acknowledge previous contributions before formulating a response or adding new information
- support him- or herself, giving reasons for an opinion or action or for innocence in the face of an accusation or criticism
- avoid belittling others
- refrain from interrupting others
- avoid belittling him- or herself
- respond to humor in an appropriate way
- greet people upon encountering them
- use persuasion as a tool to reach a goal
- negotiate or compromise to reach a satisfactory conclusion
- convey communicative intent

# Resolving a Conflict

## *Goal*

The student will apply strategies for resolving conflicts.

## *Background*

At Landmark, Charlotte Eliot has conducted sessions on conflict resolution. Her format is roughly based on Kreidler's suggestions in *Conflict Resolution in the Middle School* (1997). She poses questions on a worksheet, with space for three responses after each question. An example of her format, with one of her students' responses, follows.

### Sample Conflict Resolution Worksheet

What kinds of things cause conflicts?

1. things that bother you
2. things people don't agree on
3. money

What makes a conflict worse?

1. you just don't stop
2. not listening to other people's sides
3. my sister

What makes a conflict better?

1. thinking about what they were talking about
2. listening to people
3. don't blow things out of proportion

Teachers might also consider providing students in conflict with a framework that allows for self-appraisal. An example follows.

### When I Am in a Conflict

| Conflict | What I Do | How I Feel |
|---|---|---|
| Someone calls me a name | | |

Still another possibility is for teachers to require students in conflict to express themselves using a "because" qualifier. For example, the student

*Landmark School, Inc.*

would be required to say "I feel _____ when _____ because _____." Other conflict-resolution strategies include:

- role-playing activities

- the case study method; for example, "Here is a situation. What is a solution?"

- discussing feelings (e.g., "I feel disappointed.") rather than opinions (e.g., "I feel that you were wrong.")

Reflective listening exercises also reduce tension in a confrontational situation. The focus is on the feelings of those involved rather than the incident. If an apology is appropriate, the four steps below encourage students to think about the consequences of their actions rather than the incident. Discussion of this four-step apology is to be found in *Quantum Teaching: Orchestrating Student Success,* by DePorter, Reardon, and Senger-Nouric (1999).

- First, students *acknowledge* their actions and behaviors using "I" statements. They take responsibility for the situation. Sample "I" statements are "I acknowledge that I hurt your feelings when I said those things about you." and "I acknowledge that I borrowed your Walkman® without asking you."

- Second, students *apologize* as a way of acknowledging the impact of the incident. If students do not understand the impact of their behavior, they should ask. Sample apologies are "I apologize for hurting you and realize that I may have ruined our relationship." and "I apologize and realize that you thought someone had stolen your Walkman®."

- Third, students *make amends* to deal with the consequences of their behavior. They might say to the other person, "Is there anything I can do to make it right?" or "I want to do something to help our friendship. I would like to spend more time with you."

- Last, students *recommit* to replacing problem behavior with appropriate behavior. They might say "I agree to treat you politely." or "I agree to ask before I borrow anything from you."

The objectives below are from Kriedler (1997). Group training and discussion are necessary precursors for students to fulfill them, as these actions are not likely to occur spontaneously.

## Objectives

The student will:

- agree to solve the problem
- move away from the site of the problem
- attempt to observe four rules:
    1. do not interrupt
    2. take turns (one person tells what happened, how he or she feels, and why, then the other person tells what happened, how he or she feels, and why)
    3. do not call the other person names or put the other person down
    4. be as honest as possible
- remember that he or she agreed to solve the problem
- take turns giving ideas about how to solve the problem
- agree on a solution

# Social Communication: Resolving Conflicts in a Residential Setting or during Free Time

## *Goal*

An adult chaperone or teacher will establish and follow a routine for gaining information in a conflict.

## *Background*

Landmark case managers and supervisors complete an intake form when a student is asked by an instructor to leave class or, less often, when a student asks to leave class. The case manager usually plays a neutral role as scribe, writing down the student's version of the events that led up to dismissal from class, verbatim. Judgment is often reserved until the case manager hears the instructor's version of events.

The case manager's neutral, nonemotional behavior frequently calms a riled-up student. Repeating what the student says verbatim has two effects. First, if the story isn't exactly true, the student might squirm a little at hearing the replay and make a few amendments that get closer to the truth. Second, the inanimate intake form becomes the focus, and anger at the other person often subsides.

At Landmark, two students were in a confrontation. When a teacher asked about it, both started talking at once. Landmark strategies for avoiding this situation and effectively mediating such a confrontation are outlined below.

## *Strategies*

The adult chaperone or teacher will:

- preempt further conflict by saying that both students will get to tell their story, then pick one student to speak first, separating him or her from the other, and listen; next, separate the second student and listen to his or her story; then, bring the two students back together to discuss the situation, setting a time limit for resolving it

- use reflective listening and receptive listening strategies; for example, validate what the students are saying and structure the interaction so it is objective, concrete, and balanced

- be calm and nonjudgmental

- wait before speaking to let the students process the seriousness of the situation

- ask the students what they could have done differently to achieve a positive resolution

- clarify possible misperceptions; for example, "He actually said . . ."

- change the atmosphere, such as by adding humor or using a talk-show format to defuse the situation, in which the teacher is the host and the students are participants

# Paralinguistic Communication: Articulatory and Prosodic Features

## *Goal*

The student will effectively employ articulatory and prosodic features of voice to enhance communicative intent.

## *Background*

Some students have little or no affect (intonation or emotion) in their voices during conversation. One Landmark student who was asked to read sentences using anger in his voice replied, in all sincerity, "I can't. I never get mad." This student also had difficulty detecting varied intonation when listening to declarative, imperative, interrogative, and exclamatory sentences.

## *Objectives*

The student will:

- speak intelligibly
- speak fluently, without revisions or fillers like "uh" and "you know"
- maintain appropriate volume
- maintain appropriate pitch
- maintain appropriate voice quality
- maintain appropriate speaking rate
- categorize oral production of the four basic sentence forms (declarative, imperative, interrogative, and exclamatory)
- maintain appropriate phrasing
- maintain intonation and stress appropriate to the four basic sentence forms
- maintain appropriate intonation during oral presentations

# Paralinguistic Communication: Volume and Pitch

## Goal

The instructor will encourage the student to use a clear voice, free from tension, with appropriate volume and pitch in all settings.

## Background

On occasion, Landmark encounters students who appear unable to self-monitor for volume. Some speak too softly to be heard. Others speak too loudly for their listeners' comfort level. These students often benefit from electronic devices that provide visual feedback during oral expression, such as a device with an indicator that moves from "inaudible" to "too loud" as the student speaks. One student who habitually spoke at an excessively loud volume was trained to watch the indicator carefully and maintain his volume at the appropriate level.

A few male students have difficulty adjusting to the typical one-octave drop in pitch that occurs with the thickening and lengthening of their vocal cords at puberty. While most males suffer from tricks their voices play in the beginning stages of puberty – sudden highs and lows over which they have no control – others seem arrested in a preadolescent state. They use a high-pitched voice as a manipulative tool to achieve a desired goal. On the other hand, some children reach puberty at a later age and continue speaking at a higher pitch than same-age peers in the classroom.

## Teaching Strategies

- Generate oral expression activities in which students speaking too softly must deliver information to classmates at a sufficient volume to get the desired response. For example, in an outdoor setting, a student at the top of a hill has to deliver information or directions to students at the bottom of the hill.

- Create a video in which students (as performers) give information to viewers, such as a lesson on the proper use of seat belts. Then let students review the video and self-monitor for appropriate volume. Last, mediate a peer review of students' speaking volumes in the video.

- Respond to students using excessive volume in the classroom by speaking softly, yet audibly, thus providing a noticeable contrast.

*Landmark School, Inc.*

- Provide an electronic device (e.g., a tape recorder with a volume indicator) that students can use as a visual aid to self-monitor for appropriate volume.

- Maintain a neutral, nonjudgmental tone of voice in response to a student who appears to be using a high-pitched voice as a manipulative tool.

- Create a classroom atmosphere that is conducive to the use of development-appropriate vocal pitch.

- Discourage negative peer reactions to students using an excessively high vocal pitch.

- Refer students with atypical vocal pitch or volume to a speech-language pathologist for evaluation.

# Paralinguistic Communication: Register

## Goal

The student will use the appropriate register (tone of voice and language) with specific categories of people.

## Background

Register is readily associated with issues of behavior management. When a student uses an inappropriate tone of voice with an authority figure, the person in authority must determine the student's intent. Some students need direct instruction in the appropriate tone of voice for addressing authority figures.

Also, inappropriate register is often associated with lack of social maturity. A student who reverts to baby talk in certain situations (higher pitch and a vulnerable or whiny tone) might feel that this register gets desired results and does not realize the negative effect it has on peers and adults.

## Objectives

The student will:

- recognize and label emotions associated with specific tones of voice (e.g., cheerful, sincere, sarcastic, and angry)
- select a tone of voice and language appropriate to an authority figure
- select a tone of voice and language appropriate to a peer
- select a tone of voice and language appropriate to a child
- employ language appropriate to a situation (e.g., a ball game)
- employ language appropriate to people in a situation (e.g., when talking to the dean of students in his office)
- employ intonation and stress appropriate to a situation (e.g., reporting an accident and requesting aid for a victim)

## Teaching Strategies

The instructor will:

- maintain a distance appropriate to the context (e.g., classroom vs. residential setting), keeping in mind that he or she is always an authority figure

- model appropriate language for the setting

- refrain from escalating a confrontation by increasing his or her volume and stress to match or exceed the students'

# Paralinguistic Communication: Nonverbal Skills

## Goal

The student will enhance her or his message by using nonverbal communication skills.

## Background

In oral expression classes at Landmark, students frequently track others' presentations with a skills checklist that includes nonverbal communication phrases. The checklist serves several purposes. It improves students' observation skills, it helps students provide the speaker with constructive criticism, and it encourages students to pay attention.

A note on maintaining eye contact with a speaker: Occasionally, a listener might look elsewhere in an effort to concentrate on the content of the message. One's eyes rarely remain glued to the eyes of a speaker throughout a conversation.

## Objectives

The student will:

- maintain appropriate eye contact when speaking to one listener
- maintain appropriate eye contact when speaking before a group
- maintain appropriate eye contact when listening to a speaker
- recognize boundaries of personal space (Americans generally maintain personal space of two to two-and-a-half feet in conversation)
- accurately interpret nonverbal messages by observing facial expression, gesture, and stance (e.g., frown, tapping foot, and hands on hips)
- accurately convey nonverbal messages using facial expression, gesture, and stance
- use gestures to augment verbal messages
- angle the body appropriately toward a speaker or listener

*Landmark School, Inc.*

## Presentation Criteria

Name _____

Date _____

Day _____

| | | | | | |
|---|---|---|---|---|---|
| Posture | 1 | 2 | 3 | 4 | 5 |
| Tone of voice | 1 | 2 | 3 | 4 | 5 |
| Eye contact | 1 | 2 | 3 | 4 | 5 |
| Speaking in complete sentences | 1 | 2 | 3 | 4 | 5 |
| Expression | 1 | 2 | 3 | 4 | 5 |
| Rate of speech | 1 | 2 | 3 | 4 | 5 |
| Other: _____ | 1 | 2 | 3 | 4 | 5 |

Comments:

From Majewski, 1999.

# Evaluation

Questions _____
_____
_____
_____
_____
_____
_____

One thing I learned _____
_____
_____
_____
_____

The best part of this presentation (or one thing the presenter did well)
_____
_____
_____
_____
_____

One suggestion _____
_____
_____
_____
_____
_____

From Heddon, 2000.

*Landmark School, Inc.*

# Paralinguistic Communication: Disfluency/Dysfluency

## *Goal*

The instructor will provide a supportive listening environment for the student who lacks fluency in oral expression (e.g., a student who stutters, clutters, or lacks the ability to express thoughts fluently).

## *Background*

The distinction between disfluency and dysfluency is a minor matter for teaching goals, but relevant for diagnostic purposes. Many Landmark students are *disfluent*. Their speech is characterized by false starts, hesitations as they try to recall words, and on-line repairs during which they back up, self-correct, and start over. *Clutterers* are also disfluent speakers. They speak extremely rapidly, exhibiting hurried motor rhythms. Their speech seems to erupt in rapid bursts. As a group, they also exhibit difficulty with perception, articulation, and formulation of speech.

The *dysfluent* group consists of stutterers. *Stuttering* is a disturbance in fluency that may be characterized by prolongation of speech sounds or syllables, involuntary repetition, blocking, or other markers. A single definition of stuttering does not exist. Its incidence in the Landmark population seems to reflect that of the population as a whole – perhaps one or two percent.

Unfortunately, many educators fail to help students who lack fluency express their thoughts. How? By interrupting them, finishing their messages for them, looking away as if embarrassed by their pauses, reacting in ways that make the speakers self-conscious, and telling them to "Stop, slow down, and start over." This command frustrates students and kills the impact of the message. The manner of delivery inappropriately takes priority over the content. Such behavior in parents and other authority figures causes stutterers and clutterers, in particular, to grow extremely frustrated.

Proper treatment for stuttering and cluttering requires intense focus and substantial time. To address stuttering or cluttering superficially and fail is worse than to do nothing. These students should be referred to intensive programs run by reputable clinics. The objectives below, however, offer a few ways for instructors to provide a supportive classroom environment for students who lack fluency when speaking.

*Landmark School, Inc.*

## Teaching Strategies

- Provide templates (graphic organizers) that promote coherent delivery of knowledge and ideas, such as templates for summarizing, describing, comparing, and expressing an opinion.

- Allow ample time for the student to process and plan before expecting a verbal response.

- Maintain attentive listening behavior while the student attempts to gather and express his or her thoughts.

- Refrain from interrupting the student.

- Speak at a slower rate.

- Create an atmosphere that fosters respect for every speaker in the classroom.

- Discuss the struggles encountered by the stutterer with each classmate in private, as well as the importance of acceptance, attention, and patience to that student's success.

- Discuss strategies with the stutterer in private that he or she might appreciate for group discussions; for example, the student might want to be called on last.

- Provide cues for the dysfluent student during recitation – *only* if requested by the student.

- Refer the student to the speech-language pathologist for an evaluation or consultation.

# Bibliography of Instructional Materials

Bush, C. *Language Remediation and Expansion – 150 Skill-Building Reference Lists*. Austin: PRO-ED, 1989.

———. *500 Thematic Lists and Activities*. Austin: PRO-ED, 1996.

Davis, B. *PALS – Pragmatic Activities in Language and Speech*. Austin: PRO-ED, 1988.

Gajewski, N., and P. Mayo. *SSS: Social Skills Strategies*. Books A and B. Eau Claire, WI: Thinking Publications, 1989.

Johnston, E., B. Weinrich, and A. Johnson. *A Sourcebook for Pragmatic Activities*. Austin, TX: PRO-ED, 1984.

Kisner, R., and B. Knowles. *Warm-Up Exercises – Calisthenics for the Brain*. Book 1. Eau Claire, WI: Thinking Publications, 1984.

———. *Warm-Up Exercises – Calisthenics for the Brain*. Book 2. Eau Claire, WI: Thinking Publications, 1985.

———. *Warm-Up Exercises – Calisthenics for the Brain*. Book 3. Eau Claire, WI: Thinking Publications, 1992.

Lazzari, A., and P. Peters. *HELP 3 – Handbook of Exercises for Language Processing*. Vol. 3, *Concepts, Paraphrasing, Critical Thinking, Social Language*. Moline, IL: LinguiSystems, 1988.

———. *HELP 4 – Handbook of Exercises for Language Processing*. Vol. 4, *Defining and Describing, Written Language, Talking About Language, Word Play and Humor*. Moline, IL: LinguiSystems, 1989.

———. *HELP – Handbook of Exercises for Language Processing – Elementary*. Moline, IL: LinguiSystems, 1993.

Mayo, P., and P. Waldo. *Scripting – Social Communication for Adolescents*. Eau Claire, WI: Thinking Publications, 1986.

McConnell, N., and Blagden, C. *RAPP! – Resource of Activities for Peer Pragmatics*. Moline, IL: LinguiSystems, 1986.

Simon, C. *300+ Developmental Language Strategies for Clinic and Classroom*. Tempe, AZ: Communi-Cog Publications, 1993.

Weinrich, B., A. Glaser, and E. Johnston. *A Sourcebook of Adolescent Pragmatic Activities*. Austin: PRO-ED, 1986.

Zachman, L., C. Jorgensen, M. Barrett, R. Huisingh, and M. Snedden. *Manual of Exercises for Expressive Reasoning*. Moline, IL: LinguiSystems, 1982.

Zakim, S. *Communication Workshop*. Moline, IL: LinguiSystems, 1986.

# References

Bush, C. 1989. *Language remediation and expansion – 150 skill-building reference lists*. Austin: PRO-ED.

Cazden, C., and U. Bellugi. 1970. The child's grammar from I to III. In *Psycholinguistics,* edited by R. Brown. New York: Macmillan Publishing.

Crystal, D. 1995. *The Cambridge encyclopedia of the English language*. New York: Press Syndicate of the University of Cambridge.

Cullinan, B., ed. 1987. *Children's voices: Talk in the classroom*. Newark, DE: International Reading Association.

Cullinan, B. 1993. *Fact and fiction – Literature across the curriculum*. Newark, DE: International Reading Association.

Dale, E., and J. O'Rourke. 1971. *Techniques of teaching vocabulary*. Menlo Park, CA: Benjamin Cummings Publishing.

DePorter, B., M. Reardon, and S. Singer-Nouri. 1999. Quantum teaching – Orchestrating student success. Boston: Allyn and Bacon.

deVilliers, J., and P. deVilliers. 1978. *Language acquisition*. Cambridge: Harvard University Press.

Emerick, L.L., and W.O. Haynes. 1986. *Diagnosis and evaluation in speech pathology*. 3rd ed. Englewood Cliffs, NJ: Prentice Hall.

Fry, E.B., J.E. Kress, and D.L. Fountoukidis. 2000. *The reading teacher's book of lists*. 4th ed. Paramus, NJ: Prentice Hall.

Gardner, H. 1974. Metaphors and modalities – How children project polar adjectives into diverse domains. *Child Development* 45:84–91.

Gardner, H. 1978. *Developmental psychology – An introduction*. Boston: Little, Brown.

Gardner, H. 1983. *Frames of mind – The theory of multiple intelligences*. New York: Basic Books.

Gardner, H., M. Kirchner, E. Winner, and D. Perkins. 1975. Children's metaphoric production and preferences. *Journal of Child Language* 2:125–41.

*Landmark School, Inc.*

Gardner, H., and E. Winner. 1976. The development of metaphoric competence – Implication for humanistic disciplines. *Critical Inquiry* 5: 123–41.

Gardner, H., E. Winner, R. Bechfor, and D. Wolf. 1978. The development of figurative language. In *Children's language*, edited by K. Nelson. Vol. 1. New York: Gardner Press.

Harris, T.L., and R.E. Hodges, eds. 1995. *The literacy dictionary – The vocabulary of reading and writing*. Newark, DE: International Reading Association.

Ham, R.E. 1990. *Therapy of stuttering – Preschool through adolescence*. Englewood Cliffs, NJ: Prentice-Hall.

Jennings, T.M., and C.W. Haynes. 2002. *From talking to writing: Strategies for scaffolding expository expression*. Prides Crossing, MA: Landmark School.

Kreidler, W.J. 1984. *Creative conflict resolution – More than 200 activities for keeping peace in the classroom K-6*. Glenview, IL: Scott, Foresman.

Kreidler, W.J. 1997. *Conflict resolution in the middle school*. Cambridge: Educators for Social Responsibility.

Lakoff, G., and M. Johnson. 1980. *Metaphors we live by*. Chicago: University of Chicago Press.

Lederer, R. 1991. *The miracle of language*. New York: Simon & Schuster.

Levine, M. 2002. *A mind at a time*. New York: Simon & Schuster.

Lindamood, P., and P. Lindamood. 1998. *The Lindamood phoneme sequencing program for reading, spelling, and speech – Teacher's manual for the classroom and clinic*. Austin: PRO-ED.

McCarthy, T. 1997. *Teaching literary elements*. New York: Scholastic.

———. 2000. *Teaching literary elements with short stories*. New York: Scholastic.

McConnell, N., and Blagden, C. 1986. *RAPP! – Resource of activities for peer pragmatics*. Moline, IL: LinguiSystems.

Moats, L.C. 2000. *Speech to print – Language essentials for teachers*. Baltimore: Paul H. Brookes Publishing.

Nicolosi, L., E. Harryman, and J. Kresheck. 1989. *Terminology of communication disorders: Speech – Language – Hearing*, 3rd ed. Baltimore: Williams and Wilkins.

Paul, R. 2000. *Language disorders from infancy through adolescence – Assessments and intervention*, 2nd ed. Boston: Mosby.

Pinker, S. 1999. *Words and rules*. New York: Basic Books.

———. 2000. *The language instinct – How the mind creates language*. New York: Harper Collins Publishers.

Rosner. 1988. *Test of auditory analysis skills (TASS)*. Novato, CA: Academic Therapy Publications.

Quinn, A. 1982. *Figures of speech – 60 ways to turn a phrase*. Salt Lake City: Gibbs, M. Smith.

Semel, E., E. Wiig, and W. Secord. 1995. *Clinical evaluation of language fundamentals*, 3rd ed. San Antonio: The Psychological Corporation.

Shames, G.H., E. Wiig, and W. Secord. 1994. *Human communication disorders – An introduction*, 4th ed. New York: Macmillan College Publishing.

Simon, C. 1994. *Evaluating communicative competence*, rev. 2nd ed. Tempe, AZ: Communi-Cog Publications.

Torgesen, J.K., and B.R. Bryant. 1994. *Test of phonological awareness*. Austin: PRO-ED.

Van Riper, C., and L. Emerick. 1984. *Speech correction: An introduction to pathology and audiology*, 7th ed. Englewood Cliffs, NJ: Prentice-Hall.

Warriner, J. 1988. *English composition and grammar, Benchmark edition, Complete course*. Orlando: Harcourt Brace Jovanovich.

Weinrich, B., A. Glaser, and E. Johnston. 1986. *A sourcebook of adolescent pragmatic activities*. Austin: PRO-ED.

Wiig, E., and W. Secord. 1989. *Test of language competence – Expanded edition*. San Antonio: Harcourt Brace Jovanovich.

Wiig, E., and E. Semel. 1984. *Language assessment and intervention for the learning disabled*, 2nd ed. Columbus, OH: Merrill Publishing.

Winner, E. 1988. *The point of words – Children's understanding of metaphor and irony*. Cambridge: Harvard University Press.

Winner, E., M. McCarthy, and H. Gardner. 1978. *The ontogenesis of metaphor*. Cambridge: Harvard Project Zero and Boston Veteran's Administration.

Winner, E., A. Rosenstiel, and H. Gardner. 1976. The development of metaphoric understanding. *Developmental Psychology* 12:289–297.

Wolf, M., and D. Segal. 1992. Word finding and reading in the developmental dyslexias. *Topics in Language Disorders* 13 (1):51–65.

Yates, J., and B. Chapin. 1983. *Phonemic context articulation program*. Murray Hill, NJ: Software Research Associates.

Zachman, L., C. Jorgensen, M. Barrett, R. Huisingh, and M. Snedden. 1982. *Manual of exercises for expressive reasoning*. Moline, IL: LinguiSystems.

# Glossary

**adverb.** A word that modifies a verb (most commonly), adjective, or other adverb. A word that tells *how*, *when*, *where*, *how often*, or *how much* and usually ends in *-ly*.

**affix.** A meaningful word part (morpheme) that is attached to the root word to create a new word (e.g., *un-* + avail + *-able*).

**allegory.** A narrative or description that uses a system of related comparisons to convey a deeper meaning that lies beneath the surface meaning. In *Pilgrim's Progress*, for example, the protagonist, Christian, faces various events in his quest. Christian represents people who try to lead a Christian life, and each event stands for a problem in one's spiritual life.

**ambiguity.** The state of having various possible interpretations. **Lexical ambiguity** occurs when words have multiple meanings; for example, in the sentence "Let's run to the store.", does "run" mean "drive" or "jog"? With **structural ambiguity**, word arrangement allows for more than one interpretation, as in "Swimming off Turtle Bay, several whales were seen." Structural ambiguity usually arises from poorly constructed sentences and is rarely encountered in good children's literature.

**analogy.** A comparison based upon a partial or general similarity between two things. For example, Dudley Dursley relates to Harry Potter as Cinderella's stepsisters relate to Cinderella.

**antonym.** A word opposite in meaning to a target word. For example, "deep" is an antonym for "shallow."

**articulation.** Production of speech sounds through activation of the vocal cords and the articulators (tongue, jaws, and lips).

**aspect.** In English grammar, a term that describes whether an action is complete (**perfect aspect**), as in "Ben fished.", or continues (**continuing aspect**), as in "Ben was fishing."

**auxiliary verb.** A helping verb that adds shades of meaning to the main verb and that describes time, aspect, mood, or voice.

**cinquain.** A poem of five lines with two, four, six, eight, and two syllables in each line, respectively. A short poem form originated by Adelaide Crapsy, who adapted it from the Japanese poem form, haiku.

*Landmark School, Inc.*

**circumlocution.** An indirect, inefficient use of several words to reference a word that is beyond recall. For example; "It's in Paris, it's this tall thing, looks like an oil well . . ."

**clause.** A group of words with a subject and predicate (verb) that can be **independent** (a complete sentence) or **subordinate** to an independent clause (not a complete sentence). Here is a sample sentence: "The manta ray, which stretched to a width of twenty feet, floated above us in the Vermillion Sea." The independent clause is "The manta ray . . . floated above us in the Vermillion Sea." The subordinate clause is "which stretched to a width of twenty feet."

**cloze.** To restore omitted portions of an oral or written message after hearing or reading the remaining context.

**cluttering.** Speech characterized by excessive speed of delivery, resulting in distortion of sound and phrasing.

**conjugate.** To provide all of the inflected forms of a verb (e.g., swim, swims, swimming, swam, have swum).

**conjunct.** A word or word pair that links two propositions, such as "likewise" and "in addition." For example, "We caught several tuna; in addition, we caught a tremendous swordfish."

**conjunction.** A word or word pair that joins words or groups of words, such as "but," "either . . . or," and "because." A **coordinating conjunction** (but, and, or) joins clauses of equal importance. A **correlative conjunction** (either . . . or, neither . . . nor) is a word pair that links words, phrases, or clauses of equal importance. A **subordinating conjunction** (because, before) introduces a subordinate clause, usually an adverbial clause.

**conjunction deletion.** The process of joining clauses and omitting repeated words or phrases. For example, "Sharif played with blocks. Ben played with blocks." becomes "Sharif and Ben played with blocks."

**connotative meaning.** A meaning that arises from an emotional connection or an association with the primary or dictionary meaning.

**contraction.** A reduced form of a word or words achieved by omitting a phoneme or phonemes in speech or a grapheme or graphemes in writing (e.g., can't/cannot, o'clock/of the clock).

**denotative meaning.** The literal or dictionary meaning of a word.

**discourse.** Communication of thoughts through formal discussion. Sharing of information of an academic nature.

Landmark School, Inc.

**disfluency.** Speech characterized by pauses, repetitions, and fillers (e.g., um, uh) by people who have difficulty formulating their thoughts.

**dysfluency.** Speech characterized by stuttering, usually caused by a disturbance in the timing mechanism in the brain that controls fluency.

**dyspraxia.** "Disruption in the capacity to program voluntarily the production and sequencing of speech sounds" (Van Riper and Emerick 1984). Sounds or syllables may be out of sequence or omitted, and speech sounds garbled.

**embedded clause.** A clause nested within another clause in a complex sentence. For example, in the sentence "The whale that gently bumped our boat was a baby humpback.", the embedded clause is "that gently bumped our boat."

**euphemism.** An indirect expression of an unpleasant fact. From the Greek *eu*, meaning "good," plus *phem*, meaning "speaking." For example, in the sentence "Shamu passed away last Saturday.", "passed away" is a euphemism for "died."

**figurative language.** Word images that arise from multiple meanings and are intended to enhance or enrich a basic message.

**filler.** An interruption in fluency, usually in an effort to recall a word, that is characterized by an utterance of syllables, such as "um," "er," and "uh."

**fluency.** Speech that is articulated in a smooth manner, without repetition, circumlocution, or hesitation.

**gerund.** A verb form that ends in *-ing* and is used as a noun (e.g., sailing is fun).

**homonym.** A word with multiple meanings. A **homophone** is a homonym that is pronounced the same but spelled differently (e.g., pale/pail). A **homograph** is a word that is spelled the same and pronounced the same most of the time (e.g., bark/bark). A **heteronym** is a homograph that is spelled the same but pronounced differently (e.g., tēar as a noun/teār as a verb and cón duct as a noun/con dúct as a verb).

**hyperbole.** Extravagance or exaggeration for effect. From the Greek *hyper* plus *bole*, meaning "throwing beyond." For example, "Ben hit that ball a mile."

**idiom.** A speech form peculiar unto itself. From the Greek *idio*, meaning "not predictable" or "unlike another." Idioms are common to a particular culture or subgroup within a culture, such as teenagers, and change with

*Landmark School, Inc.*

time. An older idiom, for example, is "Don't blow your top." Today, its replacement might be "Chill out."

**imperative sentence.** A sentence that gives an order, such as "Bail out the dinghy."

**infer.** To conclude by reasoning from something known or assumed. An important skill for comprehension of literature and lectures, and even for following a conversation.

**infinitive.** A verb form that is used as a noun or modifier and is usually preceded by "to," as in "Sharif loves *to sail*."

**interrogative.** A sentence in the form of a question.

**irony.** An expression that contrasts appearance and reality. **Understatement** and **paradox** are forms of irony. For example, "What a great leader he was! He hid in his cabin throughout the storm."

**kinesthetic feedback.** Use of awareness of the motor system to self-monitor for accurate muscle movement in the execution of a task, such as in producing phonemes, writing cursively, or shooting a basketball.

**linking verb.** A verb (e.g., be, have, do) that connects the subject to the predicate (adjective or object). For example, "Eliza is cheerful." and "Nikki has a beautiful smile."

**litotes.** Understatement, especially an affirmative expressed by a negative. The opposite of hyperbole. From the Greek *litos*, meaning "plain," "small," or "meager." For example, "Staying afloat during that hurricane was no mean feat!"

**metalinguistic awareness.** The ability to reflect upon the structure of language and its underlying rules.

**metaphor.** An implied comparison between two unlike things that share a feature. From the Greek *meta*, meaning "over," and *pherin*, meaning "carry" or "transfer." For example, "The captain's *face turned to stone* as he ordered the mutinous crew member to walk the gangplank."

**metonymy.** The use of one name for another that it suggests. From the Greek *meta*, meaning "change," plus *onym*, meaning "name." For example, the question "Have you finished your watch?" on a ship means "Have you finished your turn to observe weather change or impending danger?"

**modal.** A helping verb that expresses a mood, as in "She could go.", "She should go.", and "She would go."

*Landmark School, Inc.*

**morpheme.** A meaningful linguistic unit that cannot be divided into smaller elements. For example, the prefix *pre-*, the suffix *-ed*, and even a complete word like "car."

**morphology.** The study of how morphemes are combined to make words. Provides a bridge between phonology and syntax.

**noun clause.** A subordinate clause used as a noun. In the sentence "Whoever swabs the deck will get to eat first.", the subordinate noun clause is "whoever swabs the deck."

**orthography.** The part of grammar related to the written word: letters and spelling.

**paradox.** A statement that seems incorrect or absurd but is true. A type of irony.

**paralanguage.** Aspects of communication other than words themselves, such as eye contact, facial expression, body posture, intonation, and volume.

**participle.** A verb form ending in *-ing* that is used as an adjective (e.g., flying fish).

**passive voice sentence.** A sentence in which the subject is the recipient of the action, as in "*Bruno was blown* overboard by a sudden gale."

**personification.** To give human qualities to inanimate things or ideas. From the Latin *persona*, meaning "person," "actor," or "mask," plus *fic*, meaning "make." For example, "The angry sea lashed at the crippled schooner."

**perseveration.** A psychological term for a tendency to continue an activity and be unable to stop.

**phoneme.** A speech sound (e.g., /p/, /ĕ/, /sh/).

**phonological awareness.** An explicit understanding of the speech sound system, as in recognizing a sentence, a word, a syllable, or an individual phoneme.

**phonology.** The study of the sound system of a language, including not only speech sounds, but also intonation, rhythm, and volume.

**phrase.** Two or more words acting as a unit within a sentence. For example, "in the pool" is a locative prepositional phrase (i.e., it tells *where*).

**pitch.** The tone level in speech, which is determined by the number of vibrations in the vocal cord per unit of time. The pitch of boys' voices drops an octave at puberty.

**pragmatics.** The study of how language is used in social communication and discourse.

**preposition.** A function word preceding a noun or noun phrase that can denote location (e.g., between here and the wall), time (e.g., between now and Friday), or use (e.g., with his luggage). It also can have an idiomatic meaning (e.g., between you and me).

**prefix.** An affix before the root of another word or another prefix that creates a new word that modifies the meaning of the root word or forms a new meaning (e.g., *im-* + possible = impossible).

**progressive tense.** A verb tense that indicates ongoing activity. For example, "Courtney was swinging on the trapeze." or "She is swinging on the trapeze."

**pronoun.** A word used as a substitute for a noun (e.g., it, she, he, they).

**prosody.** "The physical attributes of speech that signal stress and intonation patterns of spoken sentences, determined primarily by variations in pitch, loudness, and duration" (Nicolosi, Harryman, and Kresheck 1989).

**proverb.** A short saying that has stood the test of time and expresses a truth or useful thought, as in "All that glitters is not gold."

**pun.** A play on words that are identical in sound but have different meanings, as in responding to "Did you sail the sea?" with "No, but I did see the sale."

**receptive vocabulary.** The repertoire of words someone understands. We understand more words than we can define; however, many Landmark students show a disproportionate gap between the higher number of words they understand and the smaller number they can recall for use.

**resolution of a sentence.** Segmentation of a complex sentence, or a sentence with a complex subject or verb, into its components. For example, "Sharif and Ben went fishing." resolves into "Sharif went fishing." and "Ben went fishing."

**right-branched adjective clause.** A subordinate clause at the end of a sentence, as in "We released the dolphins *that were caught in our nets*."

**schwa.** A vowel sound (midcentral position of tongue) in unaccented syllables (e.g., around). = /ə round/.

**semantics.** "Describing the relationship between word and the world" (Gardner 1978). "The study of meaning in language, as the analysis of words, phrases, sentences, discourse and whole texts" (Harris and Hodges 1995).

*Landmark School, Inc.*

**simile.** A direct comparison between two unlike things, made explicit through use of the word "like," "than," or "as." From the Latin *similes,* meaning "like." For example, "Kimmi and Nadia swim like dolphins." and "When scaling a rock wall, Eliza is as agile as a mountain goat."

**simple sentence.** An expression of a complete thought. Usually consists of a noun or noun phrase plus a verb or verb phrase.

**stuttering.** Dysfluent speech characterized by these signs or symptoms: (1) part-word repetitions and prolongations that exceed seven percent of all words spoken; (2) the part-word repetitions are marked by at least three unit repetitions, as in "bee-bee-bee-beet"; (3) the part-word repetitions are perceived as containing the schwa in place of the vowel normally found in the syllable being repeated, as in "buh, buh, buh-beet"; (4) the prolongations last longer than one second; (5) difficulty in starting or sustaining voicing or air flow in association with the part-word repetitions and prolongations (Ham 1990).

**suffix.** An affix appended to the word root that changes its meaning or grammatical function. An **inflectional suffix** is grammatical, such as the plural marker *-s*, the regular past-tense marker *-ed*, the regular comparative marker *-er*, and the regular superlative marker *-est*. A **derivational suffix** is lexical and changes the meaning of the base form (e.g., sail + *or* = sailor).

**subject-related clause.** A subordinate clause that modifies the subject and is introduced by a pronoun (e.g., that, which, who). For example, "The captain *who struggled with Moby Dick* was Ahab."

**subordinate clause.** A clause of lesser rank than the main clause in a complex sentence. For example, "We lost the biggest fish, *although our catch for the day was good.*"

**synecdoche.** An expression that requires one to add information that has been left unsaid. For example, "Lend me your ears." means "Pay attention."

**synonym.** A word that has a meaning similar to another word (e.g., happiness/joy).

**syntax.** The study of rules governing sentence formulation.

**verb.** A word in a sentence that expresses an action or a state.

**word retrieval deficit.** The inability to recall and express a specific, known word when engaged in conversation, discourse, or writing.

# Bibliography

Adams, M.J., B.R. Foorman, I. Lundberg, and T. Beeler. *Phonemic Awareness in Young Children*. Baltimore: Paul H. Brooks Publishing, 1998.

Bernthal, J.E., and N.W. Bankson, eds. *Child Phonology: Characteristics, Assessment, and Intervention with Special Populations*. New York: Thieme Medical Publishers, 1994.

Catts, H., and A. Kahmi. "The Linguistic Basis of Reading Disorders – Implications for the Speech-Language Pathologist." *Language, Speech, and Hearing in the Schools* 17 (1986):329–41.

Clark, D., and J. Uhry. *Dyslexia – Theory and Practice of Remedial Instruction*. Baltimore: York Press, 1995.

Coles, R. *The Call of Stories – Teaching and the Moral Obligation*. Boston: Houghton Mifflin, 1989.

Costello, J.M., and A.L. Holland, eds. *Handbook of Speech and Language Disorders*, Boston: Little Brown, 1988.

Cullinan, B., ed. *Children's Literature in the Reading Program*. Newark, DE: International Reading Association, 1987.

Curtis, M. "The Best Kind of Vocabulary Instruction." *Massachusetts Primer* (1986) 15:2.

———. "Vocabulary Testing and Vocabulary Instruction." In *The Nature of Vocabulary Acquisition*, edited by M. McKeown and M. Curtis. Hillsdale, NJ: Lawrence Erlbaum Associates, 1987.

Dunn, L.M., and L.M. Dunn. *Peabody Picture Vocabulary Test – III*. Circle Pines, MN: American Guidance Services, 1999.

Farr, R., and M. Lewis. "Writing in Response to Reading." *Educational Leadership* 47 (1990):6.

Fowler, H.R., and J.E. Aaron. *The Little, Brown Handbook – Instructor's Annotated Edition*. 4th ed. Boston: Little, Brown, 1989.

German, D. *Test of Adolescent and Adult Word Finding*. Austin: PRO-ED, 1990.0

———. *Test of Word Finding in Discourse*. Austin: PRO-ED, 1991.

———. *Test of Word Finding*. 2nd ed. Austin: PRO-ED, 2000.

Gorman-Gard, K.A. *Figurative Language – A Comprehensive Program.* Eau Claire, WI: Thinking Publications, 1992.

Harp, B. "When the Principal Asks, 'Why Don't You Ask Comprehension Questions?'" *The Reading Teacher* 43 (1989):638–39.

Herz, S.K., and D. Gallo. *From Hinton to Hamlet – Building Bridges between Young Adult Literature and the Classics.* Westport, CT: Greenwood Press, 1996.

Hodson, B.W. "Helping Individuals Become Intelligible, Literate, and Articulate: The Role of Phonology." *Topics in Language Disorders* 14 (2):1–16.

Jenkins, J., B. Matlock, and T. Slocum. "Two Approaches to Vocabulary Instruction: The Teaching of Individual Word Meanings and Practice in Deriving Word Meaning from Context." *Reading Research Quarterly* 24 (2):215–35.

Konopak, B., and N. Williams. "Using the Key-Word Method to Help Young Readers Learn Content Material." *The Reading Teacher* 24 (1):89–114.

Lee, R., and A. Kahmi. "Metaphoric Competence in Children with Learning Disabilities." *Journal of Learning Disabilities* 23 (8):476–82.

Levine, M. *A Mind at a Time.* New York: Simon & Schuster, 2002.

Lindamood, C., and P. Lindamood. *Lindamood Auditory Conceptualization Test,* rev. ed. Austin: PRO-ED, 1971.

Massachusetts Department of Education. *English Language Arts Curriculum Framework.* Boston: Massachusetts Department of Education, 1997.

———. *Massachusetts Comprehensive Assessment System.* Boston: Massachusetts Department of Education, 1998.

Pence, R., and D. Emery. A Grammar of Present-Day English. New York: MacMillan Publishing Co., 1963.

Roser, N.L., and M.G. Martinez, eds. *Book Talk and Beyond: Children and Teachers Respond to Literature.* Newark, DE: International Reading Association, 1995.

Spears, R. *NTC's American Idioms Dictionary.* Lincolnwood, IL: National Textbook Company, 1988.

Torgesen, J.K. "Keys to Preventing and Remediating Reading Disabilities." Springfield, MA: American International College's Professional Development Series, October 19, 2001.

*Landmark School, Inc.*

———. "Solutions for Older Children: The Problems of Remediation of Reading Difficulties." Springfield, MA: American International College's Professional Development Series, October 19, 2001.

Trelease, J. *The Read-Aloud Handbook,* 5th ed. New York: Penguin Books, 2001.

Wallach, G., and K. Butler. *Language-Learning Disabilities in School-Age Children and Adolescents – Some Principles and Applications*. New York: Macmillan Publishing, 1994.

Wiig, E. *Steps to Language Competence: Developing Metalinguistic Strategies*. San Antonio: Harcourt Brace Jovanovich, 1989.

Williams, K.T. *Expressive Vocabulary Test*. Circle Pines, MN: American Guidance Services, 1997.

# Appendix

*Landmark School, Inc.*

# Vocabulary Word and Picture

Name _____

Date _____

Day _____

**Vocabulary word:** _____

1. How many syllables are in this word? _____

2. Definition: _____
_____
_____

3. Sample sentence: _____
_____
_____

4. Use today's word in a sentence of your own: _____
_____
_____

5. Draw a picture that reminds you of the definition of this word:

```
┌─────────────────────────────────────────┐
│                                         │
│                                         │
│                                         │
│                                         │
│                                         │
│                                         │
└─────────────────────────────────────────┘
```

*Landmark School, Inc.*

*Appendix* 289

# Vocabulary Word Map

Name _____
Date _____
Day _____

**Word** → **Definition** → **Antonyms**

**Definition** ↓ ↓ → **Sample sentence**

**Synonyms**   **Examples**

**Original sentence**

**Structure**
# of syllables _____
prefix _____
root _____
suffix _____
part of speech _____

Adapted from Moats 2000 with permission.

*Landmark School, Inc.*

# Character Analysis

Name _____

Date _____

Day _____

**Book title:** _____  **Author:** _____

**Name of character:** _____

**Physical characteristics:**

_____

_____

_____

**Personality:**  **Actions in story that give you clues about character's personality:**

_____   _____

_____   _____

_____   _____

_____   _____

**Feelings:**  **Clues from story about character's feelings:**

_____   _____

_____   _____

_____   _____

_____   _____

**Does the character change during the story?**

_____

_____

**If so, how does the character change?**

_____

_____

*Landmark School, Inc.*

*Appendix*

# Summary of an Event, Story, or Chapter

Name _____

Date _____

Day _____

Topic sentence:
(Restate the question) _____

_____

**First,** _____

_____

_____

**Then,** _____

_____

_____

**Next,** _____

_____

_____

**After that,** _____

_____

_____

**In conclusion,** _____

_____

*Landmark School, Inc.*

# Animal Description

Name _____
Date _____
Day _____

**Mammal** _____

**Name** _____

**Category/species** _____
_____

**Habitat** _____
_____

**Food** _____
_____

**Appearance**
Color _____

Looks something like _____

Size
Length _____
Height _____
Weight _____

Shape
Features/senses
Eyes/eyesight _____
ears/hearing _____
nose/sense of smell _____
mouth/teeth _____
legs, feet, claws _____
_____

**Lifestyle**
How it survives _____
_____

Natural enemies _____
_____

Family groupings _____
_____

Social community _____
_____

Unusual/quirky behaviors _____
_____

**Reproduction**
Length of pregnancy _____

How many babies _____

Babies' appearance _____

Caring for babies _____

How long until offspring are independent? _____
_____

*Landmark School, Inc.*

*Appendix*

# Setting Description

Name _____
Date _____
Day _____

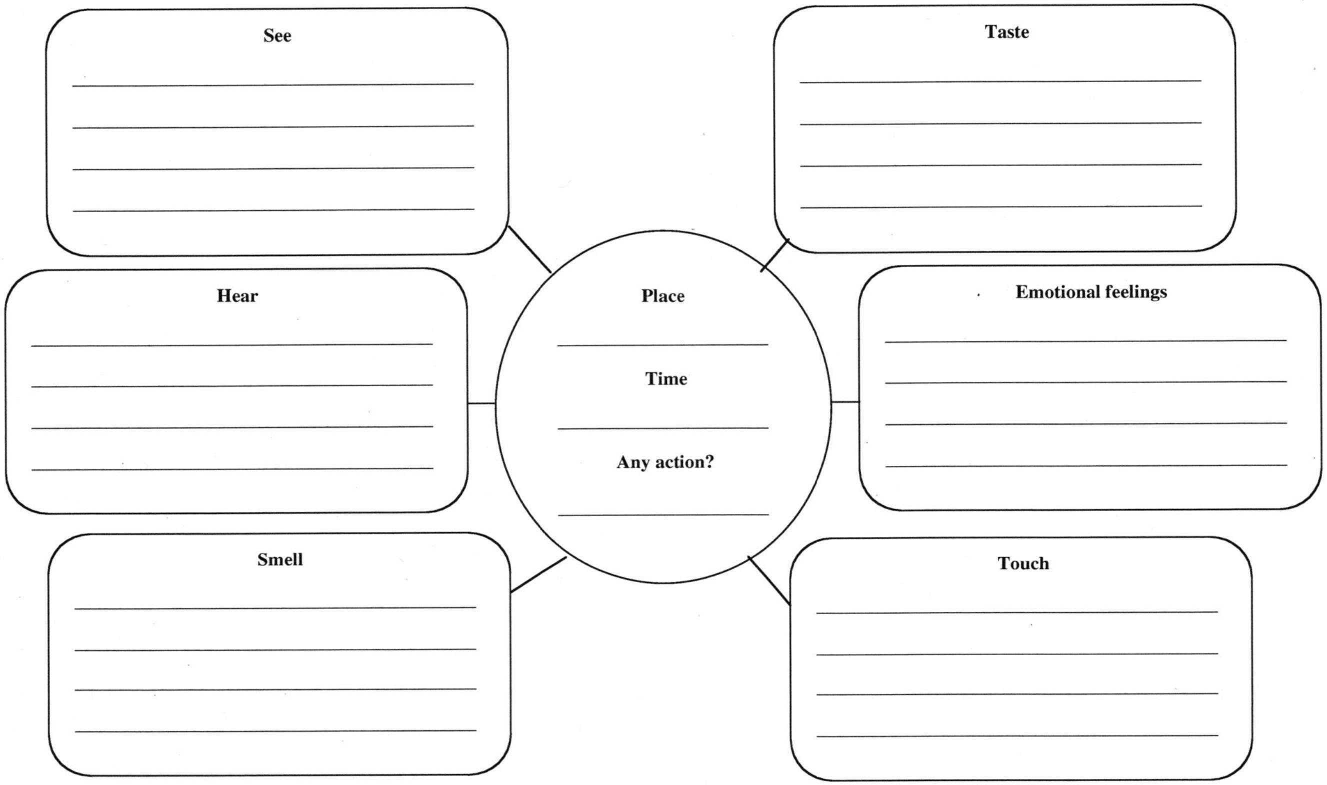

- Taste
- Emotional feelings
- Touch
- Place / Time / Any action?
- See
- Hear
- Smell

Worksheet courtesy of M. Heddon, 2000

*Landmark School, Inc.*

# Comparison and Contrast

Name _____
Date _____
Day _____

Comparison and contrast of: _____ and _____

Question: _____

Topic sentence: _____
(Restate the question)

**Similarities**

_____
_____
_____
_____

both
each
like
also
same
similarly
have in
common

Transitional sentence: _____

**Differences**

| | |
|---|---|
| ___ | ___ ___ ___ |

but
yet
however
whereas
on the other
hand
although

| | |
|---|---|
| ___ | ___ ___ ___ |

Concluding sentence: _____

Worksheet courtesy of R. Stacey, M. Heddon, B. Miller and T. Jennings, 1999.

# Process Speech (How to. . .)

Name _____

Date _____

Day _____

Introduction: _____

_____

First, _____

_____

(Why?/how?) _____

_____

Then, _____

_____

(Why?/how?) _____

_____

Next, _____

_____

(Why?/how?) _____

_____

After that, _____

_____

(Why?/how?) _____

_____

Finally, _____

_____

(Why?/how?) _____

_____

In conclusion, _____

From Jennings and Haynes 2002.

*Landmark School, Inc.*

# What's Your Opinion?

Name _____

Date _____

Day _____

Question: _____

_____

Your opinion: _____

_____

List three reasons or examples that support your opinion.

Reason/example 1. _____

_____

_____

Reason/example 2. _____

_____

_____

Reason/example 3. _____

_____

_____

Write a concluding sentence that sums up your opinion in a new and powerful way.

_____

_____

*Landmark School, Inc.*